The Private-Passive Investor
An Alternative Pathway to Financial Freedom

Copyright © 2024

All Rights Reserved

ISBN: 979-8-218-41320-0

Disclosure

This publication is protected under the U.S. Copyright Act of 1976 and all other applicable international, federal, state, and local laws, and all rights are reserved, including resale rights: You are not allowed to reproduce, transmit, or sell this book in part or in full without the written permission of the publisher.

Although the author and publisher have made reasonable efforts to ensure that the contents of this book were correct at press time, the author and publisher do not make, and hereby disclaim, any representations and warranties regarding the content of the book, whether express or implied, including implied warranties of merchantability or fitness for a particular purpose. You use the contents in this book at your own risk.

Author and publisher hereby disclaim any liability to any other party for any loss, damage, or cost arising from or related to the accuracy or completeness of the contents of the book, including any errors or omissions in this book, regardless of the cause. Neither the author nor the publisher shall be held liable or responsible to any person or entity with respect to any loss or incidental, indirect, or consequential damages caused, or alleged to have been caused, directly or indirectly, by the contents contained herein.

The contents of this book are informational in nature regarding broad topics of private market investing, and are not investment, legal or tax advice, and the author and publisher are not engaged in the provision of investment, legal, tax, or any other advice. You should seek your own advice from professional advisors, including lawyers and accountants, regarding the legal, tax, and financial implications of any investment transactions being considered.

Contents

Introduction 1

Section I: Private-Passive Investing as an Accredited Investor 6

   Chapter 1 - The Case for Private-Passive Investing as an Accredited Investor 7

      Broad Spectrum of Investment Classes Available 12

      Higher Potential Returns 12

      Private Equity 13

      Private Real Estate Syndications 14

      Portfolio Diversification and Risk 15

      Quick Summary 16

   Chapter 2 - Are You Qualified? Accredited Investor Defined 17

      Brief History of the Accredited Investor Rules 17

      The Current Definition of an Accredited Investor (As of December 2022) 18

      The Income Threshold 20

      The Net Worth Threshold 20

      Proving Accredited Investor Status 21

      Qualified Purchasers 22

      Awareness of Accredited Investor Status 23

      How Long Is the Journey to Accredited Investor Status? 23

       24

      Deficiencies of the Current Definition 24

      Quick Summary 25

   Chapter 3 - Population of Accredited Investors and Future Trends 26

      Trends Impacting Qualifying as an Accredited Investor 27

      August 2020 Amendment to Definition of Accredited Investor 29

      Changes Necessitated by the Proliferation of Crowdfunding 30

      Impact on Investors 33

      Quick Summary 34

   Chapter 4 - Favored Asset Classes of the Wealthy 36

      Hedge Funds 36

      Private Equity 38

      Venture Capital 41

      Commercial Real Estate Syndication 43

      Quick Summary 45

   Chapter 5 - Private-Passive Investing, Learning by Doing 46

      Learning by Doing 47

Public Equity Markets as Proxy for Private Equity/Venture Capital 48
Public Real Estate Markets as Proxy for Private Real Estate – Debt and Equity 50
Alternative Platforms for Non-Accredited Investors 52
Non-REIT, Regulation A Tiers 1 and 2 Offerings 53
Interval Funds 54
Finding and Investing in Regulation D, 506(b) Offerings 55
Summary of the Menu for Non-Accredited Investors in Commercial Real Estate 55
Quick Summary 56

Section II, The Education - Building Blocks of Private-Passive Investing 57

Chapter 6 - Sponsor Selection and Investment Profiles for CRE Private Offerings 58
How to Find Commercial Real Estate Sponsors 59
Commercial Real Estate Landscape 61
Real Estate Sponsor Due Diligence 62
Track Record and References 65
Attributes of Successful CRE Sponsors – Competitive Edge 66

Chapter 7 - Commercial Real Estate Syndication Offering Details 68
Leverage and Liquidity 71
Single Assets or Funds 73
Cash Flow – Distributions and Reporting Cadences 73
Important Return Metrics 74
Menu of Exit Strategies – The More the Merrier 74
Risk Management Tools 75
Investment Documentation 77
Quick Summary 78

Chapter 8 - Sponsors and Private Offerings for Private Equity 80
How to Find a Sponsor of Private Equity 83
Private Equity Landscape 84
Types of Private Equity Funds 86
Liquidity and Leverage 90
Cash Flow – Distributions and Reporting Cadences 90
Applying Lessons from Public Markets to Private Markets 91
Quick Summary 91

Chapter 9 - Crowdfunding Platforms – Democratizing Private-Passive Investing? 93
How Is Equity Crowdfunding Regulated in the USA? 94
Growth in Equity Crowdfunding Worldwide 95
How Can Crowdfunding Platforms Help Protect Investors? 95
How Can Crowdfunding Benefit Investors? 97

What are the Risks of Investing in Equity Crowdfunding Platforms? 98
How Can Investors Use Real Estate Crowdfunding Platforms to Build a Portfolio? 98
Which are the Largest Commercial Real Estate Crowdfunding Platforms? 99
The Largest Private Equity Crowdfunding Platforms 99
How Might Crowdfunding Evolve to Further Democratize Private Market Investing? 100
Quick Summary 102

Chapter 10 - The Capital Stack 104

Debt Investments in Commercial Real Estate 105
Incorporating Private Real Estate Debt into a Private Portfolio 107
Common Features Real Estate Debt Fund 107
Preferred Equity Investments in Commercial Real Estate 109
Incorporating Preferred Equity into a Private Portfolio 110
Capital Stack Considerations for Private Equity 111
Private Credit (Debt) 111
Incorporating Private Debt into a Private Portfolio 114
Quick Summary 115

Chapter 11 - Single Asset versus Funds 117

Types of Funds 119
Single Asset Investing - Pros and Cons 119
Multi-Asset Funds – Pros and Cons 120
Private Equity / Venture Capital Fund Example 120
Commercial Real Estate Fund Example 121
Fund of Funds 122
Quick Summary 122

Section III, Planning Private-Passive Strategy & Asset Allocation 124

Chapter 12 - The Private-Passive Plan 125

Private-Passive Investor Mindset 125
Private-Passive Plan Principles 128
Developing a Private Markets Investment Plan (PACER) 129
Define the Private Market Asset Allocation (PACER) 132
Memorialize Constraints on the Portfolio (PACER) 135
Execute the Private Portfolio Plan (PACER) 136
Reinvest and Rebalance Continuously (PACER) 136
A Plan for Continuous Improvement and Education 137
Quick Summary 137

Chapter 13 - Applied Plan Designs for Various Investor Profiles 139

- Starter Portfolio, $250,000 147
- Chapter 14 - Private Market Risk Factors 149
  - Commercial Real Estate Risks 151
  - Private Equity Risks 155
  - Ways for Accredited Investors to Control Risk 156
  - Quick Summary 156
- Section IV, Advanced Topics in Passive-Private Investing 158
  - Chapter 15 - Retirement Issues and SDIRAs 159
    - Self-Directed IRAs – An Account for Private Investing 159
    - More Risks and Complexity of a Self-Directed IRA 163
    - Unrelated Business Income Tax (UBIT) 166
    - Unrelated Debt-Financed Income (UDFI) 168
    - Checkbook Self-Directed IRAs 168
    - Tips and Tricks of a Self-Directed IRA 169
    - The 4% percent Rule in Retirement Planning 169
    - Private Investments and Social Security 170
    - Quick Summary: 172
  - Chapter 16 - Private Investing and Income Taxes 173
    - Private Debt Taxation 177
    - Real Estate Investment Trusts (REITs) 178
    - Specific Income Tax Implications of Private Equity 178
    - Commercial Real Estate Common Equity Taxation 180
    - State Taxes 183
    - Quick Summary 184
  - Chapter 17 - Make Investing Enjoyable Again 185
    - Is The Process Of Investing Fun And Consistent With My Values In Generating Wealth? 186
    - How Do I Avoid Stupid Investing Mistakes That Will Negate #1 And #2 Above? 187
    - Stupid Mistakes of Accredited Investors 187
- Notes 191

Introduction

Private asset classes such as private equity, private debt, and commercial real estate have historically been the playground of the wealthy elite. Private markets are massive in size and growing rapidly. Asset classes such as commercial real estate syndication, private equity, and hedge funds are included under the private market umbrella. Per the regulatory framework in the United States, investors in private offerings must satisfy the definition of an accredited investor, primarily a function of a household's net worth or annual income. The Securities and Exchange Commission (SEC) is responsible for regulating and modernizing the accredited investor framework with the primary mission of protecting investors from bad actors and the general lack of required disclosures related to private securities offerings. The heavy reliance on financial criteria to define an accredited investor sidesteps the desire to protect investors. Instead, it justifies the framework by proclaiming that the wealthy are better positioned to withstand losses in private markets. In short, the affluent have unfair advantages because they have access to private markets, and non-accredited investors are mostly locked out of these potentially lucrative opportunities. Approximately 13% of households currently satisfy the definition of accredited investors, and only a small fraction of those households actually invest in private offerings.

However, forces are colliding, changing the conditions on the playing field of private market investing. First, the ranks of accredited investors are growing each year due to actions and certain inactions of the SEC, making it easier to qualify. While it is important to protect investors, the government has a vested interest in growing the economy through small businesses having access to capital for growth. Also, as the Baby Boomer Generation enters its final act, there will be massive wealth transfers to beneficiaries that should also increase the supply of accredited investors. The demand side of the equation is also rising due to the forces of crowdfunding, technology, and fintech innovations enabled by SEC exceptions to the accredited investor standards. Demand is a function of availability and accessibility. For example, ten years ago, an investor had to go directly to sponsors of private offerings to get access. With crowdfunding sites, investors can now access a multitude of real estate or private equity offerings in one place, which fuels interest in these markets and can be useful for investor education. On top of this, frameworks and options are expanding for non-accredited investors to participate in private markets, which will further solidify the demand. No longer do investors have to be anointed as wealthy to participate, but work still remains to further democratize investing opportunities. Investors who ignore the private markets are missing out on a large universe of opportunities to grow their wealth and achieve a decent retirement.

There is little question that private markets will continue to grow, and households will have increasing access to new types of private offerings even if they do not qualify as an accredited investor. The main problem this creates is a shortfall of investor education, investing fundamentals, and planning frameworks around private markets. There are a plethora of knowledge resources and best practices for investors navigating public markets – stocks, bonds, and mutual funds. The more investors seek the advantages of investing in private equity and debt, the conditions will expand for individual investors to be taken advantage of. There has and will continue to be money lost on new platforms that promise strong returns but are doing nothing behind the scenes to protect investors against basic credit or investment risks.

Legal and regulatory professionals will argue that the recent proliferation of alternative investing platforms and crowdfunding are dangerous and that regulatory conditions should become more restrictive. Surely, Wall Street is biased and prefers the status quo. On one hand, liberalizing conditions for investing in private markets solve the problem of the unequal playing field for wealthy investors and everyone else. Democratizing access to proven access classes is a worthy long-term goal. One reason is that there is a retirement crisis in America; too many individuals are without a clear path to financial self-sufficiency in retirement. The promises of Social Security and qualified benefit plans like 401k accounts that invest in volatile public markets have not been realized. Private market strategies can help bridge this gap with higher returns, lessened portfolio risk, and decreased volatility in most cases. Increasingly, individuals are also looking for supplemental income to help them achieve financial freedom or simply plug a hole in their budgets. A private investment, passive income approach can assist these households in filling the gap between income and expenses. The problem is that investors require preparation and education in order to be ready to expand their portfolios to include private assets, as accessibility to private offerings inevitably increases in the future.

What are potential solutions? The solution to this problem is not simply to discredit private investments and that all sponsors and platforms that provide access to investors are bad actors and scam artists. This is not a problem unique to traditional private markets. The SEC framework needs to continue to modernize and adapt to changes in modern culture, emphasizing accreditation based on investing acumen and not simply wealth and changes driven by technology. Crowdfunding regulations have been improved, and will continue to seek more investor protections. Crowdfunding platforms must take the lead in providing more transparency with offerings, including transparency with their filtering or due diligence processes; otherwise, they risk being replaced by competing platforms. In addition, they must truly advocate for their customers when issues arise with large and powerful sponsors. Of course, educational resources must be developed around private markets, teaching individuals how to navigate, evaluate, and allocate capital to private asset classes, sponsors, and their specific offerings.

Throughout my W-2 career, I have had exposure to all types of investments, public and private. My career commenced as a Certified Public Accountant, cutting my teeth during the savings and loan crisis, seeing firsthand the dangers of investing in real estate. My duties later evolved into the role of treasurer for a private company, CFO for a global private company, and finally as CEO for a not-for-profit with a large investment fund. In addition to the obvious responsibility for managing the investments of these organizations, mergers and acquisitions were a dominant theme with all of these organizations. Acquisitions are essentially an exercise in private equity. Buying real businesses, fixing them up for higher profits to improve the combined enterprise, or selling businesses at a higher price down the road. Large private equity firms are vilified in the press for being short-term oriented, laying off an excessive number of employees, and being generally focused only on investment returns. The reality is that this is a basic playbook of public and private businesses alike. Growth, progress, and efficiency are essential features of capitalism, and buyouts are a necessary tool for long-term survival.

On the personal side, I was fortunate enough to accumulate a degree of prosperity during my 35+ year career within both qualified retirement plans and taxable brokerage accounts. I allocated all investable assets into the stock market, public bonds, and mutual funds, with the majority of them in qualified retirement plans with limited investment options. The advent of crowdfunding for offerings in private equity and real estate first caught my eye in 2017. This was exciting and leveraged my experience in analyzing business opportunities, but I had no framework or plan for developing a private asset allocation and how to prioritize the types of investments that I wanted to acquire. Although it did not go well initially, I hope others can learn from my mistakes.

Here's a sneak peek into the intricate paths of my financial journey: I invested in single business startups and lost. Acquired limited partner interests in venture capital funds from strong sponsors and won. Next, I expanded into commercial real syndications and found a rich universe of offerings that were diverse enough to build a portfolio that met my financial needs – income, growth, or a combination thereof. Education, experience, and capital allocation were the keys to successful investing in my case. Today, like it or not, private offerings are available to all investors – everyone requires skills and education around private markets.

I authored this book to organize my own thoughts and create a framework based on the fundamentals of two significant private asset classes – private equity (including venture capital) and commercial real estate. My mission was accomplished, as my goals and strategies changed significantly as the project progressed. For example, the benefits of private debt and the plethora of categories within private debt resulted in a more conservative asset allocation, meeting my personal goals for passive income.

My goal is to enhance the learning process for the audience of this book in a similar manner and assist them in avoiding the same mistakes I have made during my lifetime. Public or private investing should not be a casino. Investors require resources to guide their inevitable, expansive journey into private offerings. They require a basic understanding and frameworks with regard to how they allocate capital in order to thrive with a passive approach to private market investing.

Accredited investors are not a homogenous group. All differ in terms of age, risk tolerance, need for income versus growth, and optimal asset allocation. The needs of a 35-year-old recently minted accredited investor attempting to replace a W-2 paycheck with passive income differ from an investor with a $50 million net worth. Navigating the maze of private offerings for investors can be overwhelming and flat-out dangerous. This book targets those who are or expect to be accredited investors during their lifetime, as well as non-accredited investors wishing to gain education and experience in private markets through innovative crowdfunding platforms. It is about facing the expansive menu of private investment options in a responsible way. The ranks of accredited investors are growing every day, and individuals may not even be aware that they are accredited.

A vast library of literature on portfolio allocation for traditional equity and fixed-income portfolios has been published. This book, however, will not rehash this evidence. Instead, it will teach you how we can apply proven investment and wealth-building principles when the menu of investment alternatives is expanded to include private investments. It is the difference between the menus at In-N-Out Burger versus The Cheesecake Factory. This book provides a basic framework for optimizing portfolios consistent with investors' cash flow needs and overall investment objectives. It does not discard the tried-and-true rules for building wealth in public markets but, in fact, embraces these rules to apply to private markets. **This book is targeted to investors who want to learn about and diversify into the private market (alternative) asset classes, utilizing a passive approach to income and capital appreciation generation.** This does not preclude participating in the other quadrants illustrated below, consistent with investor experience, skills, comfort level, and investment goals.

	Public Markets	Private Markets
Passive	Public / Passive	Private / Passive
Active	Public / Active	Private / Active

In **Section I**, I provide an overview of private markets and investigate what an accredited investor is, why it is important, and the benefits of qualifying for this designation. The definition of an accredited investor will be reviewed in detail, and you can determine if you qualify or when you may qualify in the future. We will also quantify the ranks of accredited investors, the history of the SEC regulations surrounding accredited investors, and where we are headed in the future. Whether you are accredited now or plan to be in the future, education starts now, and we review the need to educate yourself to prepare to be an accredited investor – developing the appropriate mindset.

In **Section II**, the education begins in earnest with a detailed review of the building blocks for creating a plan to participate in private offerings, including the primary assets classes of private real estate and private equity, the sponsors of offerings, the capital stack, single asset investments versus investing in funds, and a review of the blossoming crowdfunding sector.

In **Section III**, the focus will shift to how you can be successful in private markets as an accredited investor, and all concepts could equally apply to non-accredited investors looking to build confidence in private alternative investments. Education and development of a plan or policy statement are the key areas to explore. Asset allocation is a critical activity, as it is without alternative private investments thrown into the mix. We are all unique, and defining your investment objectives is an important upfront activity. A series of templated asset allocations for various investor personas will be presented to get investors started. Finally, a more detailed review of the risks of participating in private offerings as an accredited investor will be reviewed. Private deals can be a minefield if you are unaware of the potential pitfalls.

In **Section IV**, advanced topics that accredited investors should know will be covered, including the use of self-directed IRAs versus taxable accounts. A brief review of taxation issues that investors should have a firm grasp of is presented. Lastly, there are psychological, mindset, or non-financial aspects that change when one expands one's investment horizons to include private offerings available to accredited investors. I hope this book is a valuable resource to help you achieve a higher level of wealth while avoiding common mistakes that accredited investors make.

The journey to understand and navigate private investment markets does not end here. I have established the blog at IPrivateMarkets.com for like-minded investors to consume and share information on private market investing.

Section I: Private-Passive Investing as an Accredited Investor

Chapter 1 - The Case for Private-Passive Investing as an Accredited Investor

The journey of wealth creation is aided by a system of investing savings earned actively from a job or a business. Commonly accepted principles of creating wealth in retirement accounts or taxable accounts include investing in equity indices via mutual funds or ETFs, saving 10% of income, dollar cost averaging, and diversification. Performed with discipline, these principles will take an investor to a higher level. In baseball, there are the minor leagues and the major leagues. Is there a major league for investors looking to create more passive income in an intelligent way to supplement or replace a paycheck? Is there a major league for building generational wealth? There is such a place, and it involves investing passively in private markets as an accredited investor. This book will explore what it means to become an accredited investor, the benefits, risks, the playing field, and the necessity of having a plan from the moment one commits to a private-passive approach to investing. Approached correctly, investing as an accredited investor creates greater possibilities for wealth creation, for replacing a W-2 paycheck, and for managing the risks inherent in an aggregate investment portfolio.

There is a pronounced and steady shift from public investments like stocks, bonds, mutual funds, and ETFs to private asset classes that include tax-sheltered private real estate funds, private venture debt funds, private equity funds with diversified portfolios across sectors and geographies, or limited partnerships in portfolios of RV parks across America. How about the next vintage (sorry, not wine) fund from a top-tier private equity firm? This shift entails a change from active investing, watching your portfolio value change daily, eyes glued to CNBC, and temptations to trade excessively to a passive scenario where you can enjoy your time, receive quarterly progress updates from a cadre of really smart sponsors with their pulse on the markets, collecting reliable quarterly cash flows, and exiting investments at a 3x multiple of invested capital five years later. Morphing your mindset and your money to private, passive investing is what this book is about.

The investing landscape is moving in this direction, and it is time to learn how to shift from Wall Street to Main Street's private markets. The wealth gap is wide and growing, with increased impetus for governments to level the playing field by providing more access to private investing opportunities, historically accessible only by the rich. While most opportunities are only available to accredited investors, the ranks of investors are increasing, and crowdfunding has enabled non-accredited investors to access similar private opportunities. The democratization of investing is happening, but education and planning are vital to accompany this movement in order to avoid unfortunate consequences.

What exactly are we referring to with private-passive investing? The matrix exhibited in Figure 1 below is limited to the context of investing or how we earn money outside of our core occupation. Stated another way, it compasses the methods that can be used to replace or supplement a paycheck. It is about methods of building wealth over the long term.

Figure 1

	Public Markets	**Private Markets**
Passive	Buy and Hold, buy index funds, minimize fees, the "60/40 portfolio" comprised of 60% public stocks and 40% bonds.	Passive investments in venture capital, real estate syndications, private equity. Illiquid for 3–10-year terms, with higher potential returns.
Active	Active traders in the public market. Day traders, 401k, and IRA investors that "over trade" their accounts, investing in IPOs and fads.	Flipping houses. Starting your own side business. Requiring more time, potential large reward for given the amount of active participation required.

The advice for being a "public-passive" investor has been well documented, including Warren Buffett's wisdom to buy and hold for the long term, buy low-cost index funds, minimize fees, and properly allocate assets. The majority of the classic books on investment management delve deeply into the public-passive quadrant.

The next category is "public-active" investing, and much has been written about day trading, technical analysis, options trading strategies, and timing the market. "Private-active" investing examples include house flipping, starting your own side gig, and internet businesses. The private-active quadrant could cover starting your own business as a primary source of income, and there are many resources available for entrepreneurs in this journey.

The final quadrant is the "private-passive" investor, which is the focus of this book. There have been books written that focus on pieces of the massive private markets, mostly by sponsors that are entrenched in these markets and building their brand in order to raise more capital. There has not been a comprehensive book written from an investor's viewpoint to educate investors on the fundamentals of private markets and establish frameworks for building generational wealth. Private-passive investing is still primarily the domain of accredited investors, but as we will see, not entirely. Passive income is discussed extensively in personal finance books, blogs, and podcasts. Passive income and passive growth are independent subsets of the private-passive quadrant. It does not have to be focused only on income generation.

> "Wall Street makes its money on activity. You make your money on inactivity."
> Warren Buffett, Colloquium at the University of Florida, Oct. 15, 1998

A book on passive-private investing would not be complete without a recognition and reconciliation of the ideas and methods of David Swensen. David Swensen was the President and Chief Investment Officer of the

Yale University endowment. Swensen, along with Dean Takahashi, invented what was termed "The Yale Model." David Swensen passed away in 2021. The most obvious and knocked-off element of Yale's strategy is its radical (at the time) bet on private markets. When Swensen left Wall Street and took over Yale's endowment in 1985, nearly three-quarters of the $1 billion portfolio was invested in U.S. stocks, bonds, and cash, according to the organization. Three decades later, Yale's $30 billion endowment trailed only Harvard's in size, and traditional domestic assets make up less than one-tenth of the portfolio (see Figure 2)[1]. That capital goes instead to funding leveraged buyouts and venture capitalists, to buying natural resources and real estate, and to hedge fund managers. And where Yale's portfolio has gone, America's endowments and foundations have followed.[2]

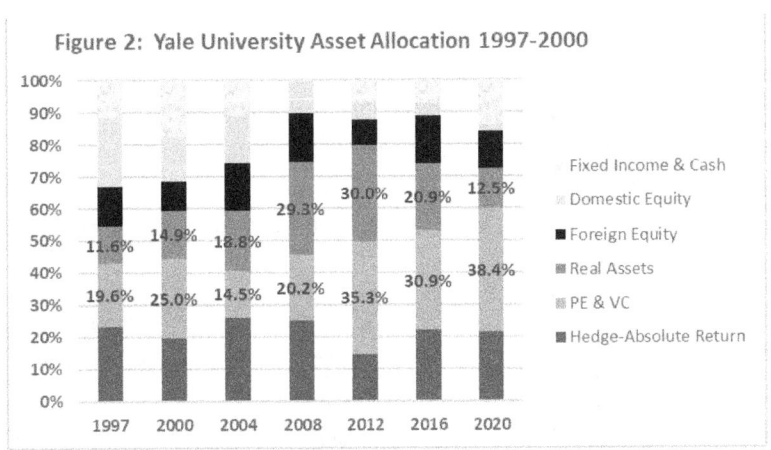

Figure 2: Yale University Asset Allocation 1997-2000

So much for the 60/40 public market portfolio allocation. David Swensen realized that private assets requiring rigorous research and no active exchange offered a premium to patient investors who could forgo the need for immediate liquidity. When he started at Yale, the endowment had 75% of its investments in public equities. Seeing better opportunities in alternative assets such as private equity, hedge funds, real estate, and natural resources – he aggressively shifted the asset mix.[3] It worked at an institutional level. Fast forward to 2023, and an increasing number of converging factors are bringing private assets into the reach of individual investors. Can individual investors replicate this success? This is where we need to "square-up" the Yale Model with reality, and hopefully, this book is a first step in that direction.

I have seen multiple references to David Swensen and his advocacy for individual investors to shift 20% of their assets to private investments. This makes sense, given what he and his team accomplished at Yale. On the other hand, I have not found a direct quote from Swensen on this matter, only the opposite. Unless an investor has access to "incredibly highly qualified professionals," they "should be 100 percent passive - that includes almost all individual investors and most institutional investors." This quote directly places us in the passive row of the quadrant, but what about private investments? I will take a conservative interpretation of David Swensen and assume his advice would place the average investor in the public-passive quadrant because they lack the sophistication to navigate private marketplaces. The world of investing is moving at lightspeed, and I hope to address the many forces that are moving private investing closer to the masses, definitely closer to accredited investors. Investing options and conditions today are very different from the past twenty years. I hope to provide the first step in education for individual investors to succeed, at least directionally, to the levels of success that David Swensen and his team achieved.

What is an accredited investor? In Chapter 2, a more detailed history and evolution of the accredited investor classification will be provided. The condensed version will suffice here. Following the stock market crash of 1929, the Securities and Exchange Commission (SEC) implemented the Securities Act of 1933 (1933 Act), requiring SEC registration for securities that are offered and sold to the public. Fast forward to today: U.S. securities regulations make it easier for accredited investors to invest in privately held companies through "exempt offerings" that are not "registered" under the 1933 Act. The definition of an accredited investor was introduced in 1978 in the context of allowing issuers to sell securities to this group of investors without requiring formal SEC registration. In 1982, Regulation D was adopted to simplify existing rules and regulations. The accredited investor definition was defined under Rule 501(a) of Regulation D, which included the following two primary exemptions from registration:

- The investor is a natural person whose individual Net Worth (defined in Chapter 2), or joint Net Worth with that person's spouse, exceeds $1,000,000 at the time of making an investment or
- The investor is a natural person who had individual income over $200,000 in each of the two most recent years or joint income with that person's spouse in excess of $300,000 in each of those years and has a reasonable expectation of reaching the same income level in the current year.

There are other exemptions today, but keeping it simple for now means that investors must satisfy only one of the above financial tests in order to qualify for investing in private securities.

If an issuer only sells securities to a group of accredited investors, then the securities would be exempt from onerous SEC registration requirements. This opened a whole new world for sponsors of new security offerings in all classifications, including syndications of real estate and private equity (equity in real businesses). The concept of the accredited investor benefits issuers by exempting them from the SEC reporting requirements that apply to public investment vehicles such as publicly traded equities. Smaller projects certainly cannot afford the costs of registration compliance. Many projects require multiple rounds of funding, and "registering" each round would be time-consuming and expensive. It has been forty years since the accredited investor definition was created. Social and political trends are moving in the direction of expanding the population of accredited investors. The details of these trends appear in Chapter 3.

From the perspective of the U.S. economy, the exempt offering regulations provide new ventures with a relatively efficient method of raising new capital, clearly having a positive impact. It is simple math to conclude a positive correlation between the population of accredited investors and economic activity. In other words, there is a political incentive to expand the ranks of accredited investors. The counterargument, rightly so, by the SEC is that investors need protection.

From the investor perspective, if they are "rich enough," then they are accredited. To get into the club, all one needs is to achieve a certain level of wealth or income. Achieve one of these criteria: you are in the major leagues. Are you ready for this challenge? Probably not, and that is why investors striving for this higher status need to be educated to succeed in the "Wild West" of private company investments. Investors need to develop the wherewithal to fend for themselves or learn which intermediaries to trust before risking their capital unnecessarily. This book is intended to be a springboard for this planning and educational process.

Becoming an accredited investor is not merely a vision of the elite. It is becoming more mainstream each year. People from all walks of life "accidentally" become accredited, whether they know it or not, every year. Most professional athletes today fit the definition after two years of salary. Employees of corporations with stock options qualify after their companies IPO or get bought out. In addition, the FIRE movement (financial independence, retire early) has created many new accredited investors due to their frugality coupled with net worth measures exceeding $1 million. Inflation itself is pushing investors up to the next level, as the SEC tests have not been indexed for inflation. Also, do not forget the Baby Boomer generation born between 1946 and 1964. It is projected that the average net worth for this group is in the range of $970,000 to $1.2 million, and the wealth transferred to heirs by 2045 will total $72.6 trillion.4   This will be a large infusion of wealth into more youthful generations that are more comfortable with alternative approaches to investing and the application of technology to solve problems.

Back in 2008, I qualified as an accredited investor instantly when the company I worked for got acquired at an attractive valuation. I clearly remember the stock market tanking in October 2008 while this deal was in the closing process. Fortunately, the deal did close, and it felt wonderful to have financial security and liquidity almost overnight. My goal at the time was to not return to a W-2 position again.

Unfortunately, I did not have a plan. I made both good and bad use of the funds over the next eight years despite not having any awareness of the opportunities available to me as an accredited investor. Good investments were paying for the college expenses of my two daughters, paying off my mortgage, and investing in my own skills. I did make some money in the stock market over this period. Bad investments included a second home on Cape Cod. As Robert Kiyosaki loves to say, a home is a liability. A second home is worse. I also acquired a small business in which my earnings were tied to the amount of time I worked.   Eight years later, I discovered the opportunities available as an accredited investor and proceeded down this learning curve. In the meantime, I ended up taking another W-2 position as a chief financial officer, which was not my intention, but it was a decision that ultimately proved valuable and gave me more time to learn about how to structure my investments for the long term. I hope that this book prepares you for the unexpected and prepares you for taking your wealth to the next level.

Again, do you want to learn how to expand your portfolio to include private assets? The answer to this question is probably not clear at this stage. A better question is, why does being an accredited investor matter? What does it mean? The most obvious advantage is that it expands the menu of investment options available to investors beyond the traditional stock and bond markets. This book will focus primarily on private real estate funds and syndications, private equity, and venture capital as asset classes that can balance a traditional portfolio and enhance the returns to build generational wealth.

Broad Spectrum of Investment Classes Available

Accredited investors have access to investment classes that the average investor generally cannot access. The Director of the SEC's Division of Corporate Finance remarked in 2018 that "Companies raised $2.9 trillion in private markets compared to $1.4 trillion in public markets..."5. For example, private investments in many asset classes, such as commercial real estate, natural resource royalties, venture capital, and private equity projects, are available to accredited investors with the minimum investment requirements.   Accordingly, accredited investors have more flexibility to customize portfolios for their unique risk tolerances and needs. The special investment characteristics inherent in these asset classes may complement traditional public equity and bond portfolios to achieve a higher degree of diversification and return.

Higher Potential Returns

Private investments can enhance portfolio returns over time. As a result, accredited investors should understand that with higher returns come higher risks, including a lack of liquidity – the ability to turn investments into cash rapidly. We will get to the details, but the expected rate of return on private market investments starts at 10% and can exceed 20% for certain asset classes. This heightens the need for a system or plan that aligns with investor needs and the ability to tolerate risk within the portfolio.

The expected rates of return in the public financial markets are well documented, with a long-term track record. As an example, the returns on public asset classes during the 15-year period ending 2020 are illustrated in *Figure 3*. Every 15-year period in history will vary depending on the dominant macro and political environment during that time. Commonly mentioned benchmarks for U.S. equities indicate a range of return on investment of 8-12%. This data corroborates these benchmarks. International equities will act similarly in real terms, but the value of the U.S. Dollar will impact the final results. Fixed income instruments generally return less than equities, in this case, about 5% less. Cash is cash, and the Federal Reserve directly impacts the level of short-term interest rates at any time, in this case, 1.16%.

Figure 3 [5]

	Return 2006-2020
Large Cap Equities	9.88%
Mid Cap Equities	9.55%
Small Cap Equities	9.44%
Diversified	7.11%
Emerging Markets	6.95%
Public REITS	5.78%
International	4.97%
Fixed Income	4.49%
Cash	1.16%
Commodities	-4.01%
Data Source: Morningstar	

The conventional approach offered by wealth managers is a 60/40 portfolio (60% equities and 40% fixed income). The return for a diversified portfolio during this period was 7.11%. For simplicity, we can say that investors might expect a 10% return from equities, 5% from fixed income, and 7% from a classical diversified portfolio.

If accredited investors were satisfied with this rate of return and the associated volatility, private investment markets would not be as large as they are today. The most sophisticated university endowments allocate a portion of their portfolios to private equity and private real estate, as evidenced by the Yale Model.

Private Equity

Returns on private equity are higher due to the higher risk inherent in the illiquid nature of such investments and, in certain cases, due to leverage and/or the underlying companies being early-stage investments. Hedge funds will not be addressed in this book since they will likely never be within reach of the average investor to participate. Hedge funds can be considered a derivative of Wall Street investments, while private-passive investing focuses on Main Street, real businesses, or real estate. **The U.S. Private Equity Index provided by Cambridge Associates shows that private equity produced average annual returns of 10.48% over the 20-year period ending on June 30, 2020.**[6] The above table of public asset returns is for a 15-year period, so there is a slight mismatch between these comparative periods. Determining the rate of return on private equity requires the valuation of all underlying assets on a quarterly, annual, or ad-hoc basis as successful exits occur. Accordingly, the returns on private equity are less volatile than the returns experienced in the public markets. Elevated risk levels should equate to higher returns over the long term. Many investors target a return of 20% for private equity, reasonable considering the nature of the investments, the lack of liquidity, potential leverage, and the fact that there is a wide disparity between the top quartile private equity funds and the median or average private equity funds. In the specific case of venture capital, a subset of private equity, the investment in early-stage companies demands an even higher risk premium. The fact is that many startup ventures will not survive.

As with individual stocks that are publicly traded, an investor never experiences the "average return" on an investment portfolio. An investment in single-company private equity deals can result in a total loss of investor principal or can produce a 10x or higher return. Therefore, a 20% expected return benchmark for a single private equity investment is somewhat useless. For most investors, if they have the capital to invest in private equity, the fund approach is recommended to smooth out this variation of returns amongst various projects in the portfolio. Investing in individual entities is a losing proposition for most investors, excluding investors who are industry "insiders," such as directors or competitors of the target company or experienced venture capitalists.

Even with private equity funds, the variability of returns can be massive and highly dependent on the quality of the fund sponsor. The 20-year return of 10.48% previously mentioned seems surprisingly low if one can invest in public markets with more diversification and earn a 10% annual return. The quality of a private equity fund manager does matter. If you break down the universe of private equity fund managers, the returns of the top quartile of managers will likely exceed 30%, the second quartile of managers will match the S&P 500, and the bottom quartile of managers will underperform. Manager or sponsor selection and diversification will be very important parts of your plan should an investor wish to allocate a piece to private equity.

Our goal is to begin to educate investors about alternative private investments, a world that has previously only been on the radar of the wealthiest members of society but will be more attainable as the members of the accredited investor class continue to swell or as the SEC continues to liberalize access to these investments incrementally. This book will make the case that with a proper plan that marries risk tolerance, need for liquidity, years to retirement, and other factors, you can potentially enhance your total portfolio return with more diversification and less risk. Education is the foundation of any such plan.

Private Real Estate Syndications

Private real estate syndication offerings are increasingly more popular and available as an alternative for newly accredited investors and non-accredited investors as well. The proliferation of crowdfunding platforms such as Realty Mogul, Cadre, Fundrise, and Crowdstreet provide a wide variety of opportunities with relatively low minimum investments in the $25,000 to $35,000 range. Investors can build a diverse portfolio of real estate by property types, strategies, and regions to meet their needs.

The expected rates of return for private real estate syndications are in the range of 10% - 20%, dependent on many factors, including property type (multifamily, office, industrial, retail), the amount of leverage, and location in the capital stack, the expected duration of the investment, and other factors. Like private equity, there is a lot of variability in actual returns depending on the acumen of the sponsor, the type of assets being acquired, the macro environment, and luck (remember Covid-19). Rarely does an investor earn an "average" return on a single asset project. Becoming financially sophisticated in this arena will increase your odds. However, real estate is generally more "forgiving" as an investment than an investment in private equity. Land is land; a building is a building. Values will fluctuate, but property values will eventually recover following downturns. What makes real estate risky is leverage, lack of contingency plans, and the lack of operator experience with the asset type.

The National Council of Real Estate Investment Fiduciaries (NCREIF) is one source of deep historical data that measures the performance of real estate assets around the world. The NCREIF Property Index (NPI) measures returns back to 1978, and the NPI tracks the performance of core institutional property markets in the U.S. Included in the NPI are multifamily, industry, office, hotel, and retail. Since inception, the NPI has returned 2.25% on a quarterly basis, or 9% annually, unleveraged.7 Granted that over a period of 40 years, there are many different macro and interest rate environments to contend with. A return of 9% is not that great if the 10-year Treasury Rate is higher. It is useful to compare the long-term performance of commercial real estate to the S&P 500 performance over common periods of time.

The returns come from the income or rents generated plus capital appreciation. A leveraged project will return more, and the risk profile will increase as well. Assuming the average leverage on real estate projects is a conservative 50%, the average return on real estate investments increases from 9% (NPI benchmark) to 18%

(NPI benchmark divided by the reciprocal of the assumed leverage percentage). Accredited investors flock to real estate syndication projects because of the potential higher returns and the lessened volatility compared to the public equity markets. Also, most investors understand what real estate assets are and how they generate cash flow.

Portfolio Diversification and Risk

Allocating a meaningful but reasonable percentage of an investment portfolio to private markets enhances returns and will provide the additional benefits that come from diversification. Private investments are not correlated with the public equity market and fixed-income markets. Investors have just experienced 2022, a frustrating year in which we witnessed stocks, bonds, and even crypto moving significantly lower in lockstep. With private assets, part of the lack of correlation is because the value of private market instruments is not measured continuously as with public equities. This does not necessarily mean that private investments maintain their value during challenging, recessionary times. It simply means that they are not marked-to-market with regularity.

Venture capital and private equity investments typically get marked-to-market when there is a recapitalization or liquidity event, such as a new capital raise round or sale of the company to a third party. That is when the capital gains or losses are realized. Unfortunately, these companies can become worthless anytime if a venture fails or they can no longer access capital. Investments in private real estate are very similar – the value only changes when a material event occurs impacting the capital structure, such as a recapitalization or sale of the project. Sometimes, there is an annual disclosure of estimated property values based on the broker's opinion of values, especially when sponsors of real estate agree to accept investments from self-directed IRA accounts.

Basically, private investments are less volatile than public markets until they are not. The only exception might be investing in alternative assets with a self-directed IRA. Sponsors allowing investors to invest within an SD-IRA need to provide an annual valuation of the assets to the investor, which is more easily done for real estate but more difficult for early-stage ventures. Also, sponsors are happy to take your money from an SD-IRA but do not always comply with providing the necessary information for an annual valuation.

As an indication, the correlation between returns in private real estate compared to other benchmarks is contained in Figure 4 below.

Figure 4 - Low Correlation Between U.S. Real Estate, Bonds, Stocks (2000 - 2020)

	Private Real Estate	Public REITs	Stocks	Bonds
Private Real Estate	1.00			
Public REITs	0.25	1.00		
Stocks	0.14	0.68	1.00	
Bonds	(0.12)	0.04	(0.34)	1.00

Correlation Data as of December 2020. Indexes represented: Private Real Estate - NCREIF Fund Index-Open End Diversified Core Equity (NFI-ODCE); Listed REITs - FTSE NAREIT U.S. Real Estate Index; Stocks - S&P 500 Index; Bonds - Bloomberg Barclays U.S. Aggregate Bond Index. Further credit to Crowdsteet C-REIT.

Because of the lack of correlation, there is the potential to earn higher returns with less units of risk with a portfolio allocation of 60/20/20 (stocks/bonds/private real estate) than a traditional 60/40 portfolio (stocks/bonds). Stocks are only 14% correlated to private real estate per Figure 4, while bonds are negatively correlated. There are also the psychological benefits of owning asset classes that do not trade daily, which creates a temptation to trade excessively, which can sabotage long-term success. In general, including private investments should smooth the ride and make it easier to stick to an investment plan, assuming the allocation to private assets is adequately diversified within itself. A major negative of private assets is the lack of liquidity, which will be addressed in depth further.

Quick Summary

1. The definition of an "accredited investor" was formally created in 1978 to permit issuers of private securities or funds to bypass the formal and onerous requirements of the Securities Act of 1933 by offering securities directly to accredited investors.
2. In essence, an individual qualifies to be an accredited investor if they satisfy one of two tests of wealth. An investor needs to have a net worth exceeding $1 million or taxable income in excess of $200,000 ($300,000 on a joint basis) in each of the prior two years. Clearly, these tests do not measure financial sophistication.
3. The wealthy have access to asset classes that the typical public market investor does not have access to, regardless of financial acumen, such as hedge funds, private equity, and private real estate.
4. Asset classes such as private equity and real estate can provide higher returns to investors, as indicated by historical performance. Returns on alternative assets are not historically correlated with public equities and bonds, providing further opportunities for accredited investors to efficiently allocate, diversify, and reduce the risk of their overall investment portfolio.

Chapter 2 - Are You Qualified? Accredited Investor Defined

Accredited investors have special privileges granted by federal and state securities laws in the USA. This special treatment originated with the regulations of the Securities and Exchange Commission (SEC), particularly Rule 506 of Regulation D. Accredited investors are a special class of investors that may participate in private investment offerings, including the following:

- Private real estate syndications and related funds
- Private equity and related funds
- Venture capital and related funds
- Hedge funds

Investors have often wondered how they can get in on new unicorn companies prior to an initial public offering (IPO) and start on the pathway to creating generational wealth. The answer to this question has historically been to become an accredited investor. Private securities offerings are exempt from the burden on issuers of the full registration and disclosure requirements contained in the SEC Securities Act of 1933 ("Offerings"), but in return, these deals can only be offered to accredited investors.

Why do the companies that issue private securities care about this exemption? The reasons are that issuers can sell securities in an unlimited amount and number of accredited investors and are under no legal obligation to make the disclosures required by the 1933 Act. Naturally, issuers make extensive disclosures consistent with industry norms to accredited investors, but no minimum disclosures are required, and the format of such offerings varies widely. Issuers need to raise capital and have a strong incentive to build offering memorandums with extensive information to "sell" investors. The standards for public issuers are much more standardized, burdensome, and stringent.

Accredited investors receive special treatment because the SEC views them as either (1) financially sophisticated or (2) possessing the financial wherewithal to absorb losses associated with these private investments. Which of these is the primary reason? The history of the accredited investor rules, and in fact, what has not been done to amend the statutes, indicate inconsistencies in the SEC position. It is not a stretch to conclude that these regulations are trending in favor of more investors qualifying as accredited in the future with relaxed financial tests or examinations that demonstrate proficiency with private investments.

Brief History of the Accredited Investor Rules

As mentioned, the need for an accredited investor definition began with the Securities Act of 1933, although it wasn't legally defined in its earliest form until Rule 242 was adopted in 1978.

As outlined in the SEC's 2015 review, the definition of an accredited investor has evolved over time:

- 1933 – After the stock market crash of 1929, the Securities Act of 1933 was implemented, and it required SEC registration for securities that were offered and sold to the public.

- 1974 – The Commission adopted Rule 146 to provide greater certainty in the application of the Section 4(a)(2) exemption, which exempts from registration "transactions by an issuer not involving any public offering." Rule 146, while it didn't explicitly define an "accredited investor," had criteria that exist in the modern-day definition (e.g., prohibited general advertising and general solicitation, offers had to be made to certain types of financially sophisticated persons, etc.)

- 1978 – Introduced the concept of accredited investors for the first time into federal law.

- 1980 – The Small Business Investment Incentive Act added the accredited investor definition to Section 2(a)(15) of the Securities Act and exempted non-public offers and sales of up to $5 million made solely to accredited investors.

- 1982 – Regulation D was adopted to simplify existing rules and regulations. Regulation D established two exemptions and one non-exclusive safe harbor from Securities Act registration. The accredited investor definition was defined under Rule 501, which included the $200k income and $1 million net worth requirements. It also originally included investors who purchased $150k or more of securities being offered.

- 1988 – SEC rescinded the $150,000 minimum purchase requirement as a qualification of an accredited investor.

- 2011 – As part of the Dodd-Frank Act, the Commission revised Rules 215 and 501 to exclude the value of one's primary residence from the net worth calculation.

- 2019 – Proposed changes to the definition based on the first comprehensive review since 1982.

- 2020 – The Securities and Exchange Commission adopted amendments to the "accredited investor" definition, improving the definition to more effectively identify institutional and individual investors with the knowledge and expertise to participate in those markets. This update is covered in more detail in Chapter 3.

The terminology used in the above historical summary will make more sense once we review what the current definition of an accredited investor is.

The Current Definition of an Accredited Investor (As of December 2022)

An "accredited investor" is: [8]

- a bank, savings and loan association, insurance company, registered investment company, business development company, or small business investment company, or rural business investment company

- an SEC-registered broker-dealer, SEC- or state-registered investment adviser, or exempt reporting adviser
- a plan established and maintained by a state, its political subdivisions, or any agency or instrumentality of a state or its political subdivisions for the benefit of its employees if such plan has total assets in excess of $5 million
- an employee benefit plan (within the meaning of the Employee Retirement Income Security Act) if a bank, insurance company, or registered investment adviser makes the investment decisions or if the plan has total assets over $5 million
- a tax-exempt charitable organization, corporation, limited liability corporation, or partnership with assets in excess of $5 million
- a director, executive officer, or general partner of the company selling the securities, or any director, executive officer, or general partner of a general partner of that company
- an enterprise in which all the equity owners are accredited investors
- **an individual with a net worth or joint net worth with a spouse or spousal equivalent of at least $1 million, not including the value of his or her primary residence**
- **an individual with income exceeding $200,000 in each of the two most recent calendar years or joint income with a spouse or spousal equivalent exceeding $300,000 for those years and a reasonable expectation of the same income level in the current year or**
- a trust with assets exceeding $5 million, not formed only to acquire the securities offered, and whose purchases are directed by a person who meets the legal standard of having sufficient knowledge and experience in financial and business matters to be capable of evaluating the merits and risks of the prospective investment
- an entity of a type not otherwise qualifying as accredited that owns investments in excess of $5 million
- an individual holding in good standing any of the general securities representative license (Series 7), the investment adviser representative license (Series 65), or the private securities offerings representative license (Series 82)
- a knowledgeable employee, as defined in Rule 3c-5(a)(4) under the Investment Company Act, of the issuer of securities where that issuer is a 3(c)(1) or 3(c)(7) private fund or
- a family office and its family clients if the family office has assets under management in excess of $5 million and whose prospective investments are directed by a person who has such knowledge and experience in financial and business matters that such the family office is capable of evaluating the merits and risks of the prospective investment

I have bolded the primary two financial criteria above that are based on "financial wherewithal," the ability to "take a hit." The other criteria involve attempting to define organizations or individuals that have the financial sophistication to evaluate private offerings, or "financial sophistication." Again, we see these two general classes of accredited investors. Over time, it appears that the SEC has come to the correct conclusion that an investor's level of income or wealth at a point in time does not correlate with having financial sophistication. This seems obvious based on my personal experience. Although I was a CPA and financial executive in the industry for decades, even that knowledge does not always equate to financial sophistication to evaluate a particular venture capital deal, for example. A professional athlete or entertainer may have the income and wealth to qualify but is much too busy making millions to understand a particular 200-page private placement memorandum. Taylor Swift clearly has both the skills and the money. In short, the current regulations define accredited investors as either insiders to the offering, those with a limited set of professional credentials, or those who have the ability to absorb losses as defined by some arbitrary numerical standards. Let's look first at these two financial criteria for individual investors before analyzing where this is all trending. As an aside, it is interesting that crypto investments in aggregate have resulted in massive destruction of value during 2022, and there were no offering memorandums or qualifications of accredited investors of any kind required in the crypto markets.

The Income Threshold

An individual with income exceeding $200,000 in each of the two most recent calendar years or joint income with a spouse or spousal equivalent exceeding $300,000 for those years and a reasonable expectation of the same income level in the current year.

As an example, I am a single investor wishing to place a $50,000 investment in a real estate syndication for multi-family apartments in 2023. I must demonstrate to the issuer that I have income in 2021 and 2022 of at least $200,000 each year and a reasonable expectation of earning this amount during 2023 when I make the investment. The income test is the simplest of the two approaches to prove to the issuing sponsor – typically the first two pages of an investor's tax return for the years in question. The expectation that I continue to earn over $200,000 during 2023 is a bit "squishier," as obviously anything can happen, such as job loss. I am not sure how much this current year's expectation provision really protects issuers or the public. It is only fair to state that the income approach is the simplest to compile and demonstrate of the two approaches.

The Net Worth Threshold

An individual with a net worth or joint net worth with a spouse or spousal equivalent of at least $1 million, not including the value of his or her primary residence.

Net worth is defined as a person's assets minus liabilities, referred to as the "balance sheet concept." Note that net worth excludes a person's primary residence, which may be the most highly valued asset that an investor owns. Stated another way, it may make the SEC feel better if a private investment goes bust; the investor will not be risking their home. To demonstrate compliance with this criterion, individuals are required to provide comprehensive details on both assets and liabilities, affirming that the resulting net worth surpasses $1 million. With regards to your primary residence, "indebtedness that is secured by the person's primary residence, up to the estimated fair market value of the primary residence at the time of the sale of securities, shall not be included as a liability…" Again, Robert Kiyosaki, in his book Rich Dad, Poor Dad proclaims that "your house is not an asset," and in this case, the SEC clearly agrees with Robert.

For an individual to determine qualification as an accredited investor, they should create a personal balance sheet like the one below by subtracting the total number of liabilities against the total assets.

Figure 5

	Allen	Brian	Carla
Primary Residence			
Home Value	$ 500,000	$ 500,000	$ 500,000
Mortgage	$ 50,000	$ 300,000	$ 600,000
Home Equity Line		$ 100,000	
Assets			
Bank Accounts	$ 500,000	$ 500,000	$ 500,000
401(k)/IRA	$ 300,000	$ 300,000	$ 300,000
Other Investments	$ 400,000	$ 400,000	$ 400,000
Car	$ 25,000	$ 25,000	$ 25,000
Total Included Assets	$ 1,225,000	$ 1,225,000	$ 1,225,000
Liabilities			
Student and Vehicle Loans	$ 100,000	$ 100,000	$ 100,000
Other Liabilities	$ 100,000	$ 100,000	$ 100,000
Underwater Mortgage			$ 100,000
Balance of Home Equity Line		$ 100,000	
Total Included Liabilities	$ 200,000	$ 300,000	$ 300,000
Net Worth	$ 1,025,000	$ 925,000	$ 925,000

As noted in the example above, Allen qualifies as an accredited investor because his net worth is more than $1 million. However, Brian and Carla do not qualify due to additional liabilities. In Brian's case, he has a $100,000 home equity line that boosts his liabilities and drops his net worth below $1 million. Meanwhile, Carla's underwater mortgage increases her liabilities and reduces her net worth.

Proving Accredited Investor Status

Over the past five years or so, it has become much easier to provide the investment sponsor with the necessary documentation to prove that you are accredited. Sponsors cannot accept an investment until they have sufficient documentation to prove that one is accredited by way of the income approach or the net worth approach. In my experience, sponsors that are not sticklers for this documentation may not be trustworthy. Historically, sponsors provided a form that the investor must have their certified public accountant (CPA) fill out to attest to the investor's qualifications. This created friction in the investment process, as a third-party CPA would have to get involved with the preparation and signing of the form. Costs would sometimes be incurred depending on your relationship with the CPA.

Today, a new group of service providers will provide the accredited attestation once you have uploaded the necessary documentation. Sponsors typically pay for this service as it serves as a convenience to their investor groups and speeds up the process of raising the capital for a project. An example is Parallel Markets, a company that provides identity services for both individual investors and institutional sponsors. As discussed further in Chapter 3, the ranks of accredited investors is growing, and there is mounting pressure on the SEC to change the definition of an accredited investor to make the standard more fair and, at the same time, expand the pool of capital to emerging enterprises to foster economic growth.

The Income Threshold is much simpler to demonstrate with third parties, as tax return information and standard documentation are readily available. The Net Worth Threshold logically requires more documentation, including attestation from the investor affirming the absence of undisclosed liabilities, to satisfy the CPA or other third party that the net worth exceeds $1 million. Unfortunately, relying solely on these two financial tests for individuals creates privacy concerns to some extent, which could reduce participation in private offerings to some degree.

Qualified Purchasers

There is another definition to mention at this point: a qualified purchaser. Sorry about that. No lack of red tape here. There are typically two frameworks, the first being that which applies to a private offering (think a startup business or real estate syndication) and the second being pooled investment funds (think mutual funds or a collection of securities). Both frameworks have their own exceptions to burdensome registration and disclosure rules for defined cases.

Qualified purchasers are relevant to fund products or pooled investments. An incomplete but short version of a qualified purchaser is an individual investor or a family-owned business that holds at least $5 million in investments (value of primary residence excluded). Qualified purchasers are likely accredited investors also. However, accredited investors are less likely to be qualified purchasers. You would think that all qualified purchasers are also accredited investors, but the accredited investor's test is a net worth threshold, which subtracts liabilities from assets. If liabilities are high enough, that could drive Net Worth below $1 million and disqualify a person from being an accredited investor.

What does this matter? Because depending on what fund sponsors are doing and how much capital they need, exceptions to the regulations will be relied upon for them to achieve their desired result.

Accredited investors are allowed to invest in 3(c)(1) funds, which the SEC defines as a "pooled investment vehicle that is excluded from the definition of investment company in the Investment Company Act (of 1940) because it has no more than 100 beneficial owners (or in the case of a qualifying venture capital fund 250 beneficial owners)." Qualified purchasers are allowed to invest in the 3(c)(1) funds open to accredited investors, as well as in 3(c)(7) funds, which are regulated by section 3(c)(7) of the Investment Company Act of 1940. These funds can have up to 1,999 investors before falling under the rules of the Securities Exchange Act of 1934 compared to the lower limits on 3(c)(1) funds. When you see a fund product that is offered to only qualified purchasers, the reason is that the fund needs to be larger in order to achieve its investment goals. I mention this because, in your quest to build a private portfolio, your hopes will be dashed a few times by the words "offering is available to qualified purchasers only." Thus, it is important to keep in mind that the SEC created the definition of a qualified purchaser to help protect investors by ensuring that only sophisticated and financially capable individuals and entities are able to invest in certain securities that carry a higher level of risk.

Awareness of Accredited Investor Status

I first qualified as an accredited investor in 2000 at age 39 based on the Net Worth Threshold. The truth is that I had no awareness of this fact at the time. This lack of awareness is normal. Approximately 3% of investors that meet the definition of accredited actually participate in private offerings.[9] Most accredited investors do not take advantage of their privileged status, knowingly or not. It was not until 2017 that I could qualify based on the Income Threshold, making it easier to prove accredited status. The point is that we all hear about venture capital, hedge funds, and syndicated real estate, but we do not know how to discover and access such opportunities.

In most cases, newly minted accredited investors will not be able to jump into private offerings immediately. There are many competing objectives for capital in the typical household, such as paying down mortgages, funding retirement, and funding children's education. It is not prudent to totally abandon public equity and fixed income markets either. Adding to the complexity is the likelihood that the typical household savings and investments are spread around in retirement accounts and taxable brokerage accounts. There is a lot to sort out when organizing a prudent investment plan.

It does seem a bit odd that when true excess capital presents itself, we can buy $75,000 cars, buy a beach house, buy property in foreign countries, but only accredited investors can allocate $50,000 to invest in a limited partner interest in a 400-unit apartment building and earn a 20% internal rate of return. But unfortunately, that is the reality of the system as it exists in 2023.

A smart approach is to learn about offerings available to accredited investors and become educated if private markets sound interesting. Develop a system for building wealth and tracking your net worth now. Many great online tools exist for tracking your income, expenses, and net worth; any system you develop does not have to be overly burdensome. When you finally reach accredited status, it is strongly recommended to start small and proceed gradually.

How Long Is the Journey to Accredited Investor Status?

With regards to the Income Threshold, when a person can achieve $200,000 in income depends on personal circumstances. According to current SEC estimates, 8.9% of households qualify as accredited investors under the individual Income Threshold of $200,000, and 4.6% of households qualify under the joint Income Threshold of $300,000.[10] It is more than one might expect and naturally growing since the threshold has never been indexed for inflation. Median household income was $67,521 in 2020 per the U.S Census Bureau, so the gap to get to $200,000 is not insignificant.[11] There are many paths to increasing income, and many authors competently address this subject. Just assuming an annual inflation rate of 3%, it would take approximately 36 years for a median household to increase their income to $200,000. This is without any salary or earnings increase beyond the rate of inflation, which is an unlikely scenario. More rapid rates of annual earning increases will shorten the journey. Without changing the securities framework, the average household will qualify as an accredited investor in approximately 30 years.

The Net Worth Threshold can be achieved more rapidly for the average household. The SEC estimates that 9.4% of U.S. households qualify as accredited investors by meeting the Net Worth Threshold. The goal is $1 million, and becoming a millionaire is not as difficult today as in the past due to inflation and underlying economic growth. To reiterate, the value of your primary residence is excluded (net mortgage balance on that residence) from net worth in this definition. There are many reasons not to become "house poor," and this is yet another reason. Also, the savings rate and the related growth and performance of your investments can play a significant role in becoming accredited in the future. In Figure 6, an investor starting with $10,000 of investments and adding $10,000 annually thereafter can realistically get to $1 million based on a savings plan alone within 20-25 years. Also, any windfalls along the way add to net worth, which is a cumulative measurement of wealth. Stock options, inheritances, cryptocurrency bonanzas, side businesses, and real estate gains along the way will shorten the journey. Having the ability to invest in private securities can also shorten that journey, but that is the ultimate Catch-22.

Figure 6; Starting with $10,000 and adding $10,000 annually and compounding at various rates

	10% IRR Value	12% IRR Value	14% IRR Value	16% IRR Value	18% IRR Value
Year 0	$ 10,000	$ 10,000	$ 10,000	$ 10,000	$ 10,000
Year 5	$ 77,156	$ 81,152	$ 85,355	$ 89,775	$ 94,420
Year 10	$ 185,312	$ 206,546	$ 230,445	$ 257,329	$ 287,551
Year 15	$ 359,497	$ 427,533	$ 509,804	$ 609,250	$ 729,390
Year 20	$ 640,025	$ 816,987	$ 1,047,684	$ 1,348,405	$ 1,740,210
Year 25	$ 1,091,818	$ 1,503,339	$ 2,083,327	$ 2,900,883	$ 4,052,721

Deficiencies of the Current Definition

The existing personal tests for being an accredited investor clearly favor the wealthy, not necessarily sophisticated investors. Successful people from all walks of life, including entertainers, scientists, and athletes, can pass the tests but most likely have limited direct private market investing experience or sophistication. Conversely, a young CPA or MBA may possess the skills to understand and prosper with private offerings but cannot because they do not earn enough or have not accumulated enough wealth yet. The current definition is a protective device against losing more money than one can afford to lose, either due to investments going sour or fraudsters operating in the private investment arena. There are definitely fraudulent operators, but there is no absence of fraud in the public markets either. And what about the accredited investors who bet their entire liquid net worth on one company? That investor no longer has any financial wherewithal to fall back on if and when that investment becomes a write-off.

So, there are definitely sophisticated and unsophisticated accredited investors, just as there are sophisticated and unsophisticated non-accredited investors. There are also some obvious inequities in the standard, such as geographical and racial inequities, since median household income varies significantly based on where you live and based on racial groups. Chapter 3 will take a deeper look at these issues and possible solutions for changing the law to expand the ranks of accredited investors logically.

Quick Summary

1. Accredited investors receive special treatment because the SEC views them as either (1) financially sophisticated or (2) possessing the financial wherewithal to absorb losses associated with these private investments.
2. Individual investors are accredited investors if they meet either the Net Worth Threshold or the Income Threshold.
3. An individual with a net worth or joint net worth with a spouse or spousal equivalent of at least $1 million, not including the value of his or her primary residence, meets the Net Worth Threshold.

4. Once an individual qualifies as an accredited investor by meeting a financial threshold, they may not retain accredited investor status if they later fail to meet the specified threshold. It is evident that the SEC does not believe that wealth makes an investor sophisticated to navigate private markets.
5. An individual with income exceeding $200,000 in each of the two most recent calendar years or joint income with a spouse or spousal equivalent exceeding $300,000 for those years and a reasonable expectation of the same income level in the current year meets the Income Threshold.
6. Investors must satisfy an issuer at the time of applying to invest in a private offering. Issuers of private securities are required to vet their investor base to ensure each investor is accredited. Investors that are accredited are not always accredited if they later fail to meet either test.
7. Most current accredited investors are either unaware that they are accredited or choose not to exercise this power by investing in private offerings.
8. It is a reasonable assumption that the median American household will meet the definition of an accredited investor at some point during their lifetime for a variety of reasons.

Chapter 3 - Population of Accredited Investors and Future Trends

Since the concept of accredited investor was introduced in 1978, the qualifying ranks have steadily increased to the present day. The SEC estimates that 9.4% of U.S. households qualify as accredited investors by meeting the Net Worth Threshold. In addition, 8.9% of households qualify as accredited investors under the individual Income Threshold of $200,000, and 4.6% of households qualify under the joint Income Threshold of $300,000. Obviously, there is some overlap in the theoretical Venn Diagram of the Net Worth Threshold and the Income Threshold qualifiers. In total, the SEC estimates that 13% of households qualify as accredited investors in or near 2019, which, in the SEC's estimation, amounts to 10 million accredited investors.12

While ten million is a considerable number, it is estimated that only 300,000 or so accredited investors, or 3% actual participate in private offerings. As one might imagine, it is very difficult to get precise numbers given the vast universe of private asset classes and sponsors. The general inference is that there is a general lack of awareness, justified fear or mystique about private offerings, or a lack of educational resources to help navigate the private offering world. Where awareness exists, there may simply not be enough liquid resources available to the newly minted accredited investors to adequately diversify in this class of investments. An investor with a $1 million net worth will be less likely to invest in alternative private assets than an investor with a $100 million net worth.

As recently as 2018, "Companies raised $2.9 trillion in private markets, compared to $1.4 trillion in public markets..."13 Private investment offerings represent a significant market, but only an elite group of investors may access these potentially lucrative private deals. This points to the inequality of the current securities registration system and also reinforces the need for the public to advance their education and sophistication with regard to private opportunities. The SEC, through their exemption framework, rightfully has the goal of protecting smaller investors who do not have the same resources as large institutional investors to evaluate and select the best investments or to defend themselves in cases of fraud. Education is the key equalizer for the future. The theme of this book is to couple better education and awareness with more innovative approaches for individual investors to piggyback on the economies of scale possessed by large, sophisticated investors. For example, allowing access to private funds through intermediaries such as financial advisors and crowdfunding platforms at lower minimum investment thresholds. From a macro perspective, the amount of funding for venture capital, private equity, and real estate syndications is only a fraction of what could potentially be available if the definition of accredited investor were expanded to include new classes of investors that do possess a certain level of financial sophistication.

What about the composition of the estimated 10 million accredited investors? There is little dispute that the current financial thresholds to join the ranks of accredited investors is a blunt instrument with inherent inequalities. The median USA household income was $67,521 in 2020, per the U.S Census Bureau. There is still a clear gap between that number and the $200,000-$300,000 thresholds required on a consistent basis to be and remain an accredited investor.

Obvious inequities in the current framework are geographical, gender, and racial. The Northeast and West regions of the USA are disproportionately represented in the ranks of accredited investors since they have higher incomes and wealth on average. Median incomes were highest in the Northeast ($75,211) and the West ($74,951), followed by the Midwest ($66,968) and the South ($61,243).[14] Where you live impacts the level of access to private investments. Per the 2020 Census, the "Female-to-Male Earnings Ratio and Median Earnings of Full-Time, Year-Round Workers 15 Years and Older" was 83%, higher than historically but still significantly different.[15] Accordingly, women are less likely to qualify as accredited investors. Median Household Income for Black and Hispanic households were $45,870 and $55,321, respectively, or 68% and 82% of the average for all households in 2020.[16] It is not difficult to project that there will be increasing political pressure on the SEC to modernize the exemption framework to address these basic inequalities in the future. To be fair, the SEC has taken steps to liberalize the definition of accredited investor over the last three years.

Trends Impacting Qualifying as an Accredited Investor

The fundamental trade-off that the SEC makes when it reviews the private market exemption framework, which includes the definition of an accredited investor, is protecting the public (retail investors) from incurring losses due to a lack of appropriate knowledge versus the need for small businesses to raise capital and grow the overall economy.

SEC Commissioner Caroline Crenshaw eloquently described the fundamental issues in her dissenting opinion on November 2, 2020, to the rule revisions of the Harmonization of Securities Offering Exemptions.

> *"Entrepreneurs, particularly very small and traditionally underserved businesses, should have efficient access to capital. We should consider whether there is a fair way to broaden access for small, diverse companies while still fulfilling our duty to protect investors. Right now, high-growth companies are increasingly deciding to remain private, benefiting groups of experienced and well-funded professional investors. It seems that "you have to start rich to get rich" in the private markets. Today, we do not fix that problem. Expanding access to the private markets as the Commission has done repeatedly recently not only fails to serve the majority's stated goal of advancing the interests of small businesses and retail investors, it opens these markets to a class of investors who do not have the capital to survive one or two failed ventures."* [17]

This quote reaffirms what is already known, that plenty of work remains to improve the framework related to private markets. Existing rules are very arbitrary, a blunt instrument, and in many respects unfair. The rich get richer. We need more creative ways to solve the problem in the future. It seems unlikely that future changes will serve to restrict private companies' access to capital, as this would negatively impact economic growth and make it more difficult politically. All the trends by the SEC and other governmental entities support the goal of **expanding** the number of accredited investors. A material exception to this generalization was in 2012 when the

SEC Amended the Accredited Investor Net Worth Standards to exclude the equity value of the investor's primary residence from the $1 million Net Worth Threshold for individuals. The SEC saw the wisdom of putting a speedbump in the path of investors betting their home equity on a new technology start-up, for example.

In fact, certain things the SEC is not doing support this outlook. One clear omission over the past 40 years has been a lack of an indexing mechanism for the Net Worth Threshold or Income Thresholds for inflation. With no indexing mechanism, more investors qualify if their incomes just keep up with inflation. The Securities and Exchange Commission updated the definition of an accredited investor in its final rules dated December 8, 2020.[18] The issue of inflation-indexed was discussed in great detail with the following arguments:

For Indexing Net Worth Threshold	Against Indexing Net Worth Threshold
Unadjusted thresholds have lowered the level of sophistication required for accredited investor status over time.	It would adversely affect certain real estate investors and be unfair to existing accredited investors.
SEC actions and inactions over the past forty years have had the effect of lessening investor protections.	Availability of information has improved since the inception of definition; financial tests are less useful in determining "sophistication."
	A significant reduction in the accredited investor pool through an increase in the definition's financial thresholds could have disruptive effects (for private markets)

In the end, they decided to leave the thresholds at existing levels. There does not appear to be any strong momentum to increase these thresholds in the foreseeable future.

The ability for issuers to advertise private offerings creates more accredited investor awareness of private offerings, and this is an example of further liberalization of private markets. The JOBS Act of 2012 (JOBS Act) liberalized advertising of private issues. Prior to the JOBS Act, the Rule 506 exemption prohibited issuers from general advertising of offerings. The JOBS Act required the SEC to allow general advertising in cases where all purchasers of the securities are deemed accredited, and the issuer takes reasonable steps to verify that all the purchasers are accredited.

Rule 506 of Regulation D is now divided into the following two offering type categories:

- 506(b) – No advertising. These are more popular in terms of issuer volume. Can accept up to 35 non-accredited investors. Non-accredited investors represented only 6% of Rule 506(b) offerings in 2015-2018, an indication of issuers' reluctance to include them due to additional disclosure requirements and costs. This is a potential way for non-accredited investors to enter private offerings, but only if they

have a pre-existing relationship with the deal sponsor. This would likely be the case with smaller real estate syndications with newer sponsors.
- 506(c) – Permits issuer advertising but only allows sales to accredited investors and requires them to perform the necessary due diligence to ensure all investors are accredited.

The ability to solicit is relatively new, and investor awareness of private offerings has steadily improved over the past decade. Every day, there is a new real estate syndication offering appearing in my Instagram feed. The negative aspect of this is that certain issuers appearing in my Instagram feed are inexperienced in the marketplace and have had known problems inside the commercial real estate sector. Education, planning, enhanced access to information, and due diligence processes that can guide and assist accredited investors will be the key to being ready to evaluate the merits of this general solicitation.

The definition of an accredited investor is also relevant to Regulation A, adopted by the SEC in 1936 and amended in 2015 by the JOBS Act (Regulation A+). Regulation A+ is an exemption from registration requirements for certain companies, providing them a competitive advantage versus having to register. As a result of the JOBS Act, there are two tiers of Regulation A offerings:

- Tier 1. Capital raise limit in one year up to $20 million.
- Tier 2. Capital raise limit in one year up to $75 million (raised from $50 million in March 2021). Tier 2 offerings have more extensive disclosure requirements than Tier 1, but they preempt state registration requirements. This makes Tier 2 much more attractive to issuers. Non-accredited investors are limited as to how much they can invest in a Tier 2 offering to no more than 10% of the greater of annual income or net worth of natural persons. So, as more AIs are generated in the future, there will be more Regulation A Tier 2 offerings as well.

Groundfloor is an example of an early-stage platform for house flipping projects. They started as a Tier 1 company and put a lot of effort into converting to a Tier 2 company to be able to sell their offerings in all 50 states. Yieldstreet REITS also appears to utilize these provisions of Regulation A. A more detailed discussion of these platforms will be provided in Chapter 5.

August 2020 Amendment to Definition of Accredited Investor

In August 2020, the SEC announced amendments to the accredited investor definition, which added new categories of qualifying natural persons (individuals) and entities and made certain other modifications to the existing definition. The most significant changes were the following:

1. Add a new category to the definition that permits natural persons to qualify as accredited investors based on certain professional certifications, designations or, credentials, or other credentials issued by an accredited educational institution, which the Commission may designate from time to time by order. Initially, this means holders in good standing of the Series 7, Series 65, and Series 82 licenses as

qualifying natural persons. This approach provides the Commission with the flexibility to add certifications, designations, or credentials in the future.
2. Include as accredited investors, with respect to investments in a private fund, natural persons who are "knowledgeable employees" of the fund.
3. Add the term "spousal equivalent" to the accredited investor definition so that spousal equivalents may pool their finances for the purpose of qualifying as accredited investors.
4. Add limited liability companies with $5 million in assets may be accredited investors.
5. Add SEC- and state-registered investment advisers and exempt reporting advisers.
6. Add a new category for any entity, including Indian tribes, governmental bodies, funds, and entities organized under the laws of foreign countries, that own "investments," as defined in Rule 2a51-1(b) under the Investment Company Act, in excess of $5 million and that was not formed for the specific purpose of investing in the securities offered.
7. Add "family offices" with at least $5 million in assets under management and their "family clients," as each term is defined under the Investment Advisers Act.

Items 1-3 above are the most relevant for a typical individual investor. In particular, item 1 opens the door for an approach in which knowledgeable or sophisticated persons can qualify by achieving relevant designations – evidence of knowledge and not rigid financial tests. I can see this expanding over time to cover CPAs, lawyers, and potentially certain post-graduate degrees. For individuals who cannot qualify based on the financial thresholds, this provision promises to be the fastest way a person can become accredited in the future. The expansion of the definition is further evidence that more individuals will have access to private markets as accredited investors in the future. As more people become accredited investors, the main concern is that they are able to build a diversified portfolio of private investments, given the lower levels of net worth and liquid assets.

Changes Necessitated by the Proliferation of Crowdfunding

I would like to return briefly to the last sentence of Caroline Crenshaw's quote from above, where she states, "*It opens these markets to a class of investors who do not have the capital to survive one or two failed ventures.*" This is a significant and justified issue. Even investors that experience failure early on with a private offering and can survive financially will be hard-pressed to return after an initial negative experience. I consider myself in these ranks. Failure causes a lot of introspection and avoidance of whatever caused that pain. A major theme throughout this book is to provide knowledge and strategies to accredited investors to avoid a major loss early on. Crowdfunding platforms are not necessarily a panacea but are an important tool in the arsenal for investors to diversify and a higher level of oversight (the platform sponsor) performing filtering duties and due diligence related to their deal flow.

The JOBS Act also accelerated the growth of equity crowdfunding. The emergence of crowdfunding platforms over the past decade is an explosive trend that is a promising source for small businesses to raise capital and for investors to have more access to private investments. Title III of the JOBS Act, implemented in

2015 and amended in 2021, allows issuers to issue up to $5 million in equity, but the transaction must be conducted through an SEC-registered crowdfunding portal. The issuer is subject to disclosure requirements at the offering and on an annual basis, but the investors can include an unlimited number of non-accredited investors. Accredited investors could already invest using crowdfunding portals, but I am sure many would welcome the increased regulation on issuers to better inform them on investment decisions. More regulation on the issuers and the crowdfunding platforms is a vital part of improving the existing system of crowdfunding for all investors.

The overall framework of exemptions that affect accredited investors has expanded over the years, as described. It is confusing, but the growth provides more exemptions and more potential opportunities for investors. Figure 7 summarizes the principal exemptions, starting with the private placement exemption of Section 4(a)(2) of the 1933 Act, which is the largest in terms of volume but impacts institutional investors only.

Figure 7: Framework of Exceptions from Registration for Raising Capital					
	Capital Raise Limit	Solicitation Allowed	Investor Status	Preemption State Registration	Intermediary Required
Section 4(a)(2)	None	No	Private placements (not to general public)	No	NA
Rule 506(b) of Regulation D	None	No	Unlimited accredited investors. Up to thirty-five sophisticated but non-AI	Yes	No
Rule 506(c) of Regulation D	None	Yes	Unlimited accredited investors	Yes	No
Regulation A: Tier 1	$20 million	Permitted	All investors	No	No
Regulation A: Tier 2	$75 million	Permitted	Non-accredited investors are subject to investment limits based on annual income and net worth	Yes	No
Title III Regulation Crowdfunding; (2015, 2021)	$5 million	Limits on advertising. Offering must offered on an internet platform through a SEC-registered intermediary.	Investment limits based on annual income and net worth. Minimum 5% of income or net worth if either is less than $100,000;	Yes	Yes, online portals

Where do we go from here? The socio-political pressures are to further liberalize the definition of accredited investors, moving more towards qualifications, sophistication, and common-sense measures. The SEC's Advisory Committee on Small and Emerging Markets (now the Small Business Capital Formation Advisory Committee) has repeatedly recommended the SEC expand the pools of accredited investors. Congress also has an interest in expanding the ranks of accredited investors. Two House of Representatives bills in 2016 and 2017, respectively, urged the SEC to revise the definition to increase access and fairness of the regulations. Both bills failed the Senate. Despite the 2020 amendments by the SEC, the definition of an accredited investor has remained relatively unchanged since 1982.

Impact on Investors

The concept of accredited investors is not likely to be scrapped in favor of allowing all investors to access private market assets. But based on the recent history and deliberations of the SEC, it will be very difficult to roll back to making the definition more restrictive. Such a rollback would not be fair to existing accredited investors, but more importantly, it would restrict capital available to small businesses and private syndication markets. The most probable scenario is that there will be further liberalization of the rules, the creation of new categories of investors that are more closely linked to proven sophistication measures, and that, ultimately, more investors will qualify and have access to private market offerings. Regulations do need to be maintained to protect investors, and the best way for investors to protect themselves is to increase their knowledge and abilities to understand the world of accredited investing.

There are two primary ways that the SEC can achieve concurrently the goals of protecting the public and fostering economic growth: (1) increased regulation of issuers in terms of enhanced disclosures and (2) expanding the number of investors that qualify for accredited status. More disclosure requirements level the field for investors willing to do the research. Excessive new disclosure requirements defeat the purpose of exempt offering provisions, which is to reduce the cost and administrative burden for small issuers. The recent expansion for Regulation A mentioned previously is an example of expanding the exemption to include new investor populations in exchange for more formal initial and ongoing disclosure requirements imposed on the sponsors of offerings.

More disclosure only goes so far in protecting investors the further down the road we proceed towards allowing retail investors access to private offerings. Today, there are 44 states that manage lottery programs in the USA. Theoretically, I think an investor with $10,000 in the bank can use it all on lottery tickets. I have not tried it. That same person cannot invest $10,000 in a private multi-family property investment, an asset class that reliably provides an internal rate of return of 10-20%. In the case of the lottery, if you read the rules and the small print, a player has all the information necessary to make an informed decision to buy the tickets. That does not make it a smart decision. And who reads the fine print on a lottery ticket other than Jerry from the movie *Jerry and Marge Go Large*? With the private multi-family deal, the SEC's concern is that the investor does not necessarily have all the vital information in the offering documents to make an informed investment decision. The standard is not so much whether the investor is making a smart decision but whether they have the data to make an informed decision. That is apparently what the SEC is concerned about. Unfortunately, most retail investors will not read the small print. Knowing this, the accredited investor concept will remain in place and evolve gradually over time.

There are a variety of creative ways in which the definition of accredited investor could be liberalized in the future. Three categories of characteristics to consider are (1) an investor's financial and business acumen, (2) an investor's individual characteristics of sophistication, and (3) an investor's specific behavior.[19] Financial acumen can be measured by professional status, investment experience, history of private investing, or professional experience in the securities industry. Individual characteristics include the investor's level of education, wealth, or income. Investment-specific behavior might be the total amount invested in private securities, the number of private transactions participated in, or involvement with a wealth advisor or financial planner.

Specifically, the following list provides possible methods for expanding the ranks of accredited investors in the future taken from academic research and SEC past deliberations:

1. Individuals who have certain types of educational backgrounds are verified by a government body.
2. Individuals who have certain business experiences and professional accreditations.
3. Individuals who invest minimal amounts. This would be simple to do but may not impact overall investment levels due to the high minimum investment requirements of private offerings.
4. Investors who have experience investing in exempt offerings.
5. Individuals who work in and are knowledgeable about private sponsors and their markets.
6. Examination for accredited investors, reducing the unfairness of allowing only the wealthy to participate in private offerings.

With its recent amendments to the accredited investor definition by the SEC in 2020, the barn door is now opened for item #2. Ditto for #3 with other regulatory changes such as Regulation A, Tier II. Personally, I think there is no better experience than that of actually investing in private offerings, and building a portfolio, and learning. Grandfathering existing accredited investors who demonstrate a history of investing in private offerings (a minimum dollars invested threshold over a defined period, such as the last 24 months) would also help in cases where an individual previously qualified under the Income Threshold but now does not, but has years of experience in private markets. Lastly an examination for accredited offerings would open the door for anyone with the desire to learn and study to become a provisional accredited investor. A premium should be placed on tests or actual experience that demonstrate knowledge and understanding of how the private markets function, as well as the associated risks and benefits. The reality is there will likely be a combination of the above methods for qualification in the future. The expanding ranks of accredited investors will represent a formidable source of new capital for creating new ventures or improving existing businesses. For investors, accredited status provides more options for creating passive income, building generational wealth, and at least a decent retirement.

Quick Summary

1. Accredited investors are a large and growing group, estimated at over 10 million.

2. The population of accredited investors is underinvested in private offerings, either lacking awareness, education, or confidence to invest in alternative asset classes.
3. The framework of exempts for SEC registration requirements has been expanding, and the definition of accredited investors has introduced new categories based on non-financial tests, such as credentialing.
4. New platforms are arriving on the scene to take advantage of the expanded framework, providing accredited and non-accredited investors with the opportunity to diversify into alternative asset classes.
5. It is possible that accredited status will someday be attainable by any person or household that obtains an appropriate credential license or demonstrates the desire to learn and pass an examination on the topic.
6. Even if an investor remains non-accredited, there are emerging new forces and technologies that will allow investors access to the asset classes favored by the wealthy.

Chapter 4 - Favored Asset Classes of the Wealthy

Accredited investors have a wide variety of private asset classes available to choose from. Four such private asset classes include hedge funds, private equity, venture capital, and real estate syndications. These asset classes will be reviewed in order of accessibility, from the most difficult for accredited investors to invest to the easiest, in my experience. There are other asset classes, basically any private opportunities with a general partner / limited partner structure. Natural resources are another example. We will focus on the aforementioned categories.

Hedge Funds

Hedge funds are investment pools that invest in alternative asset classes, utilizing alternative investment strategies in pursuit of earning high absolute returns. Hedge funds consist of the manager, or general partner, and a limited number of investors, or limited partners. The manager earns a fee based on assets managed and a performance fee. Hedge funds are not regulated by the Investment Company Act of 1940 as mutual funds are. They are part of the SEC's overall framework for private investments, as previously described.

In contrast, mutual funds are "long-only" vehicles, benefiting when the market moves higher. This is fine until events such as the global financial crisis in 2007-2009 or the 2022 inflation scare occur. Hedge funds are designed to perform much better during down or choppy markets, thus the term "hedge." Many market participants view hedge funds as a tool for diversifying an overall portfolio, not necessarily to outperform the market. This is not dissimilar to your goal as an accredited investor, to create higher returns with less units of risk for your entire portfolio by allocating a percentage of investable assets to private asset classes.

Hedge funds are shrouded in mystery and controversy. Their managers are considered the elite or all-stars of investment management, smarter than the market, and extremely wealthy themselves. It is difficult to get exact aggregate hedge fund market metrics at any given time. There were approximately 8,142 hedge funds at the end of the second quarter of 2020, excluding funds of funds, a moderate decline since this number peaked in 2015 when there were 8,474 funds.20 As of the 4th Quarter of 2022, total assets under management (AUM) for the hedge fund industry was $4.8 trillion.21 If your money were not being treated well in the aggregate, the growth in hedge funds would not continue. A top hedge fund, Citadel, describes on its website, "We will explore any territory in pursuit of an idea, taking unconventional approaches and making big, bold investments in unexpected places." Does that give you a perfect understanding of where your investment monies are going?

Cliff Asness of AQR Capital Management describes it this way, "Hedge funds are generally perceived to be the investment of choice of the rich and the informed, and they are more interesting and fun to discuss than your Vanguard index fund." Given the mystery and vagueness, do hedge funds fit into your plan to build wealth with a private-passive strategy?

Hedge fund strategies fall broadly into four main categories:

1. **Long/Short Equity**: Taking a long position in a stock that they expect to rise and a short position (betting it will go down) in a stock that they expect will fall.
2. **Relative Value:** Generally called arbitrage, strategies seek to take advantage of spreads between highly correlated securities.
3. **Event Driven:** Capitalizing on events inside a particular company and exploiting perceived pricing anomalies, including merger arbitrage.
4. **Directional:** Including strategies that take advantage of the trends in global markets and tend to be leveraged.

A detailed review of these strategies is beyond the scope of this book, but I list them to pique your interest. For a more detailed explanation, start with Anthony Scaramucci's *The Little Book of Hedge Funds*. Making it more difficult to analyze hedge funds is their use of multi-asset construction to achieve their objectives, including commodities, stocks, bonds, options, and even cryptocurrencies. A general thesis of hedge funds is that markets are inefficient. At any time, there is a rich pool of inefficiencies in the market upon which hedge fund managers practice their contrarian ways.

The common themes with all major classes of private assets are lack of liquidity and the use of leverage. As an investor, your mindset must be to tuck away your capital for long periods, and the cash inflows will come later to fund your life or to reinvest. The use of leverage to enhance returns is a key feature of many of the asset classes covered herein, with the exception of venture capital, which has enough business risk that leverage is not necessary to generate outsized returns.

Hedge fund managers typically earn an annual management fee on assets under management of between 1.0%-2.0% and a performance fee of 20% of the profits. Accordingly, for every $1 million invested, the annual fees would be approximately $15,000. If the fund makes $500,000 in profits, the manager will earn $100,000 and the investors $400,000. The fees are high, as with all private investment vehicles, but it works since the fund manager has a large stake in the fund, referred to as "eating their own cooking." High fees attract the best talent, and as long as the interests of the general partner and investors are aligned, this type of capitalism works. Similar to mutual funds, the best managers beat the market each year, but there is a large contingent of hedge funds that underperform the market.

Who are the typical investors in hedge funds? Whereas hedge funds started as a darling for the Uber wealth of the world, hedge fund investing is now an institutional game, with over 75% of assets being institutionally owned.22 Institutional investors include public and private pensions, foundations, endowments, and insurance companies. The largest single category of investors is termed "Funds of hedge funds." Fund of funds raise capital from wealthy individuals and institutions to invest in a basket of hedge funds. Herein rests the hope for the average accredited investor for getting hedge fund access in the future. This is the domain for sophisticated, accredited investors, not appropriate for individual investors with a degree of wealth but possessing no clue about investing in hedge funds.

How can accredited investors get access to great hedge funds? Hedge funds generally have a limited number of participating investors, and the minimum investment requirements can range from $500,000 to $10 million and upwards. Hedge fund investors are still an exclusive club that has access to some of the greatest minds. Accordingly, only the top percentiles of accredited investors will have access directly to the best hedge funds. If you have a portfolio exceeding, say, $5 million and can allocate up to 5% of your assets to hedge funds, your choices are (1) go through a financial advisor or (2) locate a fund of funds that will make the decisions for you. You need help, and the best approach is to leverage the skills of experts to locate and invest in hedge funds. The due diligence process alone is daunting.

The fund of hedge funds approach is interesting, but even today, it does not seem to cater to the average accredited investor. On the positive side, these vehicles provide access by aggregating funds from accredited investors with minimums as low as $50,000. They also provide diversification, as they invest in 30-50 funds, spreading the funds over multiple investment strategies. On the negative side, the fund-of-funds structure adds another layer of fees of 1-2% for the investor, but worth it versus trying to do it yourself.

If your desire for status drives you to invest in hedge funds, limit your exposure to 2% of your portfolio and seek the help of a financial advisor. Due to the large part they play in managing your money, you want to ensure any hedge fund manager is qualified to handle your money. You can review a hedge fund manager's disciplinary history, fees, and investment strategy by looking at their Form ADV. You can find this form on their website or using the SEC's Investment Adviser Public Disclosure database:

IAPD - Investment Adviser Public Disclosure - Homepage (sec.gov)

I don't see hedge funds as a reliable, predictable way to generate attractive passive income over the long term. The lack of transparency regarding what is in the portfolio concerns me. Locating a good hedge fund seems similar to chasing a hot mutual fund manager – there always seems to be a reversion to the mean at some point. Ideally, you would want a fund of funds that provides expertise and diversification benefits, and this can only be achieved with a portfolio of at least $5 million, probably more. It would be an inspiring goal for any accredited investor to be able to have a slice of their alternatives in hedge funds – a signal that you have already created generational wealth. I am doing a pass for the average accredited investor. Unlike the other asset classes covered in this chapter, hedge funds are investment funds, not real businesses that can reliably generate wealth for investors. This is a key distinction. I want to have a clear idea of the underlying assets that I am investing in. Accordingly, this book will not address hedge funds further, but developments in this space should be monitored.

Private Equity

Private equity refers to investment firms that invest in or acquire private companies that are not listed on a public stock exchange. These storied firms generally utilize a fund approach to hold a group of investments organized by vintages (i.e., 2019). These private equity funds may also buy out public companies, take them private, and then collaborate with their hand-picked management teams to restructure them for potential future growth.

The process begins with deal teams that seek undervalued businesses, public or private, that may be the result of poor management or macro events creating dislocations in the economy. Typical private equity firms have specialties in certain industries or verticals, but the largest private equity firms are industry-agnostic. Generally, they will take a controlling interest in a company, employing large amounts of leverage in the acquisition to enhance the returns for the fund while increasing the number of companies that will ultimately reside in the fund. The deal team that drove the underlying investment and advocated for the transaction remains with the project to assist management in implementing new strategies to create value over the investment horizon of five to seven years. The firm will take seats on the Board of Directors and typically will chair the Board. The team is continuously focused on the ultimate payday, the exit. Exit strategies include selling to a large corporation, taking the company public, or possibly selling the company to another private equity firm. Another "exit" option is to sell the investment to the next vintage fund for that private equity firm if more time is needed to generate the optimal value of the company. This last option, an internal recapitalization, is also not unusual in private real estate syndications.

Venture capital is a type of private equity firm that will be addressed separately. Private equity tends to focus more on mature, larger companies as opposed to early-stage ventures. Private equity also has various financing groups and can provide debt financing, equity financing, and combinations thereof. It would not be unusual for debt financing to be a gateway to increased improvement or the ultimate takeover of the target company at a later date.

At the core of a successful private equity firm's success is access to exceptional talent, including outside experts, libraries of information, vision, experience, and flexibility to strike when market conditions allow. The financial and operational aspects of any deal are crafted synergistically to optimize returns to investors. The private equity mindset is that every deal will provide an excellent return – failure is not an accepted outcome, even in a portfolio context. Deal teams are aligned on achieving the target IRR throughout the life of the investment. There are simplistically three phases of a project: one-third the acquisition phase, one-third the asset management phase, and one-third the exit phase.22

How can individual investors, accredited or not, compete with the skill of a proven private equity firm? They cannot. An important part of the plan for any accredited investor is to learn how to piggyback on the skill and expertise of any private equity fund sponsor to align your interests with theirs. A major caveat is that this asset class is still not directly accessible to most accredited investors.

How do private equity firms make money? Each vintage fund may hold 10-20 investments. The larger funds can exceed $2 billion in assets, and each deal may represent 5-10% of the total fund capital. A typical fund life would be 10 years, with a few one-year options to extend. There may even be perpetual funds for investors with even longer-term investment horizons. Private equity firms make their money patiently. The industry norm is that they earn a 2% asset management fee and 20% of the profits over a minimum hurdle internal rate of return. To exhibit their own conviction, private equity firms can co-invest and put some of their own money in a fund. In addition to this general rule, transaction fees are earned based on gross proceeds of debt and equity issuances to target companies. Exit fees based on sale proceeds may also be charged, reducing the return to the investors.

The private equity industry would not be successful if investors were not pleased with the results. The size of the private equity industry is enormous and continuously growing. Underlying this is the alignment of monetary incentives between the firms and investors. A reasonable expectation for investor returns would be 20%, net of fees. In evaluating firms in any asset class, accredited investors should always ask the question, are my returns and the returns of the sponsor aligned, and how? If you were to invest in a private equity fund as a retail investor, and the result was a return in the range of 12-14%, is the return commensurate with the risk? Probably not.

Typical investors in private equity are large institutions, including large pension funds, sovereign wealth funds, insurance companies, and high-net-worth families. It is possible for accredited investors to get access through intermediaries such as financial advisors. Large financial or wealth management advisory firms can act as feeders or aggregators of a group of large checks from accredited investors to invest in a particular private equity fund.

Investors called limited partners (LPs) fund private equity funds, with the firm or its affiliates acting as general partner (GPs) firms. LPs provide the capital for the private equity funds used to make investments. Most of the capital provided to funds comes from the LPs. LPs can expect their money to be tied up for five to 10 years, at which point they would gradually be repaid their capital and profits. LPs cannot lose more than their investment since they have limited liability.

Proof that private equity is still a game for large institutions, higher education endowments with over $1 billion in assets allocated 14.7% of their portfolios to private equity in 2020. However, endowments with under $25 million in assets allocated only 2.1% of their portfolios to private equity in 2020. 24 Note that these allocations do not include other private-passive asset classes, only private equity. Retail or individual investors need to manage their expectations with regard to private equity when developing their ideal portfolio allocation, assuming they can find opportunities to invest in private equity funds. The reality is that you will need at least $75,000-$100,000 to invest directly into a private equity vintage fund, and the money will be tied up for 10-13 years. With innovation in the crowdfunding arena, these minimum investment requirements have come down over the past decade. For portfolio allocation purposes for individuals, it really depends on your overall level of net worth and liquidity. The above benchmarks suggest an allocation to private equity of 10% or less.

There are key attributes to look for in successful private equity firms. They tend to be a tight-knit group of visionary partners that make all the important decisions. Although they become experts and focus on certain industry sectors, they have the creativity and skill to develop new areas of expertise and succeed. A competitive drive enables this mindset. The best leaders in private equity believe it is much more than making money. It is about advancing society and communities by improving their portfolio companies for the benefit of all of their stakeholders while providing strong returns to investors. Their focus is totally on outcomes in terms of the rate of return to their funds on a long-term basis.

How can accredited investors get access to private equity? Slowly, private equity is going retail, but it is still difficult to get access to for newly-minted accredited investors. The regulatory hurdles and the industry appetite for private equity to target individuals are still real barriers. Increased access to private equity funds is a trend that accredited investors need to get ahead of with awareness and education. In the meantime, access through financial advisers that pool client assets to make a large contribution to a private equity fund is a method of access. Alternatively, investing in the public stocks of the largest private equity firms is a way to get exposure to this asset class. Examples of public equities include Blackstone (BX), The Carlyle Group (CG), and the Invesco Global Listed Private Equity ETF (PSP). This will be addressed in more detail in the next chapter. Remember again, "small" university endowments with under $25 million in assets allocated only approximately 2.1% of their portfolios to private equity, and your portfolio should reflect a similar conservative allocation to the private equity asset class. Any investment vehicle aimed at the public will have to offer good diversification. Finding private equity funds that fit into a relatively small asset allocation is a challenge for individuals who are not uber-wealthy.

Venture Capital

Venture capital (VC) firms are a subset of the private equity. They just happen to specialize in start-up and early-stage businesses with significant long-term potential. What they do is very similar to traditional private equity, except they are investing in more risky nascent businesses.

How do venture capitalists make money? The practices of venture capital firms are remarkably similar to private equity. They typically create fund products sequentially numbered or in vintages. The industry norm is that they earn a 2% asset management fee and 20% of the profits on their investments, with some variations to the rule. The major difference is the expectation around portfolio performance. Since the underlying companies are at the early stage, some without revenues, the expectation is that about 30% of the investments will not be successful, 40% will muddle along, and the majority of the fund's return will come from 30% of the holdings. More risk and variability of returns occur inside a venture capital portfolio than with a mutual fund or with a private equity portfolio.

Typical investors in private equity are large institutions; however, with a smaller portfolio allocation than investors in private equity. To illustrate, higher education endowments with over $1 billion in assets allocated 10.8% of their portfolios to venture capital funds in 2020 (vs. 14.8% allocation to private equity). Endowments with under $25 million in assets allocated only .5% of their portfolios to venture capital in 2020 (vs. 2.1% allocation to private equity).25 Large institutions are more risk-averse, meaning they have less appetite for venture capital. Which investor groups fill this gap?

Wealthy individuals make up the majority of the difference, and unfortunately, more and more accredited investors are at the lower end of the wealth spectrum. I say this because single-asset venture capital deals and venture capital funds are much more accessible to accredited investors than private equity, and venture capital is inherently riskier. The return expectation should be north of 20% due to the additional risk associated with early-stage companies. Investors should set a maximum allocation in their alternative portfolios that is relatively modest in the 0-10% range. And they should stick to venture capital fund products only. Investing in any single venture is a form of gambling in which investors can expect to lose an entire stake.

How can accredited investors get access to venture capital? As I alluded to, it is relatively easy as crowdfunding sites are rapidly making venture investing mainstream. I approach this space with skepticism based on my past experience. If you want to invest in a single venture on a crowdfunding site, losses will likely be the result. Once a venture funds a round, investor relations on a post-funding basis are typically non-existent. It will be frustrating and painful if you want to find out what is going on at the company. Early-stage companies have a long-term horizon and don't have to provide any information as they build (or don't) their businesses. My first two single-asset ventures went bust. My next two are still alive, will not be unicorns, and will be my last investments in single ventures.

I have a more favorable view of venture capital funds with proven track records that accept accredited investors with minimum investment requirements of $50,000-$100,000. Crowdfunding is the subject of a later chapter, but suffice it to say that the platform matters. Do your due diligence on the platform and understand the level of vetting they do for their posted offerings. At a minimum, the information provided should cover the detailed profile and track record of the venture capital fund sponsoring the investment. I don't recommend investing in the hypothetical Acme Ventures Fund #1. Ideally, it is a later vintage with at least one vintage fully realized and closed. Venture fund sponsors will usually provide a status report or track record on all the funds being offered leading up to the current vintage.

My sample size with venture funds is small, but I invested in three in the 2018-2019 time period. All investments were offered via one excellent crowdfunding platform but quite different approaches. The performance through September 30, 2022, below should take into account that all the funds are halfway through their terms, but consider that they went through COVID-19 and the 2022 inflationary environment.

- Proven Silicon Valley VC firm, Fund vintage > #10. Invested 2019. Multiple 1.53x initial investment.
- Platform-managed collection of fifty investments. The crowdfunding firm vets the companies from their marketplace and selects fifty to include in the portfolio. My analogy is "throwing darts at a dartboard," and as expected, it has worked. Invested 2018, Multiple 1.7x initial investment.
- Specialized healthcare fund, first in a vintage. Invested 2019. Multiple 1.22x. The lack of diversification and the inexperience of the manager have hurt performance, but at least not losing money. COVID-19 should have been the most bullish thing that could have happened for this fund. It may still be. There is a long way to go.

The bottom line is that funds provide investors with the necessary diversification, which is critical to generating consistent returns in early-stage ventures. Start investing with a sponsor using the minimum required investment, and learn which proven sponsors you want to develop long-term relationships with based on actual experience. One final note: venture capital funds provide professional quarterly reporting and audits, unlike single-asset venture capital investments that leave you begging for information on their progress.

Commercial Real Estate Syndication

Commercial real estate syndicators/sponsors offer a wide variety of opportunities for accredited investors. Investors have the opportunity to create a diverse portfolio of real estate to meet their objectives, whether it is generating passive income, growth through appreciation, or a blend of growth and income. Minimum investment requirements for projects typically start at $25,000 to $100,000 or above. Crowdfunding platforms have contributed to the growth of this sector to the point where many sponsors are finding it more efficient to use crowdfunding as their primary distribution and investor relations arm. An additional unique feature of investing in commercial real estate is strong income tax benefits that are incentivized in the IRS Code. The availability of accelerated depreciation, for example, can result in large streams of tax-free passive income for many years until a project exits.

Commercial real estate syndication refers to an ecosystem where sponsors seek out properties in private transactions. To finance these transactions, debt finance is utilized for between 50-70% of the capital structure (or "capital stack"), and equity from investors makes up the remainder. All of these elements or financing together are termed the sources of capital. There can be mezzanine or preferred equity between these two capital structure components. Similar to private equity, commercial real estate sponsors view their activities in three phases: the acquisition phase, the asset and property management phase, and the exit phase. All three are important, but in real estate, most agree that you make your money on the initial purchase transaction. That being said, poor property management can also submarine a deal. Vertically integrated firms provide all operating services internally, including underwriting, property and asset management, and construction. Others may outsource some of these functions. Great sponsors are always alert for an exit, and they consider multiple potential exit strategies. Syndication sponsors should be adding value at every phase of the investment process. The more established sponsors establish funds that are numbered sequentially, similar to venture capital or private equity, providing benefits to investors and sponsors.

Similar to private equity, all investment decisions rest with a tight-knit group of partners in the business, typically an investment committee led by a strong founder. The sponsor team is continuously focused on the ultimate payday, the exit. Exit strategies include a sale to another syndicator or an institutional investor or possibly selling the investment to another fund managed by that sponsor (recapitalization).

At the core of successful commercial real estate syndicator success is access to experienced talent, focusing and developing specialized expertise in specific sectors of real estate, libraries of information, vision, experience, and flexibility to strike when market conditions allow. Sectors can include multifamily, hotels, industrial, retail, office, storage, and others. Like private equity, the financial and operational aspects of any deal are crafted synergistically to optimize returns to investors. Deal teams are aligned on achieving the target IRR throughout the life of the investment. Successful sponsors should plan for what can go wrong and prepare in advance for contingencies that invariably will arise. Multiple exit scenarios are planned, and returns are conservatively modeled. The barriers to entry for sponsors are not very high, so experience and track record mean a lot in this business.

How do commercial real estate syndicators make money? Whether the sponsor deals in single assets or funds, the economics are similar. Each fund may hold 3-10 assets. A typical fund life might be 7-10 years, with several one-year options to extend. The fees appear higher in terms of percentages than private equity because the value of any individual deal is typically smaller than that of a private equity transaction. Sponsors make their money in many ways, and the industry norms are roughly as follows:

- Acquisition fee of 1.0 – 2.0% of the gross purchase price of a property.
- Asset management fee of 1.0 – 1.5% of revenues for asset administration, compliance, accounting, and reporting services.
- A loan funding fee of 0.5% – 1.5% of bank loan proceeds
- Property management fee of 3.0 – 3.5% of gross collected revenue.
- Construction management fee of 4.0 – 5.0% of the cost of construction or renovations. Varies for development projects vs. value-added projects.
- Sponsors promote our share of profits at exit after a preferred rate of return of, say, 8% and the return of all capital to investors. The "promote" is similar to the carried interest of private equity firms (20% of profits). Unlike private equity, the promotion provisions are highly variable and depend on many factors that will be covered in more detail later on.

To signal alignment of interests with investors, sponsors typically co-invest 5-10% of the total equity proceeds. It could be argued that with the myriad of fees above, the sponsor would be just fine without profits on the deal, but in reality, if they do not develop a strong track record, they will not be able to raise desired amounts of outside capital in the future. Investors are generally looking for a 13-20% internal rate of return on commercial real estate syndications.

The typical investors in real estate syndications are everyone. Large institutions, REITS, private equity first, insurance companies, high net worth families, and accredited investors. Accredited investors have a wide variety of options, single assets and funds. Participation is typical as limited partners (LPs) on single-asset projects, with the sponsor or its affiliates acting as general partners (GPs). LPs provide the equity capital required to close on property investments. As mentioned, GPs typically co-invest alongside the LPs to signal an alignment of interests. Besides bank financing, most of the capital provided to funds comes from LPs. LPs can expect their money to be tied up for 3-10 years, at which point they will ideally be repaid their capital and their share of the profits. Refinancing of projects in the earlier years is another way that LPs get distributions on projects. LPs cannot lose more than their investment since they have limited liability.

All syndicators have websites displaying their offerings. Networking and word of mouth are the best ways to learn about sponsors. Crowdfunding sites are ripe with deals and platforms such as Crowdstreet, Cadre, and Realty Mogul. These platforms are an excellent way for investors to learn about sponsors, but it appears that most sponsors on these platforms do not sell directly to investors; instead, they choose crowdfunding as their primary method of capital raising and distribution.

Accredited investors have ready access to private real estate deals and funds. The steady expansion of the SEC regulatory framework will continue to drive new innovative approaches to investing in real estate for both accredited and non-accredited investors. Accordingly, I recommend all investors increase their awareness and education in this space. Single-asset real estate deals are much safer than their counterparts in venture capital, so a higher portfolio allocation is warranted when designing a private-passive portfolio. I still recommend starting small and focusing on funds to get experience with sponsors and to continue an investor's learning process. My experience is there are always issues with any project. It is great that these projects are not marked to market like public equities. Going through the full cycle of a project will give investors a solid understanding of the plethora of factors that impact value, short-term or long-term. For example vacancy rates may have been projected at 5%, but the actual experience is closer to 10%. Hurricanes or other acts of nature impact value, including the cost of future insurance reserves. Investors will quickly learn what inferior property management looks like. On the other hand, not all is negative. Significant increases in property values due to macroeconomic and natural real estate cycles can result in large increases in property value, as witnessed during 2021 and 2022.

Quick Summary

1. Four asset classes favored by accredited investors include hedge funds, private equity, venture capital, and real estate syndications.
2. Hedge funds are generally collections of strategies for investing in public market assets – equities, bonds, commodities, futures, and even cryptocurrencies. The private-passive approach to investing prefers investing in real businesses and real estate projects (akin to Main Street investing).
3. Private-passive investors should learn about fund offerings from private equity and venture capital sponsors with strong track records and allocate a small percentage of their portfolio to this asset class. Access to these funds is provided through reputable crowdfunding platforms with reasonable minimum investment requirements.
4. Commercial real estate syndication is an asset class that provides tremendous potential to build a diversified portfolio across many sub-asset types and investment objectives, such as income, growth, or a combination thereof.

Chapter 5 - Private-Passive Investing, Learning by Doing

"Courage is resistance to fear, mastery of fear -- not absence of fear." Mark Twain

Becoming an accredited investor is a worthy goal and one that most households are consciously or unconsciously driving towards. Once there, the menu of private investment options increases significantly. Can a non-accredited investor build the necessary skills and qualifications by participating in certain private markets in which accredited investors spend their time or in public market proxies? The answer is yes, to some degree, by getting experience in the asset classes related to private equity and real estate. The pathway to becoming an accredited investor is likely one of the following:

Figure 8	
Public-Passive ⟶	Private-Passive ↑
Public-Active	Private-Active

Going from Public-Passive to Private-Passive means building investable assets by building wealth in public markets (equities, index funds, mutual funds) until the prerequisite net worth is attained. From Private-Active to Private-Passive means pathways such as investing in rental properties or side hustles in which more active involvement is required. Once accredited, the active investing persona can be transitioned to a more passive approach to investing.

Until an investor is accredited, the best proxy for investing in private markets is to gain more experience building a portfolio of public equities that mimic private equity and commercial real estate and taking a longer-term perspective. A patient mindset is required when investing in private equity funds, and investors should work on a mindset shift in the short term, a shift from checking prices every day to long-term results. The other major asset class is private real estate projects and funds offered by syndicators. Investors need to educate themselves on how to build a portfolio using the best proxies, such as public real estate investment trusts or REITS, both publicly traded and non-publicly traded types.

When we discuss the private investment plan creation process in Section III, one of the first steps is to determine asset allocation. Asset allocation is a very personal thing, depending on many factors. Thus, we will stick to the framework and not specific investment recommendations. Investors will need to decide how much of their overall portfolio, including retirement assets, will remain invested in traditional public equity and fixed income and how much to allocate to private investments available only to accredited investors. For example, let's use a conservative 25% allocation of the overall portfolio to private markets. As experience is gained in private markets, investors will learn their comfort level with private markets and can adjust this allocation accordingly. Remember, the Yale Model illustrated an allocation to private markets to a staggering 70% of total assets under management.

Learning by Doing

The discipline of managing an optimal portfolio allocation is a critical skill. In this regard, investing is never entirely a passive exercise. An investor must always be seeking to learn, do the research, and to simply be curious. Without those characteristics, private market investing could be a painful exercise. Practice the discipline of allocating a portion of your overall investable assets into private market alternatives and learn how to manage this small portfolio. The idea is to visualize that you are an accredited investor today and develop a plan for that segment of your portfolio in order to commence the long road to developing the necessary skills to be a private-passive investor. Even if you only have less than $100,000 to invest, you can begin to organize your finances to achieve accredited investor status faster and with confidence. There is a chance you will find this approach comfortable and successful enough that no adjustments will be necessary once accredited status is achieved.

Figure 9

	Target Allocation of Entire Investor Portfolio		
	Public Markets	Private Markets	Total Investments
$	300,000	$ 100,000	$ 400,000
	75%	25%	100%

	Target Allocation to Private-Passive Portfolio		
	Real Estate	Private Equity/VC	Total Investments
$	70,000	$ 30,000	$ 100,000
	70%	30%	100%
	Proxies	Proxies	
	Public REITS (traded)	EFTs	
	Public REITS (non-traded)	Mutual Funds	
	Alternative Platforms	Portfolio of Stocks	
	Achieve diversification within each segment		

Private real estate opportunities are more readily available to accredited investors than private equity or venture capital unless you have a large amount of wealth and access to a financial advisor or wealth manager. In the above example, the allocation of the "Private Markets Portfolio" is 70/30 real estate to private equity. The actual allocation will be purely a personal decision based on your comfort level and understanding of the various asset classes. Per Figure 9, $100,000 is allocated to the Private Market Portfolio and subsequently allocated 70% to real estate and 30% to private equity (broadly defined). How can you put this money to work in a way that enables you to learn these asset classes without undue levels of risk? To fully mimic the experience, you should plan for a five to seven-year holding period because active trading is not part of the experience or mindset in private markets.

Public Equity Markets as Proxy for Private Equity/Venture Capital

When an investor qualifies as accredited, they should not jump directly into private equity or venture capital single-company offerings. This is more the territory of the uber-wealthy, and the minimum investments can be high. Progress is being made on this front, allowing retail investors more access at lower minimums. It will be exciting to see the changes that occur in this asset class over the coming decade. Once accredited, an investor may have access to venture capital or private equity funds with proven sponsors and with minimum investment amounts within their budget.

My recommended approach is focused on funds, leveraging proven sponsors who know what they are doing and have a strong track record. Funds are typically sold in vintages (by year), so an investor can diversify over time with the same sponsor. Investing in single-asset deals is possible today through crowdfunding sites, but only for accredited investors. OurCrowd is an example of such a platform. I do not advocate single-issuer deals for the typical investor, so in preparing to be an accredited investor, I will not include single issuers as part of the Private Markets Portfolio.

If the plan is to allocate a portion of your accredited investment portfolio to private equity or venture capital, get educated by investing in public proxies and exposing yourself to the best educational resources. If you are the type of investor that "learns by doing," it is very difficult to mimic the experience with small amounts of capital when operating in private markets. Even when you become accredited, it is very difficult to find good opportunities in private equity and venture capital without going through a financial advisor or unless you are uber-wealthy. I won't lie; it is still difficult for non-accredited investors to access private markets. The choices are public market proxies and new online platforms that take advantage of exceptions to the SEC regulations and the JOBS Act of 2012. Momentum continues to this day to further democratize investing for all.

In public markets, it is much easier to diversify and learn as you go. Let us return to the hypothetical $100,000 Private Market Portfolio above ("Alternative Portfolio") per Figure 9. Further, there is a sub-allocation to private equity or venture capital of 30% because this asset class has a long successful track record. My recommended approach is to invest in funds or a small portfolio of stocks in the public equity markets. This is because when you become an accredited investor, you will want to invest in vintage funds from great sponsors in this space. So, we want to allocate $30,000 in the Alternative Portfolio to advance our education and experience within this asset class as best we can.

Much has been written about portfolio construction for individual investors and is beyond the scope of this book. Public market wisdom and principles apply equally to private markets, including the following:

- Diversify – Try to utilize funds, such as ETFs or mutual funds, or small portfolios of stocks that are directly involved in the businesses represented in the private market portfolio.
- Determine the level of risk desired in the portfolio. Chapter 10 gets into the capital stack and where investors want to be positioned inside the capital stack. Private investors may wish to be 100% in debt investments to generate income, 100% in equity for growth, or somewhere in between. Non-accredited investors can build a portfolio of private investments to achieve any of these objectives through public market proxies or alternative platforms that do not require an investor to be accredited.
- Dollar-cost averaging is an investment strategy where an investor divides the total amount they want to invest into regular, smaller investments made over a period of time instead of investing a lump sum all at once. This technique reduces the risk of buying at the peak of a market, helps average out volatility, and can help investors maintain discipline and avoid making impulsive investment decisions based on market movements.
- Do not trade or try to time the market.

Figure 10 provides a sampling of public market proxies for exposure to private equity and debt. There are also additional options if you have access to the London Stock Exchange or other non-USA exchanges. This list is not all-inclusive. Research the public players in private equity, create a small basket of stocks, and learn from their news, as well as quarterly and annual reports. Build a diversified portfolio. The most significant challenge will be to morph your mindset to the illiquidity of private markets. The public market proxies are very liquid, and the temptation to trade will exist. When invested in private offerings, you will not be able to exit until the sponsor allows you to do so.

Figure 10
Examples of Public Market Proxies for Private Equity Investing

Large Bracket PE Firms		Private Debt Companies	
BX	Blackstone	BXSL	Blackstone Secured Lending Fund
KKR	Kohlberg Kravis Roberts & Co. L.P.	KKR	Kohlberg Kravis Roberts & Co. L.P.
CG	The Carlyle Group Inc.	BIZD	VanEck BDC Income ETF
ARES	Ares Management Corporation	ARCC	Ares Capital Corporation
OWL	Blue Owl Capital	OBDC	Blue Owl Capital Corporation

A final point: My investment career is now approaching 40 years. If I had simply invested all my taxable and retirement funds in the S&P 500 rather than getting cute with individual stocks and changing allocations, my net worth would likely be significantly higher today. The younger an investor, the more this makes sense. However, I have come to realize that private markets can be approached to directly meet an investor's objectives at various stages of life, and enhanced returns can be realized if willing to accept the lack of liquidity in these markets. An investor must exhibit planning skills and patience.

Figure 10
Examples of Public Market Proxies for Private Equity Investing

Large Bracket PE Firms	
BX	Blackstone
KKR	Kohlberg Kravis Roberts & Co. L.P.
CG	The Carlyle Group Inc.
ARES	Ares Management Corporation
OWL	Blue Owl Capital

Private Debt Companies	
BXSL	Blackstone Secured Lending Fund
KKR	Kohlberg Kravis Roberts & Co. L.P.
BIZD	VanEck BDC Income ETF
ARCC	Ares Capital Corporation
OBDC	Blue Owl Capital Corporation

Do not forget private debt options, as illustrated above. These equities will offer attractive yields consistent with private debt and should exhibit much less volatility relative to common equity positions. Private debt is a key tool for investors with an income strategy orientation.

Public Real Estate Markets as Proxy for Private Real Estate – Debt and Equity

One method of preparing to invest passively in private real estate syndications prior to becoming an accredited investor is with public real estate investment trusts or REITs. REITs have been around for more than fifty years. Congress established REITs in 1960 to allow individual investors to invest in large-scale, income-producing real estate. REITs are efficient individual investors who earn a share of the income produced through commercial real estate ownership. They provide instant diversification for investors, relieving them from having to purchase a collection of properties. Public REITs are advantageous since they allow an unlimited number of unaccredited investors to invest in them.

I recommend that real estate have a large allocation within an Alternative Portfolio to reflect the many opportunities available within this asset class once you become accredited. You will want to identify specific fund opportunities that meet your investment goals. By going through this process of educating yourself on REITS, you will learn about powerful streams of passive income that can be generated and the instant diversification that REITs provide for a portfolio.

Fortunately or unfortunately, there are different types of REITs you may invest in. At this stage, some types of REITS will be available to you. The actual selection of REITs for your Alternative Portfolio comes down to personal goals and objectives.

To qualify as a REIT, a company must have the bulk of its assets and income connected to real estate. It must distribute at least 90 percent of its taxable income to shareholders annually in the form of dividends. A company that qualifies as a REIT is allowed to deduct from its corporate taxable income all the dividends that it pays out to its shareholders. Because of this special tax treatment, most REITs pay out at least 100 percent of their taxable income to their shareholders and, therefore, owe no corporate tax.26

There are essentially three types of REITS:

1. Public, Traded REITs

2. Public, Non-Traded REITs
3. Private REITs

Before you become accredited, publicly traded and public non-traded REITs are available on the menu for investors. Private REITs issue shares that are neither traded on national exchanges nor registered with the SEC but rather issued pursuant to one or more of several exemptions to the securities laws set forth in regulations promulgated and enforced by the SEC. These exemptions include rules set forth under Regulation D, permitting an issuer to sell securities to "accredited investors," and Rule 144A, which exempts securities issued to qualified institutional buyers (QIBs).

In 2017, Blackstone (BX) introduced the Blackstone Real Estate Income Trust, an open-ended private REIT designed to deliver private real estate asset management to institutional investors and wealthy individual investors through financial advisors. It is the behemoth of private REITS.

Figure 11 – Summary of REIT Characteristics			
	Public Traded	**Public Non-Traded**	**Private**
Available only to AIs	No	No	Yes
SEC Registration	Public traded REITS are registered with the SEC and regulated	Public, non-traded REITs are regulated and required to file with the SEC	Private REITs are not registered with the and not regulated by the SEC
Listed on exchanges	Yes	No	No
Minimum Investment	One share on an exchange	A non-traded REIT typically starts around $1,000 but may vary	A minimum investment amount of anywhere between $10,000 to $100,000.
Liquidity	Redemption programs vary by company and are often limited.	Redemption programs are often limited and vary by company.	Very liquid and may be traded every business day, which means they are easy to redeem
Performance Information	A wide range of public information is available both by the company that owns and manages the REIT, and independent sources	There are required SEC filings and performance reporting is publicly available. Long term perspective needed	Typically, there is little to no public information released about private REITS
Examples	AIV, KIM, O, REG ticker symbols on NYSE	Realty Mogul Funds	Crowdstreet C-REIT BREIT (Blackstone REIT)

Alternative Platforms for Non-Accredited Investors

Publicly Traded REITS

The public stock exchanges are the platforms for publicly traded REITS. REITs are portfolios of real estate projects that are owned and managed by the REIT. There are also EFTs that contain a portfolio of REITS for even more diversification. For example, VNQ tracks a broad index that captures much of the US real estate market.

The major difference between owning public REITs to the private real estate that accredited investors access is that public REITs are liquid. That creates the temptation to sell or trade-in and out of investments. This is not what accredited investors do, accordingly, investing in public REITs will provide investors with the opportunity to develop a long-term mindset while striving for a 3-5-year holding period. Trading costs are minimal, volatility is greater than in private markets (because of the liquidity), and the expected returns are comparable. Private real estate investments also have tax advantages, discussed later in this book, that REITs may not provide. Overall, public REITs are the best vehicle for learning about commercial real estate. It is important to take a deeper dive into your holdings to increase your knowledge base in preparation for becoming accredited. In other words, do not simply invest and forget. Read the quarterly reports that public REITS provide to continue the learning process and while holding the REIT positions.

Public Nontraded REITS

Public nontraded REITS more closely reflect the types of private investments that accredited investors seek in the commercial real estate sector. The lack of liquidity more closely reflects the reality of private syndicated real estate funds. Until recently, public nontraded funds were difficult to get into without being very wealthy, accredited, and with the assistance of a financial advisor. The Blackstone REIT is a prime example of such a large and private nontraded REIT. The fees seem high, but this is, of course, typical and reflects the higher expected performance.

Modern platforms are starting to change this by bringing previously unreachable real estate funds into the reach of the public. Realty Mogul is an example of a modern platform that manages two non-traded REITs – an Income REIT and an Apartment Growth REIT. Both have a reasonable minimum investment requirement of $5,000. There are restrictions on liquidity for the first three years, quarterly dividend distributions for cash flow, and the intent of generating long-term capital gains.

As introduced in the previous chapter, Regulation A is an exemption from registration for public offerings that has made it easier for emerging alternative real estate platforms to raise capital and ultimately help investors. Regulation A has two offering tiers: Tier 1, for offerings of up to $20 million in a 12-month period, and Tier 2, for offerings of up to $75 million in a 12-month period. For offerings of up to $20 million, companies can elect to proceed under the requirements for either Tier 1 or Tier 2. There are certain basic requirements applicable to both Tier 1 and Tier 2 offerings, including company eligibility requirements, bad actor disqualification provisions, disclosure, and other matters. Additional requirements apply to Tier 2 offerings, including limitations on the amount of money a non-accredited investor may invest in a Tier 2 offering, requirements for audited financial statements, and the filing of ongoing reports. Issuers in Tier 2 offerings are not required to register or qualify their offerings with state securities regulators.

Section 401 of the Jumpstart Our Business Startups Act (JOBS Act) called for the expansion of Regulation A to assist small businesses with access to capital. Issuers utilizing this provision are by definition "small," but some of the platforms are very interesting. Crowdfunding platforms are migrating to Tier 2 in order to serve a nationwide customer base. It is important to note that individual investors are limited to investments of no more than 10% of the greater of annual income or net worth. Yieldstreet provides a REIT option for nonaccredited investors, similar to Realty Mogul.

I do not have direct investing experience with these funds, but the trend of platforms such as these emerging to provide more options to investors is encouraging. Regulatory changes are assisting this move to democratize investing. Do your research; there are plenty of disclosures telling you what properties are held in the fund, the fees, and the fund strategy. Start small with any new platform and raise your stakes when you have more confidence in the platform based on your experience in terms of transparency and total return.

Non-REIT, Regulation A Tiers 1 and 2 Offerings

Regulation A Tier 2 offerings are emerging that allow a non-accredited investor to invest in and develop portfolios of debt or equity investments in real estate assets. Groundfloor is an example of such a financial product for individual investors that allows non-accredited and accredited investors to participate directly in real estate investment loans on a fractional basis. Developers borrow funds from Groundfloor to acquire and ultimately fix-and-flip single-family residential property. Investors can invest in these projects for as little as $10 per project, with interest rates generally around 10-12% (as of 2023) and project terms of 6-12 months. I have experience as an investor on Groundfloor, but this is not financial advice or an endorsement.

With any new platform in the real estate space, it is important to differentiate between debt or equity instruments that are secured by real estate or investments in the company or sponsor itself. The latter is true venture capital, and you need to get paid for the units of risk you are taking, typically north of 20%. Anytime an investment mentions "to be used for general corporate purposes," you are investing in a business and not a specific real estate project that is supported by the value of such real estate. Concerns with these new offerings are at least four-fold: (1) the going concern of the venture itself, (2) the default rate, especially if the borrower base are individuals without long track records, (3) the cost to the company of pursuing a large number of foreclosures and (4) pervasiveness of loan term extensions (i.e., the timing of liquidity for investors relative to the platform's expectations).

An example of a platform outside of real estate is Masterworks. Masterworks is a platform that allows investors to buy shares in high-end artworks. The application provides access to art investment opportunities that were previously only available to wealthy collectors and institutions. Through Masterworks, investors can buy shares in individual works of art, which are then owned by a special purpose vehicle (SPV) that manages the artwork on behalf of the investors. Investors can then sell their shares on the Masterworks platform or hold them as a long-term investment. Investing in art has its own set of risks, but this is yet another example of how the SEC's changes in the regulation framework are providing more access to previously unreachable asset classes.

Testing new, unique platforms is important, following basic due diligence on the platform company. Make sure you can develop a diversified portfolio to mitigate the defined risks. Also, Regulation A Tier 2 companies have some filing requirements with the SEC. You should be able to locate financial statements on the sponsor company that would indicate ongoing concern issues by the sponsor's auditor.

Interval Funds

Investment companies and related funds are governed by a different set of rules, the Investment Company Act of 1940, as amended (the "Investment Company Act" or "1940 Act"). Uber wealthy accredited investors have access to special funds offered by the very large mutual fund companies that ordinary persons cannot access. Interval funds are one such type, and new platforms are attempting to provide non-accredited investors with access to this structure.

A closed-end fund is a type of mutual fund that issues a fixed number of shares through a single initial public offering (IPO) to raise capital for its initial investments. Its shares can then be bought and sold on a stock exchange, but no new shares will be created, and no new money will flow into the fund. In contrast, an open-ended fund, such as most mutual funds, accepts a constant flow of new investment capital. It issues new shares and buys back its own shares on demand. An interval fund is a type of closed-end fund with shares that do not trade on the secondary market. Unlike typical closed-end funds, an interval fund's shares are not typically listed on a stock exchange. Although interval funds provide limited liquidity to investors by offering to repurchase a limited number of shares on a periodic basis, investors should consider shares of interval funds to be an illiquid investment.

The illiquid nature of investments in the accredited investor arena is a constant theme and requires a mindset shift for "new money" investors. It is part of the tradeoff for getting higher returns over the long term. One example of an interval fund structure that non-accredited investors can access is Fundrise. I have not used Fundrise. When I first signed up for their platform for learning purposes, I recall doing it through their app, which is nice. However, like certain other new financial tech products, the first thing they want you to do is transfer money from your bank account, and then you can learn about what to invest in on the platform. I like to do it the opposite way. Since then, I have discovered that the desktop version of the application nicely lays out the options for investing before asking for money. Fundrise has an interesting offering that provides a nice graduation path from non-accredited investors to accredited. By the time this book is published, I plan to invest with Fundrise as their income-oriented products look attractive for my situation. As is typical with these types of products, investors considering this need to be thinking about tying up their money for long periods of time.

Finding and Investing in Regulation D, 506(b) Offerings

As described in Chapter 3, up to thirty-five non-accredited investors may invest in private offers under Regulation D, 506(b) exemption to the 1933 Act. However, these deals are hard to find and you must have a "pre-existing" relationship with the sponsor and be both sophisticated with this type of private offering and be suitable to the investment. This is problematic for sponsors to document; thus, it is hard to find sponsors willing to utilize this code exemption.

When considering alternative investments and platforms available to non-accredited Investors, consider the following:

- Be cautious and skeptical.
- Do not be a guinea pig – wait until the platform is more mainstream with at least a five-year history, ideal through various interest rate conditions or business cycles.
- Understand if you are investing in true real estate assets or the business of the sponsor – avoid the latter.
- Start small, learn, and gain experience on the platform.
- Ask yourself if the return is commensurate with the units of risk you will be incurring.
- Expect that liquidity may not be able to be advertised by expected maturity dates for single asset projects.

Summary of the Menu for Non-Accredited Investors in Commercial Real Estate

Buying your own apartment building or house for rent places an investor in the private-active quadrant per the framework in Chapter 1. If your goal is to eliminate the hassle of direct ownership of rental property, you will desire to migrate to the private-passive quadrant. Below are listed the types of passive income vehicles that I would utilize to gain experience with commercial real estate. The whole idea of being an accredited investor is to be an informed passive investor, making the optimal decisions as to which assets to purchase when to purchase, and which online distribution platforms to utilize.

Pulling it all together, the allocations in Figure 12 below provide an example of crafting a private portfolio for non-accredited investors. If your plan is to focus on real estate as an accredited investor, you can ignore the "private equity" component and focus on the private real estate sub-allocations. For example, you would focus on the suballocation +/- 5% column for real estate (i.e., multi-family 25%, etc....). The real estate allocations are rough approximations of the NAREIT NPI composition, representative of the overall market cap of REIT investments. Certainly, if you feel more comfortable with a particular asset class, the allocations can be adjusted to meet your comfort level or personal experience. Furthermore, it is highly recommended that one sticks with fund products in these markets for the diversification benefits until you have enough experience and capital. Technically, I consider the public equities of private equity firms to be fund investments since the underlying assets are essentially a diversified set of private investments in many sectors of the economy.

Figure 12: Sample "Private Market Portfolio" for Non-Accredited Investors

AI Asset Class	Non-AI Proxy Class	Sectors	Example Investments	Primary Allocation	Sub Alloc +/- 5%
Private Equity	Public Equities			30%	
		Private Equity	PSP, BX, CG, KKR, GCMG, ARES		40%
		Large Cap	VTI, VOO, SPY		40%
		Mid Cap	IJH, VO		10%
		Small Cap	IJR, VB		10%
Private Real Estate	Publicly Traded REITS			70%	
		Multi-family	AVB, EQR, ESS, MAA		25%
		Industrial	PLD, DRE, EGP, FR		20%
		Hotels	HPT, RHP		5%
		Retail	O, SPG, KIM		10%
		Office	ARE, BDN, BXP		20%
		Alternatives	Realty Mogul, Fundrise, Groundfloor		20%

Obtaining experience in alternative private platforms is important at this stage, rather than just being entirely invested in securities traded on public exchanges. Listed above are Fundrise, Groundfloor, and Fundrise, and these platforms will reflect to a high degree the modern crowdfunding applications that accredited investors are utilizing. They allow the investor to be more involved in the process of selecting private funds and projects. These platforms will further your education with the asset classes that accredited investors are utilizing.

Quick Summary

1. Preparation, education, and simulated experience in asset classes and private investments that accredited investors utilize is critical preparation for the non-accredited investor.
2. Investors should consider allocating 20-25% of their entire portfolio to alternative asset classes utilized by accredited investors.
3. Investing in public proxies for private asset classes is a strategy that can be part of an overall education of private markets. Public companies that specialize in private equity, as well as EFTs and REITS, are reasonable proxies for managing an Alternative Portfolio prior to accredited status.
4. It is highly recommended that fund vehicles be utilized during the early years of their journey into alternative private assets.
5. Don't forget the proxies that invest in private credit offer high dividend returns and lower volatility.
6. Alternative platforms are emerging that can give non-accredited investors a closer experience with the types of investments that accredited investors are involved in. Do your research, understand the risks, and bet small to get experience with these platforms that are unique in bringing Wall Street to Main Street.

Section II, The Education - Building Blocks of Private-Passive Investing

Chapter 6 - Sponsor Selection and Investment Profiles for CRE Private Offerings

Undoubtedly, many readers will claim that passive investing is never 100% passive. There is significant work that investors need to perform upfront, and nothing is more critical than sponsor (manager or general partner) selection. Asset allocation and selection of individual offerings or investments are secondary. When you pick a poor or inexperienced sponsor, you have to live with that decision for five years or more. Some investments can go down the drain faster than that, especially when dealing with fraudulent behavior. My first investment in venture capital was a greenfield brewery project – the entrepreneur is now in prison.

From Chapter 4, the private assets covered herein were narrowed down to commercial real estate syndications, venture capital, and private equity. All three of these asset classes have a lot in common with regard to sponsors, mainly that the sponsor is actively involved in running a business. Real estate syndicators don't just buy real estate; they actively manage the business of that real estate until a subsequent exit. Private equity and venture capitalists are very actively involved in managing the improvement or growth of their portfolio assets. In contrast, hedge funds manage portfolios of public assets in the same way mutual funds manage financial assets. What is a sponsor's history and track record? Is the sponsor experienced in managing the businesses or projects they are investing in? This chapter will focus on commercial real estate sponsors, and Chapter 7 will take a deeper dive into the details of evaluating specific commercial real estate offerings. Chapter 8 will cover issues specific to sponsors of private equity and venture capital.

Three factors are important for any private investment, including the market, the property or business, and the sponsor. Experienced sponsors have already made and learned from their mistakes. Nobody can consistently predict market cycles, but it helps to have sponsors who know how to manage cycles when they come. Great sponsors have institutional knowledge embedded in their DNA regarding specific industries or segments of the market, using conservative leverage, matching the type of debt with the operational risk of the project, and executing a plan that blends the financial and operational strategies to achieve outsized returns. In private markets, outperformance over the long run is highly dependent on selecting sponsors that perform in the highest tiers of their respective asset classes. We need to increase the odds of success by locating and investing with the upper quartile of private offering sponsors or at least avoiding the bottom quartile.

The end result of this due diligence process is the development of an "approved sponsor listing" in the asset classes and sub-asset classes that a private-passive investment plan requires. If a sponsor is not on the list, it's a no-go. I continuously modify this list based on my experience. Adding a sponsor to the list is the culmination of a disciplined process steeped in due diligence. For any new sponsor, I bet as small as possible and then continue my learning from the "inside." When you get excited about private offerings, every deal advertised looks like a shiny nickel. Your eyes move to the project, the location, the internal rate of return of 30%+, and temptation calls. When I feel this emotion, I immediately move to the sponsor and remind myself that this is the first item to investigate. A short list is perfectly fine as long as the approved sponsors are tested, have an established track record in the sectors represented in your plan, and are aligned with your objectives and values. Contained on my list are sponsors whom I have not yet transacted with as I wait for new capital to match the new offerings they might offer in the future. Figure 13 is the first step in the private-passive framework in the shaded area, finding proven sponsors.

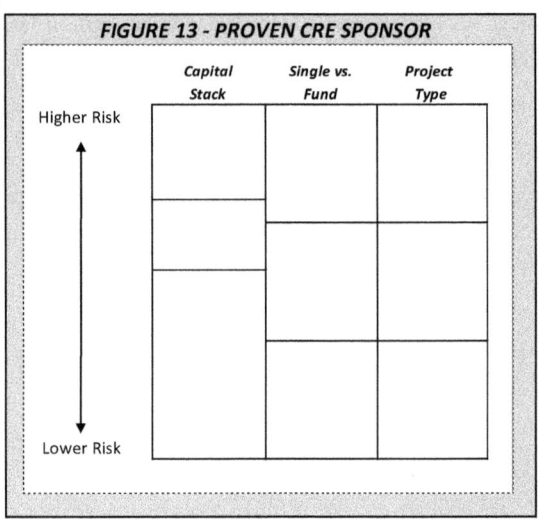

How to Find Commercial Real Estate Sponsors

I am broadly using the term sponsor to include the roles of project syndicator and operator. A real estate syndicator is a person or a company that pools capital from multiple investors to invest in real estate projects. The syndicator typically acts as the managing partner and oversees the acquisition, management, and sale of the property. In return for their services, the syndicator typically receives a percentage of the profits generated by the investment. A syndicator is responsible for structuring a deal and raising funds but is not accountable for executing the business plan. An operator is responsible for all aspects of property and asset management and business plan execution. Generally, sponsors serve as both syndicators and operators, as many are vertically integrated entities. I will continue to use the term "sponsor" to refer to the entity responsible for taking your investment, executing the business plan, and delivering the expected internal rate of return over the project lifespan.

How do you find sponsors and start building your authorized sponsor list? Below are suggestions for building a sponsor pipeline:

1. **Networking:** Finding investors in the market and making connections. The network expands quickly when utilizing all the methods below and expands more quickly once you are invested in the private markets.

2. **Podcasts:** This is a great method for learning about commercial real estate. The guests on podcasts occasionally are private-passive investors, and they provide their contact information to follow up with them. Certainly not an exhaustive list, but I find the following podcasts beneficial:
   a. Best Real Estate Investing Advise Ever with Joe Fairless
   b. Real Estate Strategies Podcast with Ken McElroy
   c. Bigger Pockets Real Estate
   d. Millionaires Unveiled
3. **Conferences:** Annual conferences are unbelievably valuable for making connections, such as:
   a. National Multifamily Housing Council
   b. Best Ever Conference
   c. MFIN Conference
4. **Meetups:** There are groups on Meetup.com that deal with this exact subject matter from the comfort of your own home.
5. **Mastermind Groups:** Groups for investors (commonly known as Limited Partners or LPs) as a networking tool for locating quality sponsors in commercial real estate.
6. **Crowdfunding Platforms:** This is a valuable resource for learning about the industry and specific sponsors and opportunities. You can listen to live or recorded webinars on each offering, which reveal a lot of information about sponsors and their track records. Crowdstreet.com is excellent in this regard, as are others as well.
7. **Advertisements:** Nowadays, the sponsors of 506(c) offerings find you. Once Instagram or Facebook, for example, figures out your interest in commercial real estate syndications, the ads will miraculously appear. Still, I am a bit wary of discovering sponsors in this manner. Call me old-fashioned. The sponsors that are my proven "go-to" sponsors do not advertise on Facebook (yet).
8. **Commercial Broker's Websites:** If you are interested in a particular location or region, you can investigate commercial brokerages in that region and ask them who they trust and recommend.
9. **Sponsor Websites:** Once you have located sponsors for further due diligence, review their particulars on their website. If they do not have a website, that might be a red flag.
10. **Following the Breadcrumbs:** Once you get involved in researching syndicators, it will lead you down different paths. For example, my focus is concentrated on large multifamily projects and portfolios thereof. An excellent sponsor had an offering for a portfolio of properties with a 25%+ projected internal rate of return (IRR). It sounded great, but at that point in time, I was looking for more safety and income. During the webinar on the project, they mentioned the name of the provider of the preferred equity tranche on the deal that was projected to earn 15-17% IRR with much more safety, as the preferred investors would get paid before the common equity holders. I located this sponsor of the preferred and invested there instead.

Commercial Real Estate Landscape

Some measures of the commercial real estate landscape are necessary at this point to make the process of identifying sponsors more logical since most sponsors tend to specialize their activities within these four dimensions. The activity of locating sponsors will work synergistically with your investment plan, which is the subject of Section III of this book.

Property Type

There are five main property types and multiple subtypes in the commercial real estate arena, as follows:
- Multifamily
- Industrial
- Office
- Retail
- Hospitality

Examples of subtypes within the broader multifamily category are student housing, build-for-rent communities, and mobile home parks. RV Parks are part of hospitality.

Geographical Region

To be consistent with the NCREIF National Property Index, I will refer to the four main regions of the USA. Real estate is a global business, and geographical boundaries can be extended as necessary to achieve your personal goals. To provide a frame of reference, Figure 14 provides an idea of the size and scope of the property types and geographical dispersion in the USA:

Figure 14 [27]

RE Type	West	South	Midwest	East	Total	% Type
Multifamily	$ 92,108,085,195	$ 80,351,761,712	$ 16,571,892,689	$ 73,047,279,547	$ 262,079,019,143	28.1%
Industrial	146,089,384,664	62,445,527,016	25,143,918,291	65,686,855,546	299,365,685,517	32.1%
Office	91,141,869,650	30,294,473,493	13,783,208,102	104,976,898,224	240,196,449,469	25.7%
Retail	57,299,963,776	32,047,804,863	10,766,443,172	28,372,043,418	128,486,255,229	13.8%
Hospitality	623,575,868	458,100,000	398,900,000	1,490,772,096	2,971,347,964	0.3%
Total	$ 387,262,879,153	$ 205,597,667,084	$ 66,664,362,254	$ 273,573,848,831	$ 933,098,757,322	100.0%
% Geo	41.5%	22.0%	7.1%	29.3%	100.0%	

Investment Profile

Sponsors tend to specialize in particular investment profiles within property types and geographical boundaries, but not always. The economic cycle or market conditions may dictate changes in strategy. For example, in 2022, the market for development was favored over "value add" as existing owners (and potential sellers) slowly recognized or failed to accept the falling market values of their properties.

- **Core Investments**: The least risky offering and more stable cash flow. This generally translates into the lowest internal rate of return (IRR) because there are few ways for the sponsor to improve the property. These investments are usually found in established and attractive major markets. With core investments, think of reliable passive income. In mutual fund parlance, it falls in the income bucket.

- **Core-Plus Investments, or Blend of Core and Value-Add**: It is similar to the world of growth and income investments such as mutual funds. With core-plus investments, think of a nice blend of income with growth potential. In mutual fund parlance, it falls in the growth and income bucket.
- **Value-Add Properties**: Require fixing up and/or in need of better management. By improving the property, the sponsor is able to raise rents, attract better tenants, or lower operating costs. With value-add projects, think of higher returns and moderate risk. In mutual fund parlance, it falls in the growth bucket.
- **Opportunistic or Development**: The pinnacle of elevated risk/high reward. They either require significant rehabilitation or ground-up development. These projects might also be taking advantage of dislocations in the economy or market. Examples might be investing in hotels or office properties in the aftermath of the Covid crisis in 2021-2022. With this category, there is little immediate cash flow but higher potential returns in the future. In mutual fund parlance, it falls in the capital appreciation bucket.

Investment Structures

This dimension addresses what is termed the "capital stack," the topic of Chapter 10.

- **Debt**: The least risky part of the capital stack or structure is the claims of the preferred equity and common equity holders, which are subordinate to the debtholders. Debt is typically secured by the property itself. Because it is safe and defensive, the expected returns are approximately 6-10%.
- **Preferred Equity**: Preferred equity has priority over common equity, either by being first in line to receive the cash flow, first to receive the return of capital, or both. Medium risk, with expected returns of 8-14%.
- **Common Equity**: The riskiest and potentially attractive place in the capital stack, subordinate to the claims of debt holders and preferred equity holders, with expected returns of 10-20% depending on the other variables in the offering.

Real Estate Sponsor Due Diligence

What do great commercial real estate sponsors look like? These are substantial enterprises with all business functions and staffing covered. They have a track record of consistently creating a lot of wealth for themselves and investors. An established industrial real estate developer purchased the building where my company was located five years ago. This new owner, the industrial property developer, occupied a full floor of this three-story downtown suburban office building. They renovated the common areas as well as their office space, which were extremely elegant with no detail sparred. Their office was fully staffed with a distinguished owner and a well-defined executive team. Let's just say that this was not a garage start-up but a real enterprise. And speaking of garages, their side of the indoor garage was occupied by a Tesla, a Bentley, a Porsche – you get the idea. Our side was stocked full of Hondas and Toyotas.

My point is two-fold. Real estate development and management is a lucrative business, and investors have the opportunity to participate in this success. Secondly, sponsors can run the gamut between a small handful of executives to formal enterprises such as our landlord. For me, I would rather gravitate to the proven, larger sponsors. Upstart sponsors will either become the next great enterprise or they will fail due to inexperience or loss of investor trust.

Performing detailed due diligence on commercial real estate sponsors and their projects is essential, and many excellent checklists exist to guide you in the process. Accordingly, I am not going to recreate the wheel in this book. Great sources of checklists include Bigger Pockets Real Estate, legal counsel websites that specialize in real estate, and a well-organized checklist developed by Brian Burke in The Hands-Off Investor: An Insider's Guide to Investing in Passive Real Estate Syndications. The following discussion is about the critical processes investors should undertake to vet sponsors for inclusion on their approved sponsor list.

The process of sponsor evaluation starts with gathering information on the experience and credentials of the key executive and their executive team members. Do the lead executives have a strong background in commercial real estate, either with the current sponsor and/or predecessor firms? Not all sponsors do. I have seen key executives who were marketing executives in technology companies immediately before launching a commercial real estate syndication business. It is important to understand who will be responsible for underwriting acquisitions and executing the investment strategy following the acquisition. The team should have significant relevant experience and be able to handle the demands of particular real estate sectors and associated business plans. What types of business plans have they executed that are relevant to their current offering? Development projects are very different from multifamily value add projects. Zoning and permitting require unique skills. A sponsor should present their entire team on their website to provide investors with an appreciation that all necessary functions are covered by seasoned personnel.

At a high level, the due diligence process involves reviewing a sponsor's website, checking references, and scheduling a call with the target sponsor. Depending on the firm, this would be with the key executive or the investor relations director. They should want to talk to you as well to understand your objectives and potential fit with the type of projects that they offer. A two-way conversation is essential to understand if there is what amounts to a long-term marriage. I have never experienced a sponsor in venture investing or real estate that avoids an introductory call to explain an offering and to understand your needs and objectives as an investor. Even the sponsors who eventually committed fraud did this – perhaps they were too eager. If a sponsor is simply willing to take your money, move on.

A sponsor's team requires that all key functions are competently managed. An investor should have a clear picture of the level of experience of all key executives and how long their management team has been together. Starting at the top, there are one or two key executives who are responsible for the success of syndication activities. Who are the key executives, and how is the risk of succession managed if they cannot fulfill their obligations? What is the size of the staff, and how established is the firm? Are they vertically integrated? Basically, this means they have internal capabilities around acquisitions, asset management, property management, construction, and administrative functions. The more control they have is generally better, but eliminating sponsors that are not vertically integrated is not mandatory. Outsourcing key functions to best-of-breed service providers is a great strategy in business, and real estate syndication is a business. What functions are outsourced, which firms do they partner with, and for how long? Your ultimate goal is to gain comfort around how they operate, and what is the leadership "value system" in which they operate?

Key functions of a real estate sponsor include the following:

- Acquisitions and underwriting refer to the processes of locating properties in the markets in which they operate. Most sponsors should have a network of firms and resources assisting them in locating suitable properties, preferably "off-market" opportunities. The more established firms will have a veteran "on the beat," a person who knows everyone and has trusted relationships. Underwriting requires someone with experience in building models that reflect the realities of the investment type and market. A model is only as good as its underlying assumptions, and a good underwriting process generates informed assumptions. Understand how this works.

- Asset management refers to the function of continuously optimizing the property to generate the highest operating cash flow and investor returns. Adjustments to the overall strategy are inevitable at various points in the life of the project. They interface with executive management and daily property management to affect the strategy and ultimately to maximize the net operating income that is generated from the project.

- Property management is the process of continuously managing the property at a micro level. Finding new tenants, collecting rents, implementing policies prescribed by asset management, property maintenance, and managing all daily operations. This function is commonly outsourced to smaller sponsors; in this case, you should understand the qualifications of the property management firm in that local market. If outsourced, gain an understanding if the sponsor's plans to bring the function in-house in the near future. Transitions in property management are never easy, particularly if the sponsor is creating this function from scratch.

- The investor relations function is a very important function for investor satisfaction so that investors return for future projects. From experience as an investor, this can be a deal breaker for continuing to invest in future projects of a sponsor. There should be a regular cadence to reporting to investors, which should be no less than quarterly. Ask the prospective sponsor to provide an example of how their regular reports are formatted. The variation in reporting styles is incredible. Many sponsors will simply provide a quarterly financial statement and notification of how much the quarterly distribution to investors will be. This is really not sufficient. The best sponsors will report actual results versus the underwritten assumptions for key variables of the property, such as revenues and net operating income by property. Without this, an investor has to constantly refer back to the acquisition model to see if a project is on-track. Unfortunately, some sponsors report whenever they feel like it, sometimes having a six-month gap between reports. It is important to understand who the investor relations contact is and have a

rapport prior to investing. If they are not forthcoming with all your questions in the initial interview, do not invest.
- Legal and accounting functions can be outsourced or, internal, or a combination. Most successful sponsors must rely on external firms for key functions; this is a strength and not a weakness. Audits may be required, and external auditors obviously have to perform the audits. Understand what functions outside accountants perform, who generates the annual K-1 tax reporting, and the date that investors can expect to receive K-1s. Ask who the outside legal firm is. Has the sponsor changed legal or accounting firms during the last 3 years, and why?
- If an investor plans to invest in a self-directed retirement account (SD-IRA), does the sponsor accept this type of arrangement? Many sponsors do not, which, in my opinion, is a reasonable position to take due to the extra administration that is required for SD-IRA compliance. It may be that the best sponsors that have strong investor rosters are the same sponsors that do not need to accept SD-IRA investors. Specifically, will the sponsor provide an annual valuation as required for investors to mark the value of their investment to market? If not, this is potentially a very expensive problem for investors to have a third-party prepare an independent valuation, if not an impossible task without access to key data. There is a separate chapter later on related to using self-directed IRAs for your private-passive portfolio.

Track Record and References

Request that the sponsor provide you with their track record. The track record is usually divided into two categories: realized investments (exited) and existing investments. Track record documents provide a wealth of information, including the extent of their history, the types of properties and shifts thereof through their history, and, naturally, the returns from these investments. Experience in a geographic market should be discernable, indicating that they have hands-on knowledge of key model assumptions in that market and how to deal with changing local market conditions. Fields of data that you should see include:

- Project name
- City, State
- Property type
- Dates of acquisition and sale (if realized)
- Purchase price
- Sale price
- Internal rate of return (IRR) hereinafter defined.
- Equity Multiple (e.g., if $1 million is invested in a project, and $2 million is returned to investors, the equity multiple equals 2.0x)
- Notes or explanations

Track records should realistically have some failures. If not, perhaps the sponsor has not been tested through full market cycles and/or financial crises. I certainly prefer to partner with sponsors that have been through battles in the past and have an appreciation of the necessity of risk management when entering each and every deal. Recently, I invested in an opportunistic office building project with a long-time enterprise sponsor whose track record indicated 37 realized projects over 17 years, including 2 failed investments. There was a foreclosure of a retail project caused by the Global Financial Crisis and a loss incurred on a mixed-use property more recently during COVID-19. It is worth repeating that things will go wrong in private markets, and it is important to understand the DNA of any sponsor. I proceeded with this particular project, as it was clear to me that the sponsor was the beneficiary of a distressed situation created in the office market due to Covid-19. Buying up other sponsors' messes is usually a good strategy.

Asking the sponsor to provide references is a reasonable request. A short call to discover another investor's experience with a sponsor, including the strengths and weaknesses of the sponsor, is advisable.

With regards to your interview with the sponsor, ask how they reacted to challenging projects and what actions they took to protect investors' principles. Have they ever lost investor principal, and why? Could this situation have been prevented upfront with a more conservative capitalization or additional risk management techniques? Attempt to form a holistic picture of the sponsor's history. Finally, ask them upfront about the criminal history of key personnel, specifically whether there is any history of fraud or securities violations. Sponsors are supposed to disclose this in their offerings but rarely do. Just Google "real estate syndication fraud" if you don't think fraud with syndications is real.

Attributes of Successful CRE Sponsors – Competitive Edge

The elite sponsors of commercial real estate consistently exhibit the following attributes:

1. There is a laser focus on not losing investor principal. Before any acquisition, they perform sensitivity analysis, plan for contingencies, and may have multiple exit strategies.
2. They focus on particular property types and geographic regions and move towards mastery in each deal within their niche. Larger enterprise sponsors can successfully manage multiple divisions, so it is important to analyze their track record in specific property types or profiles.
3. They have an understanding of and appreciation for the cycles inherent in commercial real estate. For example, during 2022, the "smart money" was not chasing multifamily properties when the market started to crack. Certain other syndicators seemed to continue to close many deals despite the disconnects that were appearing in the market and the difficulty of underwriting acceptable returns with higher interest rates. In time, we will see what the correct approach was. As previously mentioned, excellent sponsors pull back the curtain on their opinions regarding the macro climate in their regular investment reports to investors. Factual data on a specific investment is nice, but the great sponsors share their thoughts regularly on what they are seeing in the market and how they are approaching it. For them, it's a relationship with investors, not just a transaction.
4. Sponsors are always looking to grow and become vertically integrated with their primary functions. They should be striving to achieve enterprise status with maximum efficiency and economies of scale.

5. For smaller sponsors, being nimble and specialization are nice attributes and should not be discarded. For example, an emerging sponsor that has a consistent track record of investing specifically in multifamily class B or C units with a value-added investment profile in a particular defined region can be an excellent choice.
6. They delight investors.

The general due diligence process for sponsors is one of the more critical aspects of private-passive investing. Please take your time and use outside resources as necessary to ensure you develop the highest quality sponsor group to partner with on a long-term basis. Of course, there are many specifics that you must also know about sponsors to ensure they are a good fit for the investment strategy that meets your objectives and risk tolerance. This will be further explored in Chapter Twelve. In the next Chapter, we will stick to the commercial real estate sector and discuss offering the basic structure of offerings that investors will need to understand in developing and executing their private alternatives strategy. For example, if your strategy is focused on multi-family in a specific region of the USA, your sponsor search needs to focus on this subset of sponsors.

Quick Summary

1. Find the sponsor first and then the investment. A great, experienced sponsor is everything. Maintain a list of approved sponsors to keep you on track and focused. Selecting a poor sponsor at the outset may prematurely end your private-passive journey.
2. The ranks of commercial real estate sponsors are growing rapidly, and it is becoming easier to find them. Selecting proven sponsors that align with your investment goals, need for liquidity, and values is an active process.
3. Sponsor selection and passive-private strategy development have to be developed in concert.
4. Do your due diligence on sponsors of interest through detailed interviews, review of website materials, and with references. Ask other sponsors for recommendations (outside of their core markets). I will follow a sponsor through their investor meetings and updates for over one year prior to investing with them.
5. Understand the key functions that a commercial real estate sponsor performs and be satisfied that they have all bases covered. Know the sponsor's track record in the property types and geographies that fit your investing plan.
6. Update your customized list of "approved sponsors" as your needs change over time and you learn from past investments.

Chapter 7 - Commercial Real Estate Syndication Offering Details

In the last chapter, private-passive investors were introduced to general due diligence processes that are necessary to evaluate sponsors – their experience, trustworthiness, and functional capabilities. Of course, it is important to mesh our strategy and portfolio allocation with our research in uncovering excellent sponsors. If your comfort level resides in multifamily properties, there is no need to interview sponsors specializing in other property types. The next level of due diligence is to better understand a sponsor's area of focus and the typical structure of their offerings. Analyzing commercial real estate offering structure is a fundamental building block for investing in private-passive alternatives.

The importance of having a long-term plan is very important to guide your review of offerings. The commercial real estate asset class offers an incredible array of choices, and each offering can appear fantastic when first announced. Everyone understands real estate, its tangibility, attractiveness, and utility. Spending a lot of time upfront to design a plan that meets your income needs and long-term goals is fruitless if you do not operationalize this plan. It is your North Star. Each investment is a 3 to 10-year commitment. It takes a long time to get back on track if you wander off course with your portfolio constituents. Your plan will encompass the following parameters as introduced in Chapter 6.

Property Type
- Multifamily
- Industrial
- Office
- Retail
- Hospitality

Geographical Region
- West
- Midwest
- South
- East

Investment Profile
- Core
- Core Plus
- Value-added
- Opportunistic or Development

Investment Structures

- Debt
- Preferred Equity
- Common Equity

This chapter will focus on the investment profiles, and accordingly, the private-passive framework expands, as shown in Figure 15.

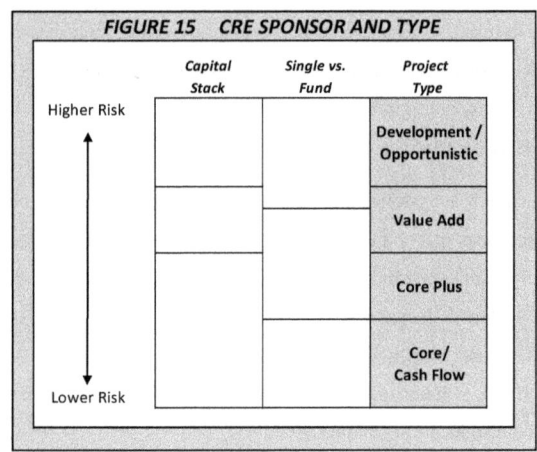

Certain combinations of variables, such as multifamily, value-add, and common equity, will offer more opportunities than you can possibly review. For some combinations of variables, funds will be your only choice for investment (but a good choice). Your plan will dictate which sponsors are interviewed and selected. Vet the sponsor first, ensure that these sponsors have their fingers on the pulse of the market environment, and then start reviewing their offerings for alignment with your plan. Learn a sponsor's "bread and butter"; where have they had most of their success? Sponsors may change their areas of focus as time passes, so seek to understand why. For example, a sponsor may have started in retail and now focuses on office properties. How has it gone so far, and does the sponsor have experience in a particular metro area? Economic conditions can temporarily change how sponsors bring deals to the market. In 2022, bank financing tightened during the period of the Federal Reserve's restrictive monetary policy. Due to this and how investors were reacting to the environment, we saw a lot more preferred equity offerings (a safer alternative compared to common equity) to fill out the capital stack for a project and provide more security for investors. In summary, reconcile how an offering aligns with the sponsor's track record provided in Chapter 6.

The size of an offering is another important variable to understand. All things being equal, smaller offerings relative to a sponsor's average transaction size will "fill up" faster. In other words, investors have to act quickly to secure an investment. Some sponsors do an excellent job keeping prospective investors updated on the progress towards achieving 100% commitments in their deals. Crowdfunding sites tend to do this very well. Top decile sponsors tend to fund their offerings very rapidly. My first investment commitment with a sponsor that I identified was voided because I did not fund the deal fast enough. Communication is key, as is understanding how a sponsor operates in the fundraising process. There is a pecking order as well. Larger investors and those with a more established relationship with the sponsor are likely to have priority.

Also, be wary of deals that extend their deadlines beyond their target commitment due date. This could be a red flag. I have a phobia of sponsors proceeding to close with the equity component of the capital structure less than the requirements of their business plan. This could indicate that the sponsor can insert equity classes senior to the Class A common and dilute the interests in the investment you just funded. Undercapitalized projects are never a good thing. Much more common during late 2022 and early 2023 for most sponsors was an inability to raise funds fast enough due to investors as a group being cautious due to the macroeconomic environment. Investors were funding deals that did not close for another long period or not at all, creating an opportunity cost during that period. Continuous dialogue is recommended with the investor relations contact with the sponsor once you have committed to determining the progress of the offering and when funds are due. Once the funds are sent, it is generally a "done deal," especially if you ever hope to work with this sponsor again.

Minimum investment requirements vary from sponsor to sponsor. Generally, you can find $25,000 minimums on crowdfunding platforms but higher minimums of $50,000 and up when investing directly with sponsors. A minimum of $100,000 is common for larger sponsors. This is a real impediment for recently accredited investors. It is true that sponsors would prefer to have fewer, more informed investors in their syndicates because it makes investor relations an easier process to manage. As you are starting out, diversification is important for the passive-private investor. Ask the sponsor if they will accept a $50,000 investment (when the minimum is $100,000) as a way to build the relationship. A few months ago, I was reviewing the profile of a multifamily sponsor in Texas that I accidentally discovered when trying to research a debt fund with a very similar name. I proceeded to have interviews and was very impressed by their organization. This particular sponsor ran a series of funds, and the next fund was scheduled to open in early 2023. I don't remember why, but it was not until the very end of our meeting that I asked casually what the minimum investment requirement was for the fund, certain they would be honored to take my money. The response was $500,000. It never even occurred to me, as most funds set the minimum at $100,000. I have not tested the negotiability of this; perhaps one day, I will. I have seen other sponsors proactively adjusting their minimums downward as economic conditions slowed during the 2022 inflation and interest rates spike. For a first transaction with a given sponsor, I recommend investing the minimum and using the next few years to continue your due diligence with this sponsor. When starting out in private investments, greed is not good.

A hot topic during 2022 with the escalation in interest rates (and corresponding theoretical compression of property values) was the issue of upfront deposits or earnest money. A buyer negotiates the deal with the seller and then has to fund a significant deposit, similar to purchasing a house. The issue involves whether the deposits are refundable or non-refundable, as the buyer then proceeds to raise the common equity to close the transaction. When multifamily property values were stable or increasing each year, transactions tended to close on schedule. However, in mid-2022, the market did a complete pivot as financing rates soared in historic increments. Deals unraveled due to the sudden difficulty of raising debt financing. In this situation, was the investor money that was raised by the buyer "on the hook" for any nonrefundable deposits? This is worth asking about before investing, especially with sponsors who have shorter track records and who have not experienced full economic cycles with respect to real estate.

A final topic to address when reviewing deal specifics is the amount by which the sponsor co-invests alongside the common equity investors, a further indicator of alignment of interests. Investors need to evaluate these issues of alignment of interests in totality, including the co-investment amount, fees, and promotion, which will be addressed later in this chapter. Sponsors should co-invest at least between 5-10% of the common equity raise as an indicator of confidence in the transaction. It may also be that the lender requires the sponsor to co-invest a certain amount. Investors need to understand the sponsor's position with regard to the co-investment amount on any project.

Leverage and Liquidity

There can be no doubt that the key distinguishing features of private-passive investing are lack of liquidity and leverage. Leverage, or using debt to enhance the yield of equity investments, is what makes the expected returns on private investments so attractive. Real estate is a clear example that most people understand since mortgages are a key part of adult life.

I will delve more deeply into the capital stack in a later chapter, but suffice it to say that this stack is the composition of the sources of funds used to finance a real estate project. The debt component is typically 50-70% of the funds raised and is referred to as the loan-to-value ratio (LTV). Higher LTVs are riskier. The equity investors contribute the difference of 30-50% of the total capital required in most cases, but the capital stack can be much more complex than that. The sponsor may invest 5-10% of the total common equity requirement as a co-investment. Chapter 10 will address the debt component of the capital stack in detail, but let's address two key factors – the sources of debt and fixed rate vs. floating rate issues. Both of these topics are extremely hot during 2023.

Ask the sponsor how they source their debt and the relationships they have. By the time offering documents are presented to investors, they should have pinpointed the lender and terms supporting the offering. There are typically two sources:

- Commercial lenders, banks, etc.
- Government-sponsored entities such as Freddie Mac or Fannie Mae. Sponsors that can secure GSE debt tend to be the more established, reputable sponsors, so this is another clue in your due diligence.

I have invested in a few multifamily fund projects and have experienced both sources of financing. Borrowing terms for commercial real estate projects can be up to ten years, with a potential period of interest-only payments of up to 5-6 years. Besides knowing the source of the financing, ask about who is providing the guarantees on the debt, if any. This may be another clue regarding a sponsor's lack of experience or reputation if onerous guarantee requirements exist on a project. More interesting of late has been the re-emergence of the fixed vs. float rate debt decision, as rates have soared during 2022.

Fixed-rate debt is set by the lender closely preceding the closing date. The rate is established as a spread (bank profit) over an index, such as the 10-year US Treasury Rate. Fixed-rate debt provides predictability to the borrower. Floating-rate debt adjusts periodically, generally from a monthly reset to an annual reset. Floating-rate debt rates are usually set at a lower nominal level than fixed-rate debt at any given time, making it more interesting when general interest rate levels are stable or falling.

Given the predictability of fixed-rate debt, why would a sponsor choose floating-rate debt? In the case of development projects or projects with a very high value-added component, floating-rate debt is the convention for lenders. Stated another way, fixed-rate debt is typically only an option for purchasing existing properties but not for additional costs of improving the property subsequent to closing. Secondly, for fixed-rate debt, there is a substantial prepayment penalty on borrowers that repay early, a common scenario since most operators plan to sell or refinance their projects within five years. This penalty, called yield maintenance, can be substantial and a major deterrent to using fixed-rate debt.

Accordingly, the use of floating-rate debt to finance a real estate project is common. Sponsors "protect" themselves and their investors by purchasing an interest rate cap, a fancy derivative contract that caps how high the interest rate can go. The sponsor must pay the interest rate cap upfront in exchange for this future protection. Lenders will oftentimes require that an interest rate cap be purchased. The cost of the cap will depend on many factors, including the term of the cap (how many years), the current shape of the rate selected (how close it is to the current floating rate, if the floating rate is 2% and the cap rate is 2.5%, it will be expensive). The bottom line is that if rates fall, the cap investment expires worthless (just like insurance), and if rates rise, the cap provides protection to the extent that the floating rate exceeds the strike rate of the cap contract. Understand the sponsor's strategy for financing and the use of interest rate protection contracts prior to committing equity capital to a project.

As one sponsor recently told me, floating-rate debt is the correct decision most of the time; it works great until it doesn't. This is another way of saying that over the long-term if you run simulations, floating rate debt will work out better than fixed rate debt the vast majority of the time. However, when 2024 happens, and the Federal Funds Rate increases by 500 basis points, it is certainly a problem. An underlying property's net operating income can be performing as planned, but the increased interest expense associated with higher interest rates can wipe out any distributions to investors for a period of time. Interest rate caps help, but unfortunately, lenders often require a borrower to re-establish reserves to purchase the next interest rate cap when the term of the initial cap is less than the term of the loan. This creates a double whammy for sponsors and investors. Despite that, the issue is not dissimilar to investing in the stock market and using rear-view mirror psychology. Investors would have loved to sell all their stocks in January 2022, even though stocks will generate a nice return over the long run. Floating rate debt strategies are not bad per se if the project is solid and generates cash, and its use may generally work over the long term. Continually investing with a proven sponsor over time (i.e., investing in each vintage fund) is a solid strategy because the final results should "even out" over time and through various economic and interest rate cycles.

Having multiple "go-to" sponsors is also helpful with regards to the interest rate issue. This was not intentional on my part, but I have been participating in another multifamily fund since late 2021 with an enterprise sponsor that used fixed-rate GSE debt of 2.8% for ten years. Looks genuinely nice in the rear-view mirror. And the debt is assumable. Perhaps diversifying sponsors based on their funding sources should be a consideration in how you invest in commercial real estate.

Lastly, investors must appreciate that commercial real estate private investments are illiquid. The expected term is usually 3-5 years, but do not count on it. When interest rates rise as they did in 2022, activity freezes as buyers and sellers feel each other out. Sellers cannot sell or refinance. There has been no better place to observe this than Groundfloor, the provider of fix-and-flip loans on single-family housing projects. Groundfloor offers these debt investments to non-accredited investors with rates of 10-12% and expected terms of up to 12 months. Repayments on my account have essentially stopped, with the majority of loans in extended or default status. This does not mean I will lose principal, but it simply means that it will be years before the money comes back to me since foreclosure processes are very slow. Patience is a virtue for private-passive investors.

Single Assets or Funds

As you scope out sponsors that meet your investment plan requirements, you need to understand if the sponsor offers only single-asset (i.e., one apartment building) offerings or fund offerings (i.e., a fund of, say, 5-10 apartment buildings). Fund products are popular today, and the trend of successful syndicators moving to fund products is well established. The pros and cons will be addressed in Chapter 11. If you are committing to fund products to spread your risk and achieve a goal of generating steady passive income, funds are a very attractive option for investors.

Cash Flow – Distributions and Reporting Cadences

For each prospective offering, understand when cash distributions will commence, how often they will be paid, and what the estimated yields will be for each year into the future. Fund products should provide a guide for what the cash-on-cash yield will be each year. The reporting cadence is critical as well. Understand how often reports will be provided and ask for a sample report. In my opinion, just a file of profit and loss information on each property is insufficient, as there should also be a color commentary on the market that impacts the investment. If all that is reported is good news, this is not realistic. Sponsors need to report the good and the bad, and the commentary needs to be provided on time, at least quarterly.

Important Return Metrics

1. **Internal Rate of Return (IRR)**

IRR is a measure of how profitable an investment is on an annualized basis over the term of the investment. It factors in the initial investment and the timing of cash flows, including the final exit value and when they occur. It is really an annualized measure of return. If you achieve an IRR of 15%, you can compare this measure to what you would have earned in a savings account, such as 1% per annum. An IRR of 0% means you eventually got your money back. A negative IRR means you lost part or all of your investment principal. This metric is a key measure of success or failure in an investment and is easily comparable to other investment alternatives. Microsoft Excel has the IRR function to assist you in calculating your own IRR. I utilize my personal finance software, Quicken, as the ultimate independent source of the final IRR since it knows the exact dates of cash in and cash out. IRRs are all relative. High is not good, and low is not necessarily bad. The differences can occur due to market factors, investment risk profiles, and project execution by the sponsor.

2. **Cash-on-cash (COC)**

COC is a measure of cash flow as a percentage of the amount invested in an opportunity, typically calculated on an average annual basis. This is important for investors who are relying on the periodic cash flow for retirement, to replace a W-2 paycheck, or for similar reasons.

3. **Multiple on Invested Capital (MOIC)**

The formula is (Realized Value + Unrealized Value) / Total Amount Invested. For investors, this is the gross multiple of how much money they have made relative to how much money they have invested. A value of 2x means investors have doubled their money (to date).

4. **Net Operating Income (NOI)**

NOI equals the property gross income minus operating expenses for any accounting period, typically reported as an annual or last twelve months total. Hopefully, NOI is positive for your investments, as it is a major component of the property's cash flow used to pay distributions. Financing costs are excluded from the definition of NOI.

5. **Cap Rate**

The quotient of NOI divided by the purchase price of the property is the Cap Rate. If the annual NOI is $1 million and the purchase price is $10 million, the Cap Rate is 10%. This is an important metric both when purchasing a property and selling a property. This metric is good for comparing properties, noting that the cap rate will differ amongst property types, property quality, profits, and geographies. Typically, sponsors should (in my opinion) estimate an "Exit Cap Rate" that is higher than their entry cap rate, making their projected IRR more conservative in light of the fact that nobody really knows what the exit cap rate will be (until realized).

Menu of Exit Strategies – The More the Merrier

A sponsor's game plan for exit is clearly to sell the property for a strong multiple in the future, irrespective of who the buyer might be. It could be a sale to another sponsor operating in the same markets or an institutional buyer. For value-add investment profiles, the renovations may be enough to target buyers that operate in a higher class of properties, thus expanding the universe of buyers and lowering the exit cap rate.

I like to find projects that could potentially be refinanced in a manner that buys out limited partners at a multiple, consistent with investor expectations. This could be an internal recapitalization such as "selling" the property or properties to another fund of the same sponsor. This would be termed an intercompany sale or internal recapitalization. For example, sponsors that offer fund products may decide that a single property should be rolled into a fund. In this case, a third-party valuation is obtained, and the property is transferred at this value. This model is commonplace in the development profile when the project moves through various funding phases. Investors may or may not be able to exit a particular development phase, depending on the terms of their agreement with the sponsor, through a recapitalization and new bank financing. In theory, each phase of the project, from permitting to final construction, adds value to the property, and different investors may participate in each phase. In multiple cases, I have been pleased to make a nice 20-25% IRR on projects that were not even sold to a third party. A recapitalization can also be external when a sponsor arranges with a large private equity firm such as Goldman Sachs to buy out the existing limited partner interests. As an investor, you should know if your sponsor has the connections and experience in executing external recapitalizations, as it is another tool for them to create positive returns for limited partners.

Extending the hold period is a clear alternative for any real estate project, especially when projections are not met for any reason. Longer hold periods can generate cash flows over longer terms and can also help preserve your principal. In one development project in Boston, the town issued a moratorium on new construction (of a particular mixed-use development), delaying construction for 18 months. While inconvenient, the project was still completed at an IRR equal to the original projection – it just took longer. There are tax benefits to holding for longer periods as well.

During sponsor-offering webinars, listen to this type of contingency planning related to any project. Experience is talking. Converting properties to another property type is another option that I have heard mentioned as a contingency plan prior to the initial closing. Examples might be converting a student housing property to a multifamily or converting an RV park to a multifamily property.

Risk Management Tools

Sponsors have many tools to manage project risk. If not obvious, ask them directly or on the offering webinar. Examples of methods include the following:

Conservative financing in terms of loan-to-value, fixed rate, or variable rate plus cap.

Sponsor buying existing property at a price representing a high cap rate relative to the market in that area, indicating a possible distressed sale.

Project rents that are at or below market rents in the area or underwriting to keep rents lower for longer to add an element of conservatism to the projected returns.

- Ability and willingness to extend the hold period to optimize IRR.
- Higher sponsor co-investment indicates alignment of interests and confidence in the project.
- Solid reserves going into the project.

Lastly, sensitivity analyses are helpful to understand the margin of error in any offering. The project's IRR sensitivity to the exit cap rate is an example that is important to know.

Fees

In Chapter 6, we discussed the fees that are associated with private offerings of commercial real estate. Back in the old days, the 2 and 20 fee structure (2% annual asset management fee plus 20% of profits) mirrored that of private equity. Today, the fee structure has morphed into one in which there are more fees, and a share of profits model that has evolved to serve the unique requirements of investors and sponsors more tightly.

Promote / Waterfall

Real estate sponsors, as is common with all private investments, generally earn a percentage of the profits, the "promote," after investors have achieved a specific level of return, the "preferred return." Promote is equivalent to the "carried interest" of private equity but can extend higher than the 20% carried interest and be more complex. The structure of the "promote" is unique depending on property type, how established and successful the sponsor is, and other factors. Understanding the terms of the "promote" is critical to assessing the sponsor's incentives and any potential conflicts of interest between a sponsor and its investors.

A "waterfall" is the formula for how the profits from a deal are shared. Figure 16 is an example of a typical waterfall structure. First, investors get their capital returned, then a minimum rate of return of 10% before the sponsor gets any share of the profits. Second, profits between a 10% and 15% IRR get split, with 75% going to the investors as a group (pro-rata basis) and 25% to the sponsor. Third, profits between a 15% and 20% IRR are split with 65% to the investors and 35% to the sponsor. Lastly, profits above a 20% IRR are split 55% to the investors and 45% to the sponsor. You can see that sponsors have a lot of incentive to generate higher profits. That is generally good, but it does not mean it will actually happen. Unforeseen macro events and bad decision-making can spoil the dream, and incentives for risk-taking may change during the course of any investment.

Figure 16

	Investor	Promote
Return of Capital		
Preferred Rate of Return - 10%	100.0%	0.0%
15%	75.0%	25.0%
20%	65.0%	35.0%
Thereafter	55.0%	45.0%

Ask yourself if the fee structure feels reasonable in your gut. Is it overly complex? High fees are a normal feature of private placement offerings, and in return, the net returns should more than compensate for this fact. Also, more established sponsors tend to have higher fees, and this can be a clue for the prospective investor. Consider this when comparing fees among sponsors that otherwise meet your criteria to invest with.

Investment Documentation

The primary investment documents are presented below. The intent here is simply to create awareness at a high level of the documents that investors will need to review closely before investing. There could be chapters devoted to tricks and traps related to these documents.

Investor Presentation

The investor presentation is the main sales document of the sponsor. The sponsor puts their best foot forward to get investors into the deal. Basic information is presented, such as the property or properties, their locations, the total offering size, sources and uses of funds for the project, estimated IRR, equity multiple, and cash-on-cash return. In its best light, the executive summary will cover the opportunity, the financial aspects, and the related timetable and "hold period." Each property will be presented in detail, including mapped locations and lots of pictures. Depending on the project, a listing of "sales comparables" and "rent comparables" will be presented relevant to the property in the offering, providing support for the financial pro forma, which provides the income statement projections for each year of the estimated hold period for the investment. The presentation should include a clear description of the waterfall structure. Sometimes, sponsors will present sensitivity analyses for key variables such as the exit cap rate.

Private Placement Memorandum (PPM)

The PPM discloses the essential features of the offering, what you are investing in, how it works, and its risks. Post-investment, this document gets filed away but is useful for referring back to as progress is reported back to investors. Not an all-inclusive list, the types of information found in PPMs are as follows:

- Introduction and offering terms.
- Investor suitability requirements
- Investment objectives and distributions
- Use of proceeds and fees
- Description of the capital stack, including loan terms, preferred equity, or priority equity
- Sponsor background and key personnel
- Risk factors. This should be a lengthy list.
- Call provisions. There should be a voluntary capital call provision to allow limited partners to protect their investments.

Operating Agreement

The limited liability company (LLC) operating agreement covers the activities of the project on a post-investment basis. Real estate syndications are typically structured as LLCs due to the flexibility that this structure provides, the limited liability provisions, and the ability to designate a managing member or manager. The manager typically does not need approval from the investors to carry out regular duties as long as the manager is acting within the authority given by the LLC's operating agreement. The operating agreement covers the following:

- The legal name of the manager
- Rights of limited partners
- Process for changing or removing the manager.
- Manager duties and responsibilities and related liabilities
- Provisions around capital contributions, additional contributions, withdrawals from the business, and the formula for calculating capital account balances. Withdrawal provisions should mirror the waterfall structure in the other offering documents.
- Taxation provisions and elections
- Maintenance of books and records

Subscription Agreement

A subscription agreement is an agreement that defines the terms for an investor's investment into a private placement. The rules for subscription agreements are defined in SEC Rule 506 (b) and 506 (c) of Regulation D. A subscription agreement is between a company and a private investor to sell a specific number of shares at a specific price, and it documents that investor's suitability for investing in the LLC partnership.

Additional Processes

1. Investors should attend the sponsor's online seminar on the offering. Listen to their questions and the questions of the other investors in that forum. In general, the questions asked during these webinars indicate that your fellow investors are a well-informed and experienced group. Use it as a learning experience.
2. Carefully review the offering documents and seek help from legal and tax counsel as required.
3. Step back and review the risk/return profile of the offering. If a 10% IRR, is it really that safe? What are the risks? If there is a 30% IRR, the risks should be obvious due to its high operational risk or excessive leverage. You should understand why the expected return is so high.
4. How does this offer stack up with other offerings being reviewed? Just as real estate sponsors look at hundreds of deals before securing an attractive property, so should you. There will always be another deal coming, and opportunity costs are omnipresent. Be patient.
5. Seek counsel prior to investing until you have the requisite experience in these markets.

Quick Summary

1. Your plan for investing in private assets should be your North Star – don't be distracted by sponsors and offerings that don't meet your objectives.
2. Private commercial real estate offerings currently provide the best landscape for building a portfolio that reflects your risk tolerance, portfolio allocation, and requirements for diversification across all aspects of the domain.

3. It bears repeating: choose your "authorized sponsors" carefully. Start with the very experienced subset. Investors need to diversify optimally given the constraints of the sponsor list, your available capital, and your overarching investment plan.
4. Private market investments have high fees. This is just the way it is because you are dealing with real businesses that are doing real work to create value for investors and themselves. Satisfy yourself that your interests are aligned with the sponsor's interests with respect to the promote structure, the sponsor's co-investment, and fees levels. Take comfort in the fact that sponsors that do not align their interests with their investors will not be in business for the long term.
5. Seek professional assistance in the document review process until you have gained enough sophistication and experience.
6. Invest the minimum with new sponsors. This investment will be the beginning of a new extended period of due diligence with that sponsor.

Chapter 8 - Sponsors and Private Offerings for Private Equity

Why can't the SEC figure out a way to approve certain fund structures for private equity and venture capital for non-accredited investors? The average investor can buy lottery tickets and can even invest in start-up companies on crowdfunding sites, but they cannot invest in proven fund vehicles that provide diversification benefits, mitigate single-asset risk, and provide stabilized (and higher) returns. There has to be a reasonable way for investors to access such funds in taxable or retirement accounts. Congress is hellbent on allowing 401k plans to offer cryptocurrency! Hopefully, this will change, at least in retirement accounts. Private equity and its venture capital subcomponent represent the best of capitalism, Main Street business requiring debt and equity capital to grow. Founders utilize the private-active component of the quadrant to build businesses that generate employment and solve societal problems.

Figure 17

	Public Markets	**Private Markets**
Passive	Wall Street. SEC makes it easy to invest here.	Main Street. Accredited investors and institutions operate here. Average investor has limited access to invest passively in private equity.
Active	Wall Street. SEC makes it easy to invest here.	Main Street. Entrepreneurs create businesses here.

Access to private equity is coming to the masses at a measured pace. Go small, go slow. Learn. This is where the existing SEC private investment framework needs to evolve to allow every investor access to private equity or venture capital fund products. Liberalizing the rules to democratize private investing might include the following three elements: (1) limits on how much investors can invest, (2) parameters around fund diversification, (3) that investment be made through a regulated entity such as a financial advisor or crowdfunding/fintech sponsor that vets the underlying fund sponsor(s) in the same way that mutual fund managers perform due diligence on stocks they add to their portfolios. Effectively, feeder funds managed by regulated entities could be funded by non-accredited investors. Imagine a future where Vanguard acquires or develops a feeder fund platform to allow its retirement customers to participate in private equity funds on its network, up to 25% of the customer's aggregate retirement account balances at the time of commitment to the offering. At present, primarily accredited investors and the uber-wealthy can benefit from adding private equity to their private-passive portfolios.

Why go through all this trouble again? Because risk-adjusted returns for private equity and venture capital funds are better than investing in the S&P 500. In general terms, limited partners (LPs) typically consider their investment in a venture fund successful if it returns at least three times their committed capital and more than 25% IRR after 10 years.

The metrics for evaluating private equity are similar and more abbreviated than those used for private real estate.

Internal Rate of Return (IRR)

IRR is a measure of how profitable an investment is on an annualized basis over the term of the investment. It factors in the initial investment and the timing of cash flows, including the final exit value and when they occur. It is really an annualized measure of return. If you achieve an IRR of 15%, you can compare this measure to what you would have earned in a savings account, such as 1% per annum. An IRR of 0% means you eventually got your money back. A negative IRR means you lost part or all of your investment principal. This metric is the ultimate measure of success or failure in an investment.

Multiple on Invested Capital (MOIC) or Total Value to Paid-In Capital (TVPI)

The formula is (Realized Value + Unrealized Value) / Total Amount Invested. For investors, this is the gross multiple of how much money they have made relative to how much money they have invested. A value of 2x means investors have doubled their money (to date).

The legendary investor David Swensen and his team's success at Yale University was due in part to shifting the portfolio allocation more towards private investments, from 19% to 38% allocation. Figure 18 provides evidence of this shift and strong anecdotal evidence that this strategy has merit; otherwise, why would the portfolio move in this direction? Again, I have not found direct evidence that Swensen recommends that individuals move into private investments; on the contrary, he did recommend a public-passive approach to individual investing. However, the world is changing with new innovations that will liberalize access to private-passive investment vehicles. It is really interesting how Yale University's allocation to public equities has declined over the past decades to a mere 2.3% allocation in 2020. Given the success of Yale over the decades, should we question the common advice of investing 60% of a portfolio in public equities and 40% in public fixed income?

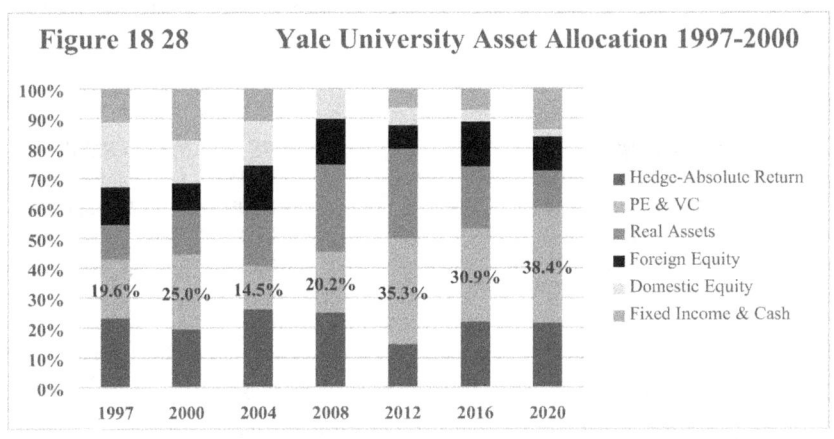

Figure 18 28   Yale University Asset Allocation 1997-2000

Risk-adjusted returns are historically better, as illustrated in Figure 19.

Figure 19 (1986-2020) [29]

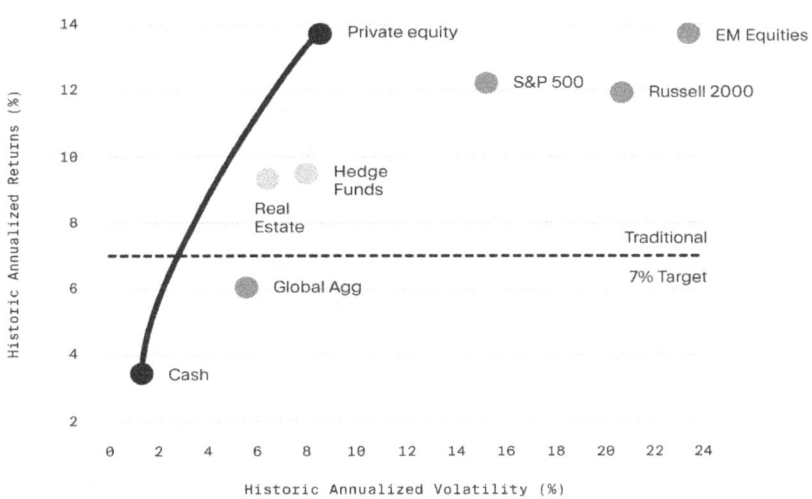

Similar to commercial real estate, the best risk-adjusted returns are reserved for top-tier private equity firms. The average returns for private equity as a "pool" (weighted private equity index) have consistently outperformed the median return, meaning the largest funds far outperform the average private equity fund. Stated another way, if you randomly select a private equity sponsor, it is likely that the returns will be at or below the "indexed returns" for the asset class. Figure 20 illustrates this point. Finding and riding the coattails of the most significant fund sponsors is worth the effort in researching. Find the firms with the best, most consistent track records. The holy grail for private-passive investors would be an index fund for the private equity fund universe weighted by market cap.

Figure 20 [30]

Historical Period	Pooled Net IRR	Median Net IRR
5-Year Average (2016-2020)	27.8%	11.2%
7-Year Average (2014-2020)	26.0%	12.6%
10-Year Average (2011-2020)	23.3%	13.6%
20-Year Average (2001-2020)	18.1%	11.2%

Further corroboration of the favorable performance of private equity and venture capital was the landmark study published in 2003 in the National Bureau of Economic Research by Alexander Ljungqvist and Matthew Richardson.[FN] The researchers found that private equity generated substantial excess returns related to the S&P 500. Specifically, for funds started between 1981 and 1993 (the "mature" funds in the dataset), internal rates of return averaged 19.81 percent, net of all fees. In contrast, investment in the S&P 500 index under an identical time schedule of cash outflows yielded 14.1 percent. The excess average (mean) returns of 5.7% percent per annum were deemed to originate mainly due to the extreme illiquidity of private equity investments. Interestingly, the median excess return was lower at 4.1%, as one would expect due to the many funds that underperform the market. A third-quartile private equity fund outperformed the S&P 500 by 13.8%!

We can argue all day whether the private equity return premium is 2% or 6%. Directionally, we have strong evidence that private equity will outperform the S&P 500 over the long term. Unfortunately, private-passive investors cannot index their investments to earn an average return in private equity. Success will depend on execution and will vary significantly by an investor. These are the main lessons with private equity – on average, the returns will be better than public equities, but an investor needs to identify fund sponsors that are regularly performing in the third or fourth quartiles of the overall private equity market. Stated another way, a typical individual investor should avoid private equity funds without a track record or a track record below the median of the competitive set.

How to Find a Sponsor of Private Equity

First, the approach recommended for investing in private equity or venture capital is with funds offered by excellent, established sponsors. We are talking about firms with the substance of Blackstone, Cinven, Insight Partners, Oaktree, Harbourvest, and Apollo. If you are thinking about investing in the next great single-asset unicorn, such as Uber or Google, you are on your own. Accordingly, the question becomes how we find the funds from the top quartile of private equity firms. Also, this is a global arena, and the search for excellent fund opportunities will extend beyond the borders of the USA. Have an open mind to expanding your targeted geographic scope for this asset class, but keep in mind that USA investors will be subject to some degree of currency risk related to investments in foreign companies.

The process of locating great private equity firms with offerings available (and fitting in with your overall plan) is the reverse of the process recommended for commercial real estate. First, you need to find the funds and then determine if they are offered by a successful private equity firm. The methods for locating opportunities with great sponsors are the following:

Financial Advisor: Financial advisors or wealth managers can provide access to private equity. As quoted from Forbes Magazine, private markets are now widely available for advisors and many of their individual clients because of today's much lower minimum thresholds. For advisors, today's easier access to private markets allows them to greatly expand their capabilities and enhance their competitive positioning.[31]

Crowdfunding Platforms: Crowdfunding aggregators that have processes to identify or target the best funds so that they can bring them to individual investors.

Invest in a Portfolio of Public Stocks of Private Equity Firms: Especially if a private-passive investor cannot devote at least $75,000 to a fund through a crowdfunding platform, put together a portfolio of at least five of the largest private equity enterprises, such as Blackstone. There are also private equity index ETFs, but make sure you have a good idea of the specific holdings inside these ETFs. Using this strategy has the benefit of instant liquidity, but this is also a potential negative since the mindset for private-passive investing involves locking funds up for ten years in order to earn higher returns.

The average investor needs to work with intermediaries such as these to access this valuable asset class. You cannot just call Blackstone with the $50,000 you are trying to put to work.

Private Equity Landscape

Private equity firms classify their vintage funds by sector, geography, and investment strategy. The assets within one fund provide some diversification, but if you seek to have more than one fund, further diversification benefits can be achieved by paying attention to these variables.

Sectors

- Technology and software
- Healthcare
- Business services
- Industrials
- Consumer discretionary
- Software services
- Financial
- Telecoms
- Consumer staples
- The intrepid "Other" category

Geographical Region

- USA
- Europe
- Asia
- A global index would consist of 60% USA, 30% Europe, and 10% Asia.

Investment Strategy

There are four main investment strategies associated with private equity. The staging or progression of companies along this continuum is illustrated below.

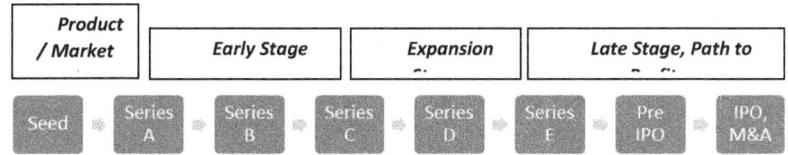

Venture Capital – minority interest in early-stage companies.

Growth Equity – minority interest in expansion or growth-stage companies.

Buyout Equity – controlling interest in mature, post-IPO companies.

Infrastructure - Infrastructure funds invest in public assets and services that are essential for a functioning society, such as power, transport, water, and waste. These funds benefit from consistent, long-term returns, low volatility, and low correlation to the wider market, making them an attractive addition to a private equity portfolio.

Private credit - Private credit is where a non-bank lender provides loans to companies, typically to small and medium-sized enterprises that are non-investment grade. This topic is covered in more depth in Chapter 10.

The private-passive investment framework expanded to include the private equity and venture capital asset class, as shown in Figure 21.

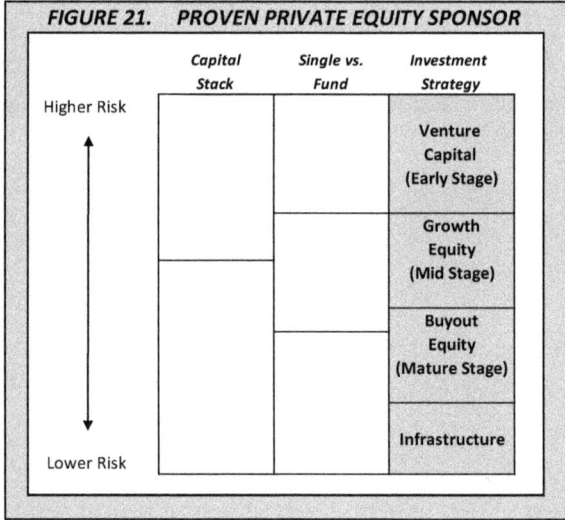

Vintage Diversification

Another dimension of diversification with private equity funds is time. Since new vintages are introduced approximately every three years, an investor can participate in each vintage of a given sponsor in order to smooth out the variability of returns due to regular business cycles.

Types of Private Equity Funds

Figure 22

Fund Type	One PE Sponsor?	Investing in Multiple Funds?	Decision Maker for Target Companies
Traditional private equity vintage	Yes	No	The PE Firm
Co-investment fund	No	No	The Platform or Advisor, and the PE Firm
Fund of Funds	No	Yes	The PE Firms
Passive PE index funds	No	Yes	The PE Firms

For each of the four types above, there will be a crowdfunding platform or financial advisory firm that sponsors the offering. The private equity fund or lead venture capital fund, if that is the case, is responsible for managing the individual companies in the fund.

1. Traditional Private Equity Fund

Private equity funds are typically offered in vintages every 3 years approximately. Each vintage is labeled with a Roman numeral (I, II, III, IV). The fund raises a designed amount of capital in the billions. Feeder funds participate in the offerings by aggregated investments from accredited investors or qualified purchasers. An investment period is defined, typically five years, to invest all of the funds raised. The fund life might be ten years, with two or three optional one-year extensions to allow for ample time to fix and grow the businesses held in the portfolio. These are very illiquid, long-term investments. Private equity firms focus on one or multiple sectors of the economy, such as technology and/or healthcare; such sectors are clearly defined in the offering materials. Each fund focuses on a given strategy, for example, buyout or growth-equity. Some funds are multi-strategy. The top-level private equity firms understand their lane and stick with the strategies and sectors where their expertise rests. The geographical reach of the fund will also be described in terms of USA, Europe, Asia, or global. Each fund should list investing parameters or restrictions, examples as follows:

- Limit on single company exposure (15-20%)
- Limits on geography allocation (such as no more than 50% outside of the USA)
- Limits on firm stage for multi-strategy funds (such as no more than 10% in early-stage)

The targeted number of investments would be 15-25, providing adequate diversification. Fees are the 2% management fee and 20% carried interest after an 8% hurdle rate for the investors is achieved. The sponsor should co-invest alongside the investors in the amount of 3-5% of the fund.

Investing in a single firm vintage fund can be a simple and great strategy for the investor as long as the sponsor has a strong track record with past vintages. It is an even better strategy to align your investments to participate in every vintage fund of a trusted sponsor since they come up every three years or so. This provides "vintage" or time diversification so that the returns are normalized across business cycles. Similar to commercial real estate funds, you don't need to make this overly complex. One or two trusted sponsors is usually all that is required to succeed, depending on the size of the portfolio.

2. Co-investment Fund

This variation consists of one feeder fund created to invest in many companies alongside private equity managers. The fund size might be around $50-100 million, with the intent of investing in anywhere from 10-50 companies across multiple strategies. Within the fund, you might have deals with KKR, Genstar, Blackstone, and TPG – you won't really know until the investment period has been completed. A typical co-investment fund would have a relatively shorter investment period of 1-2 years and a term of seven years with two to three extension options. Examples of two financial platforms (crowdfunding) that offer these types of funds are OurCrowd and Moonfare.

A great feature of a co-investment fund is the diversification across strategies, sectors, and geographic regions. A fund of ten companies is adequate for diversification purposes. Another benefit co-investment funds provide is giving the investor exposure to excellent companies at lower fees. Returns can be enhanced because of the rapid deployment of funds (one year vs. five years for traditional private equity funds). The good news is that you can find co-investment funds for as little as $75,000 minimum investment. A disadvantage is that the deal selection is up to the financial platform sponsoring the deal. There is no discernable track record until the platform itself successfully comes full cycle on a series of such co-investment funds. You can take comfort that the underlying lead private equity firms are doing what they do best. The only question is the capability of the investment team of the platform company to work with the top tier private equity firms and source decent transactions. Is there real skill and experience behind these investment decisions, or is it more a dartboard approach with an eye toward building a nicely diversified portfolio?

3. Fund of Funds

Similar to the "fund of funds" concept for hedge funds (Skybridge Capital), the concept is also being adopted in private equity. Think of it as buying a mutual fund that invests only in other mutual funds in the public markets. It may sound a bit silly in this context since we are taught that mutual funds are already a diversified instrument. The difference in private markets, and private equity in particular, is that any single fund's performance is a function of (1) how each portfolio company operates, plus (2) the skill and ability of the private equity fund to identify great acquisitions and to manage these acquisitions throughout their life cycle. In fact, you are betting primarily on the private equity firm. If you could invest simultaneously in 5-7 private equity funds of high quality, wouldn't that be nice?

Financial advisors may have access to these types of products historically, but digital platforms are now enabling accredited investors to access fund of funds products. This is an exciting development and a trend that will continue. This product is ideally suited for a future when the regulatory environment loosens to allow individual investors access to private equity, with guidelines offered through third parties with the sophistication to make decisions on what is appropriate for those investors (plan sponsors, digital platforms, financial advisors).

Fund of funds can specialize in any investment strategy, be it venture capital, growth equity, or buyout funds. With all of these, the digital platform's investment committee serves the function of asset acquisition – which funds to include in the portfolio. The platform would employ a rigorous due diligence and fund selection process. They would start with the list of top private equity firms and work with them to arrange a portfolio of 5-7 portfolios that are scheduled to launch in this vintage year. An example of parameters of a fund of funds might include the following:

- 5-7 funds, with current vintages being launched.
- Represents over fifty underlying portfolio companies.
- Fund closing in six months (fast).
- Ten-year life, with two or three one-year extensions.
- Minimum investment: $75,000-$200,000.
- Accredited investor or qualified purchaser.
- One-time acquisition fees of .5%-1.0%.
- Annual fees of .5%-1.0%.
- Carried interest – no, but find out definitively in your due diligence.

The disadvantage is that the investor does not get to choose the funds. As most investors are not experienced in these matters, this is more likely an advantage. Also, there is an extra level of fees for the digital platform since they do not wish to work for free. The clear advantage is the increased diversification benefits and the potential for earlier distributions since there are more underlying companies in the portfolio (more early exit potential). Investors should get a smoother, more reliable IRR that meets the 20%+ expectation from investing in private equity and venture capital.

4. Passive Index

"My regular recommendation has been a low-cost S&P 500 index fund," Buffett wrote in his 2016 Berkshire Hathaway annual shareholder letter. The holy grail in public-passive investing is the index fund. Active investing cannot beat passive; do not try to pick winners. Will the equivalent of index investing find its way into private-passive investing, in particular private equity? There have been promising developments on this front, but mostly with the largest platforms that target institutional investors and financial advisers, which ultimately could benefit the individual investor. It is reasonable to assume that a direct-to-accredited investor platform will arise in the foreseeable future.

Per the NewVest website, "NewVest is an institutional fintech platform of index funds that provide passive exposure to private markets in the same manner that ETFs and Index Funds provide passive exposure to public markets." This caught my eye, and I discovered it through what I consider another reputable digital platform, OurCrowd. In its press release dated January 31, 2023, NewVest announced the launch of its inaugural product, the Private Equity 50 Index Fund ("PE 50"), the first-ever private markets index fund. NewVest's mission is to transform private market investing by helping to improve access to private markets and optimize portfolio construction for all investors and private markets investment programs. One of the many nice features is that the PE 50 is a weighted index, meaning the largest private equity firms are given a higher weight. This would solve the problem mentioned earlier in this chapter, that the average return for the private equity markets is higher than the median return – i.e., the largest firms tend to outperform the average. The PE 50 intends to include the passive capital-weighting of the 50 largest global PE funds, including Blackstone, Apollo, TPG, Bain Capital, Hellman and Friedman, and many others.

OurCrowd's listing of NewVest PE 50 is, unfortunately, for qualified purchasers only, with a $100,000 minimum. If available to accredited investors, count me in. The NewVest digital platform targets institutional investors and financial advisors. Nonetheless, the convergence of technology and more flexible regulation is rapidly bringing private market innovations to the masses. We are still in the first inning, and it is important that educational resources keep up with developments in the private markets to provide investors with the promise of equal access to all private asset classes in the future.

Liquidity and Leverage

Make no mistake, commitments to private equity and its venture capital subclass are long-term in nature. Given the current uncertain economic backdrop in 2022, illiquidity was the most common issue or concern cited by the Moonfare investor community in their 2022 investor survey. The truth is that in turbulent economic times, investors operating in the public equity and bond markets would be well served to take a long-term approach to building wealth and not be juked out of the markets in uncertain times.

Older investors may want to pause based on this fact to evaluate their interim cash flow requirements and estimated lifespan versus the expected life of the fund. The term structure of these funds is typically 10 years with multiple options for 1-year extensions. Venture capital typically takes longer to produce distributions than all other forms of private equity, as confirmed by 2020 Pitchbook data. In fact, distributions in venture capital funds tend to be the most frequent and robust during Years 11 and 12 for VC funds, and only half of these vehicles fully liquidated by Year 14.32 Although this timeline has been shrinking in recent years, it is still important to be aware of it.

Leverage is what juices the returns for private equity investments and, accordingly, funds. Venture capital funds are less likely to employ debt since there is enough business or operational risk to justify the higher returns. Just be aware of how leverage is used and how it might impact the performance of any fund you select.

Cash Flow – Distributions and Reporting Cadences

Unlike their counterparts in commercial real estate, where the cadence and quality of reporting varies, established private equity firms are staffed with formal external reporting departments. The standard of quarterly and annual reports is and should be excellent. Annual reports should contain audited financials, and knowing who the fund auditors are is good information. Private equity firms should be proud to disclose this.

The typical comprehensive quarterly report is provided within 60 days of each calendar quarter and would include reports as follows:

- A summary from the General Partner.
- Financial statements, including balance sheets, portfolio of Investments, statements of operations, statements of partnership capital, statements of cash flows, and notes to the financial statements. The year-end report would include an auditor's opinion as well.
- Supplemental schedules may include a portfolio overview, a summary of portfolio movements, investment activities, valuation adjustments, realized gains and losses, IRR and TVPI calculations, and fees and carried interest calculations.
- New Investment Summaries – good reports will provide a condensed business plan for each new investment made during the quarter.
- Current activity reports which provide information on new capital events for companies in the fund's portfolio.

Getting experience with a top-notch private equity firm provides a wealth of information through their quarterly reports. Studying these reports will make you a better investor in time, or "sophisticated," as the SEC would say. There is nothing like seeing an IRR of 40% after five years, for example and knowing that a public index fund would earn 10% on average.

Applying Lessons from Public Markets to Private Markets

A major theme of this book is to apply proven lessons from the public markets as you look to operationalize a strategy in the private markets. The truths are universal.

Figure 23

Lesson from Public Markets	Adaption to Private Markets
Buy and hold; do not trade excessively	This is an automatic discipline in private markets since these funds are illiquid and have a ten-plus year term. Do not enter investments casually. Money is made on the entry.
Diversify	Focus on private equity or venture capital funds from top 50 PE firms. Avoid investments in single companies in your formal investment plan. Watch for concentrations of risk in sectors, and geographies. For example, select a venture capital fund and a buyout fund (strategy diversification).
Dollar cost average to smooth out the highs and lows in your cost basis	Start as small as possible with funds. Also, consider a strategy of investing in each vintage of a private equity or VC firm that you trust, every three years, to smooth out volatility due to normal business cycles.
Passive investing beats active investing	It is exceedingly difficult to be an active investor with a fund strategy in private markets. Owning the market to a greater degree means buying a fund that indexes the private equity market or buying a fund of funds to achieve greater diversification. Once your chips are down, you have no choice but to be passive.

Quick Summary

1. Disciplined investors operating in the private markets should shy away from single-company offerings and focus only on private equity and venture capital funds.
2. Select proven funds, top 50 venture capital, or private equity sponsors, or use a platform that provides the sponsor filtering with their own due diligence processes. Larger, more established private equity firms have historically outperformed the median funds.
3. Private equity is slowly becoming more accessible to accredited investors through intermediaries and digital crowdfunding platforms.
4. Lessons from public markets need to be applied to private markets, particularly diversification, long-term buy and hold, and dollar cost averaging.
5. Keep it simple. Start small, pick one or two sponsors with proven fund vintages, and stick to what works.

Chapter 9 - Crowdfunding Platforms – Democratizing Private-Passive Investing?

A crowdfunding platform is an online marketplace or brokerage service that connects startups, small businesses, or real estate sponsors with potential investors who are interested in investing in the business project in exchange for an equity stake. Equity crowdfunding allows businesses to raise funds from a large number of investors, typically through the Internet, rather than seeking funding from a few large investors or going public with an initial public offering (IPO).

On a crowdfunding platform, businesses typically create a profile and attempt to raise funding for their project, outlining their funding goals, business model, and potential for growth, income, and total return. Potential investors can browse through these profiles and decide whether they want to invest in the business. The investment process typically takes place through the platform, which oversees the legal and administrative aspects of the investment.

In exchange for their investment, investors typically receive an interest as a limited partner in the business or real estate project, which entitles them to a share of the profits and a limited say in how the business is run. Equity crowdfunding platforms typically charge the sponsor or business a fee for their services, which may include a percentage of the funds raised or a flat fee. From the sponsor's point of view, crowdfunding is a different way of marketing syndication offerings that traditionally had been offered directly to accredited investors. For example, CrowdStreet charges sponsors due diligence and placement fees in connection with the private placement offerings, ranging from 1% to 5% of the total offering size, and affiliates of CrowdStreet charge sponsors' services and technology fees.32 It is worth noting that there is nothing to prevent sponsors from directly or indirectly passing along this cost to investors.

Crowdfunding platforms will need to prove to investors that, over the long term, they can deliver quality investment options and attractive risk-adjusted returns. My instinct is to be skeptical, and accordingly, it is my normal policy to invest the minimum amount with new sponsors on a given platform only after completing my due diligence. Never assume that the crowdfunding platform will do your due diligence for you. A commonly asked question to a sponsor distributing an offering through a crowdfunding platform is, "Why are you offering this deal through the crowdfunding portal versus directly to investors?" The answer invariably is to the effect that outsourcing fundraising and investor relations to a third-party platform can be more effective and efficient. Or the answer might be that they want to diversify their investor base, and they love individual investors. Another likely reason is that the cost of capital is less expensive for them. The top real estate sponsors on my approved list do not (yet) distribute via a crowdfunding platform. However, increasingly reputable or "enterprise" sponsors are migrating to such platforms because it effectively allows them to outsource the fund-raising functions of the sponsor so they can focus entirely on their principal functions of locating projects, underwriting, asset, and property management functions.

I favor the offerings of funds, including those managed by the platform itself. Large platforms such as OurCrowd and CrowdStreet offer their own proprietary funds that leverage the platforms' experience with the sponsor community and obviously provide diversification benefits. Why initially invest in a fund offered by the platform? Because investors will be able to diversify their portfolios while learning how a grouping of crowdfunding offerings will perform over time. Anecdotally, they will likely find that the performance of the majority of the offerings within a fund will underperform the targets in their underwriting materials. Crowdfunding is a good idea in theory, but in practice has been painful to many investors. If the attraction is too strong, utilize a minimum investment in a fund product and make your own conclusions after five to seven years.

How Is Equity Crowdfunding Regulated in the USA?

Equity crowdfunding in the USA is regulated by the Securities and Exchange Commission (SEC) under the framework of the Jumpstart Our Business Startups (JOBS) Act, which was signed into law in 2012. The JOBS Act created or updated exemptions to the traditional registration requirements for securities offerings, including Regulation Crowdfunding (Reg CF) and Regulation A+ (Reg A+).

Regulation Crowdfunding allows small businesses to raise up to $5 million per year from individual investors through crowdfunding platforms registered with the SEC. The regulation imposes various requirements on the issuer, the intermediary platform, and the investors, such as financial disclosures, limitations on the amount that can be invested by an individual, and restrictions on the resale of securities. Under Regulation Crowdfunding, non-accredited investors are subject to investment limits when investing in crowdfunding offerings. There are no limits on the amount an accredited investor may invest in offerings under Regulation Crowdfunding.

If you are a non-accredited investor, then the limitation on how much you can invest depends on your net worth and annual income.

- If either your annual income or your net worth is less than $124,000, then during any 12-month period, you can invest up to the greater of either $2,500 or 5% of the greater of your annual income or net worth.
- If both your annual income and your net worth are equal to or more than $124,000, then during any 12 months, you can invest up to 10% of your annual income or net worth, whichever is greater but not to exceed $124,000.

Regulation A+ became effective in June 2015, and it allows businesses to raise up to $75 million per year through a streamlined public offering process. This regulation also imposes various requirements, such as disclosure and reporting requirements and limitations on the amount that can be invested by an individual. Regulation A, Tier 2 individual investors are limited to the aggregate purchase price for an investment in an offering to 10% of the greater of annual income or net worth.

In addition, equity crowdfunding is subject to state securities laws, known as "Blue Sky" laws, which vary from state to state. Some states have implemented their own crowdfunding regulations or exemptions, which issuers must comply with in addition to federal regulations.

Overall, the SEC and state regulators closely monitor equity crowdfunding to ensure compliance with the applicable regulations and protect investors from fraudulent activities.

Regulatory changes in Crowdfunding have opened the door for the democratization of investing and is the best way for non-accredited investors to participate in early-stage ventures. The net impact of increased regulation over crowdfunding is certainly a net positive, attracting higher quality crowdfunding platforms, more reputable underlying business ventures, and more competition in this arena.

Growth in Equity Crowdfunding Worldwide

Equity crowdfunding has grown significantly worldwide over the past decade as a result of the increasing demand for alternative sources of financing and advancements in technology that have made it easier to connect investors with businesses or real estate projects seeking funding.

According to a report by Statista, the global equity crowdfunding market size was valued at $7.8 billion in 2020 and is projected to reach $28.8 billion by 2026, growing at a compound annual growth rate (CAGR) of 24.4% from 2021 to 2026. In the United Kingdom, the world's largest crowdfunding market and the longest history dating back to 2010, crowdfunding volumes increased from £272 million in 2016 to £549 million in 2020.[33] This growth has been driven by the increasing popularity of equity crowdfunding platforms, which allow limited partnerships to raise capital from a large number of individual investors through digital platforms.

The growth of equity crowdfunding has been particularly strong in Europe, where regulatory frameworks have been established to support the industry. For example, the European Union's MiFID II regulations have facilitated cross-border investment by standardizing investor protection and disclosure requirements across EU member states. In the USA, the regulatory changes provided by the JOBS Act have resulted in relaxed minimum investment requirements for accredited and non-accredited investors alike and increased the size of offerings allowable under the regulatory exceptions. All signs point to larger and better crowdfunding markets on a global basis in the future.

How Can Crowdfunding Platforms Help Protect Investors?

In the early days of crowdfunding, lower-quality entrepreneurs, on average, tended to gravitate to equity crowdfunding platforms.[34] One can only hope that the growth of the industry has attracted higher-quality operators of crowdfunding sites and that regulation has dissuaded bad actors. Future growth in this powerful form of financing will ultimately depend on how well these platforms do their job of protecting investors as best they can. Crowdfunding platforms can help protect accredited investors in several ways:

1. **Verification of Accreditation:** Crowdfunding platforms can verify that investors who claim to be accredited investors meet the criteria established by the Securities and Exchange Commission (SEC). This can help prevent non-accredited investors from participating in investment opportunities that are only available to accredited investors.

2. **Disclosure Requirements**: Crowdfunding platforms can require issuers to disclose information about the investment opportunity, including financial statements, business plans, and other relevant information in a uniform format. This can help investors make informed decisions about whether to invest in a particular offering. Transparency and uniformity of disclosures is vital. Commercial real estate crowdfunding earns good marks on these fronts due to the uniform nature of real estate itself. Equity investments in real businesses is where the real problem rests, as disclosure formats and depth are anything but uniform.

3. **Due Diligence**: Crowdfunding platforms can conduct due diligence on issuers to ensure they are legitimate and that their offering is not a scam or fraudulent. This can help prevent investors from losing money in fraudulent schemes, at least in theory. In the past five years, I have seen start-up equity offerings in which the lead entrepreneur was sanctioned by the SEC, and such information was not disclosed. Also, it is important to understand what percentage of deals the crowdfunding platform accepts and what their due diligence process is. The more selective the platform is, the higher the quality of offerings travel through the funnel.

4. **Categorize Sponsor or Entrepreneur Experience**: Crowdfunding platforms can extend their due diligence to summarize and classify the sponsor's track record and experience for investors. For example, CrowdStreet has created the sponsor experience categories of Emerging, Seasoned, Tenured, and Enterprise to provide investors with a quick label to understand the sponsor's experience. Of course, if applicable, the detailed track record of a sponsor or entrepreneur should be disclosed to corroborate the ratings.

5. **Investor Education:** Crowdfunding platforms can provide educational resources for investors to help them understand the risks and rewards of investing in private offerings. This can help investors make informed decisions and avoid making costly mistakes.

6. **Provisions of Fund Product**: Crowdfunding platforms can strive to offer funds as well as single-asset investments to help protect investors with (1) professional management or asset selection and (2) natural diversification benefits.

7. **Escrow Services**: Crowdfunding platforms can hold investor funds in escrow until the offering is closed, and the funds are released to the issuer. This can help prevent issuers from misusing investor funds or running off with the money. I thought this was rather trite, but an episode involving Crowdstreet and Nightingale Group in 2023 illustrated the importance of escrowing investor funds. Nightingale raised $53 million from Crowdstreet investors to close on a large office value-added project. The Atlanta Financial Center, in November 2022, and the deal still had not closed as of July 2023. This event resulted in a complete change in policy by Crowdstreet. Per Crowdstreet, "We are

reaching out to share a recent change to the investment funding process. Starting June 1, 2023, all offerings launched on the CrowdStreet Marketplace utilize third-party escrow accounts, with the goal of providing an additional layer of investor protection through the transaction process."

Overall, excellent crowdfunding platforms perform a lot of useful functions for investors and sponsors. One item you do not typically see from crowdfunding platforms is a feature that tracks the progress or outcome of each of their offerings. The offering is posted, it gets funded, and then it will appear as a "past funded" (not a hyperlink to more detail), but no outcome information. It would be nice for investors to see progress, future rounds, a field for "in progress vs. exited," and realized IRR. It would be even better if this post-funding data functioned as a database to allow investors to do their own filtering, answering questions such as "What is the average or median IRR for a sponsor on the site or by sector or property type?" In short, crowdfunding platforms can help investors in many ways, but I have seen no evidence that they can deliver even average returns to investors over the long term.

How Can Crowdfunding Benefit Investors?

Real estate crowdfunding can benefit both accredited and non-accredited investors as follows:

1. **Access to Real Estate Deals**: Real estate crowdfunding platforms provide investors access to a variety of real estate deals that they may not have been able to invest in otherwise. This allows investors to diversify their portfolios and invest in a range of different properties with varying investment strategies.
2. **Lower Minimum Investments:** Real estate crowdfunding platforms often have lower minimum investments than traditional real estate investments, making it easier for investors to get started with real estate investing.
3. **Passive Income**: Real estate crowdfunding allows investors to earn passive income from rental properties without the hassle of being a proprietor. Investors can earn rental income from properties that are managed by the platform, and they do not have to deal with property management or maintenance issues.
4. **Potential for High Returns**: Real estate crowdfunding can provide investors with the potential for high returns. Investors can benefit from capital gains by investing in properties that are expected to appreciate in value. Attractive returns are basically the reward for the lack of liquidity in private markets. Personally, my greatest wins to date have not been delivered through crowdfunding platforms.
5. **Portfolio Diversification**: Real estate crowdfunding allows investors to diversify their portfolio with real estate assets and can further diversify these real estate assets by investing in funds or accumulating a grouping of single asset offerings. Real estate can act as a hedge against inflation and can provide investors with a stable source of income.
6. **Transparency and Due Diligence**: Real estate crowdfunding platforms provide investors with access to detailed information about the properties they are investing in, including financial projections, market analysis, and property details. This allows investors to conduct their own due diligence and make informed investment decisions. In addition, investors' peers interacting within the platform can be an

amazing source of information and knowledge. It is standard practice for sponsors to hold a webinar with question-and-answer sessions for each capital raise within the platform. I have found other investors' questions and concerns to be very insightful, occasionally putting the sponsor on the defensive and influencing my investment decision. The community effect of crowdfunding platforms is real.

Private equity crowdfunding's benefits are the same listing as above.

What are the Risks of Investing in Equity Crowdfunding Platforms?

Equity crowdfunding platforms can offer a way for individuals to invest in startup companies and other ventures that may not be available through traditional investment channels. However, as with any investment, there are risks associated with investing on equity crowdfunding platforms. The following are potential risks:

- **Lack of Liquidity:** Most importantly, crowdfunding private investments are generally illiquid, meaning it may be difficult to sell your shares and realize a profit or minimize losses.
- **Limited Information:** Startups and other ventures that raise funds through equity crowdfunding platforms may not have a track record of financial performance, which can make it difficult to evaluate the potential risks and returns of the investment.
- **High Failure Rate:** Startup companies and other ventures have a high failure rate, and investing in them can be risky. Even well-conceived and well-executed businesses can fail due to unforeseen circumstances.
- **Fraud:** Like any investment, equity crowdfunding is susceptible to fraud. Investors should carefully vet the companies they invest in and be wary of any red flags or suspicious activity.
- **Dilution:** As a company raises additional rounds of funding, the value of each individual share may decrease due to the dilution of the ownership structure.
- **Regulatory Risks:** Equity crowdfunding platforms are subject to regulation, and changes in the regulatory environment could impact the ability of investors to participate in these offerings or the terms and conditions of the investments.

It is important to carefully evaluate the potential risks and rewards of any investment opportunity, including those offered through equity crowdfunding platforms. Investors should also diversify their portfolios to manage risk and avoid over-concentration in any one investment.

How Can Investors Use Real Estate Crowdfunding Platforms to Build a Portfolio?

Real estate crowdfunding platforms can provide investors access to a wide range of real estate investment opportunities previously only available to large institutional investors. To build a real estate portfolio using crowdfunding platforms, here are steps an investor can follow:

1. The first step is to determine your investment goals, such as the need for predictable cash flow, desired return on investment, the investment duration, and the level of risk tolerance.
2. There are many real estate crowdfunding platforms available, and each has its unique features, investment minimums, and fee structures. Investors should research and compare various platforms to find the one best suits their needs.
3. Once you've found a platform, you'll need to start browsing investment opportunities. Look for investments that align with your investment goals and fit within your budget.
4. Before investing in any opportunity, it's essential to conduct due diligence. This can include reviewing the investment's financial statements, property details, market data, and other relevant information.
5. It's crucial to diversify your investments to reduce risk. Instead of putting all your money into a single project, consider investing in multiple projects across different platforms, property types, and geographical locations.
6. After investing, it's crucial to monitor your investments regularly. This can include reviewing financial statements, attending investor meetings, and staying up-to-date on market trends and changes. This is a critical element of an investor's continuing education in commercial real estate syndications.

Overall, using real estate crowdfunding platforms can be an excellent way to build a diversified real estate portfolio. However, as with any investment, it's essential to do your research and due diligence before investing.

Which are the Largest Commercial Real Estate Crowdfunding Platforms?

There are several large commercial real estate crowdfunding platforms operating in the market today, including:

1. **CrowdStreet**: This platform provides investors with access to a wide range of commercial real estate investment opportunities, including multi-family properties, office buildings, and industrial warehouses.
2. **RealtyMogul**: RealtyMogul offers a variety of investment opportunities, including equity and debt investments in commercial real estate projects such as office buildings, retail centers, and apartment complexes.
3. **Fundrise**: This platform offers a diversified portfolio of commercial real estate assets, including apartments, office buildings, and mixed-use developments.
4. **Cadre**: Cadre offers investors access to a variety of institutional-grade commercial real estate investments, including multi-family properties, office buildings, and hotels.
5. **ArborCrowd**: ArborCrowd offers a range of commercial real estate investment opportunities, including multi-family properties, office buildings, and retail centers.

It's important to note that the size of these platforms may change over time as new platforms emerge and existing platforms grow or contract. Crowdfunding for commercial real estate is a rapidly growing and evolving phenomenon. Success in navigating this arena depends on discovering proven sponsors. The more platforms, the more careful an investor needs to be. As the quantity of offerings expands, it is logical to conclude that aggregate quality deteriorates. It is important to seek experienced counsel until you have developed the education necessary to separate the wheat from the chafe.

The Largest Private Equity Crowdfunding Platforms

Prominent equity crowdfunding platforms globally are:

- **Seedrs** - A UK-based platform that offers equity crowdfunding for startups and growth companies.
- **Crowdcube** - Another UK-based platform that offers equity crowdfunding for startups and growth companies.
- **StartEngine** - A US-based platform that offers equity crowdfunding for startups and small businesses.
- **Republic** - A US-based platform that offers equity crowdfunding for startups, small businesses, and real estate projects.
- **Wefunder** - A US-based platform that offers equity crowdfunding for startups, small businesses, and real estate projects.
- **Fundable** - A US-based platform that offers equity crowdfunding for startups and small businesses.
- **AngelList** - A US-based platform that offers equity crowdfunding for startups and small businesses.
- **MicroVentures** - A US-based platform that offers equity crowdfunding for startups and small businesses.
- **Equitise** - An Australian-based platform that offers equity crowdfunding for startups and growth companies.

These platforms are regulated by the Securities and Exchange Commission (SEC) and require investors to meet specific accreditation requirements. As with any investment, it's important to do your due diligence and consult with a financial advisor before investing in private equity offerings on crowdfunding platforms. Private equity crowdfunding is global in nature, so it is important to not limit your scope to USA-based platforms and investments. Your focus should be on the quality of offerings that the platform is able to attract. Furthermore, I prefer institutional quality deals and fund options. Three of the most interesting global platforms for private equity are:

- OurCrowd is an Israel-based platform that offers equity crowdfunding for startups and growth companies.
- Moonfare is an investment platform that offers individuals and institutions access to private equity and other alternative investment funds. The platform allows investors to invest in a diversified range of funds managed by some of the world's leading private equity firms.
- Newvest is an online investment platform that allows individuals to invest in venture capital funds and startup companies. The platform aims to democratize access to VC investing by allowing individuals to invest in early-stage companies with low minimum investment amounts.

How Might Crowdfunding Evolve to Further Democratize Private Market Investing?

Crowdfunding specialized digital platforms are a vital ingredient to democratizing investment opportunities to reach accredited and perhaps non-accredited investors in the future. These platforms perform important services for the sponsors of offerings, but as we have discussed, they should perform many vital functions for investors as well. The most important of which is creating a marketplace that aggregates high-quality offerings from great sponsors and making these offerings discoverable by investors.

How Can Crowdfunding Grow Rapidly and in a Responsible Manner in the Future?

There is little question that growth will continue based on the actions of the SEC in recent years, making it easier for startups to raise higher amounts of capital through crowdfunding and providing additional exemptions for non-accredited and accredited investors to participate in these offerings. The UK experience started before the USA experience in crowdfunding, and the UK has continued to exhibit strong growth and is changing how small companies are capitalizing themselves. In an academic paper by Jensen, Marshall, and Jahera with Auburn University, the following conclusions were made:

1. Allow non-accredited investors to co-invest alongside accredited investors.
2. If a public policy goal is to create jobs, the USA may want to consider giving a tax break to investors that invest in startups similar to the UK.[35]

Clearly, growth in this realm is desired by all parties as long as investors are protected as much as possible by either becoming sophisticated themselves or piggybacking on other investors or firms that are accredited and sophisticated.

A trend for the coming years is a consolidation of these digital platforms to give them the scale, increasing their prominence, and making this industry mainstream. Most crowdfunding platforms today are themselves venture-backed. As this industry consolidates, there has to be a regulatory and business model to increase investor participation with private investments responsibly. Let us take this one step further. A significant amount of investable assets for accredited and non-accredited investors alike are located in retirement accounts, IRA, or 401k accounts. What if platform consolidation resulted in retirement account sponsors taking these platforms to the next level and integrating them into retirement plan offerings? Of course, this would require federal regulators to evolve their frameworks, which are already moving in this direction anyway.

Let's Illustrate this with an Example: A 401k plan administered by Fidelity, Vanguard, or Empower, three of the largest 401k plan administrators in the USA. Suppose an employee had a $500,000 balance that they could invest in the typical fare of mutual funds or target date funds. What if one of these 401k sponsors acquired a rising crowdfunding platform as a business line and expanded its reach and capabilities alongside a more liberalized regulatory framework? These 401k sponsors could perform all the key functions performed by current platforms, including verification of accreditation (if required), disclosure, due diligence, categorization of sponsor experience, investor education, provision of fund products, and escrow services. Imagine if an investor were allowed to invest in private offerings in an amount no greater than 20% of their 401(k)-account balance at the time of commitment to one or more fund offerings from excellent private equity or commercial real estate sponsors. Is a mutual fund different from a private equity fund from Harbourvest, other than the frequency of mark-to-market of the underlying investments? In fact, Vanguard and Harbourvest are already working together to provide additional options for institutional investors such as non-profits. Why not extend these capabilities to individual retirement accounts with well-defined limits?

Fortunately, the changes appear to be forthcoming. In May of 2020, the U.S. Department of Labor (yet another voice in the regulatory framework surrounding private investments) issued an Information Letter on the topic of private equity in defined contribution plans such as 401(k) plans. In the DOL press release, it was stated that the Information Letter addresses private equity investments offered as part of a professionally managed multi-asset class vehicle structured as a target date, target risk, or balanced fund. Adding private equity investments to such professionally managed investment funds would increase the range of investment opportunities available to 401(k)-type plan options. The Information Letter, however, does not authorize making private equity investments available for direct investment on a standalone basis. Currently, (defined benefit) private pension plans likely can invest in private equity, and now the door is opening for this asset class to be included in defined contribution plans. It is a start. Chairman of the U.S. Securities and Exchange Commission, Jay Clayton, commended the Department's efforts to improve investor choice and investor protection, saying the Information Letter "Will provide our long-term Main Street investors with a choice of professionally managed funds that more closely match the diversified public and private market asset allocation strategies pursued by many well-managed pension funds as well as the benefit of selection and monitoring by ERISA fiduciaries."

Today, just as individuals select investment options inside 401k plans, equity mutual funds that never beat the S&P 500 and can potentially fall in value significantly like they fell 15-20% in 2022, investors someday may select from a menu of plan investment options that included private equity although they will not be able to choose specific sponsors or offerings. Private equity and commercial real estate funds have proven track records as asset classes, and yet they are off limits to hard-working employees who need help saving enough money for retirement. All the trends are moving in the direction of bringing private asset classes to defined contribution plans; the question is how long it will take to develop an optimal framework with well-constructed protections. Crowdfunding, co-investment, and investment limits are three pieces of this puzzle for democratizing opportunities to build wealth for all citizens.

Quick Summary
1. Crowdfunding has experienced strong growth worldwide. The crowdfunding industry has stronger roots outside of the USA, and the USA regulatory changes are catching up with changes to the regulatory framework that benefits companies raising capital and investors seeking to invest in private markets.
2. Crowdfunding platforms should be a layer of protection for investors due to the key functions these platforms theoretically perform for both issuers and investors. However, bad things still often result. If the allure is strong, I recommend utilizing fund products that are arranged by the platform that offers

diversification. Invest the minimum amount, and you will become educated overtime on the quality of deals on the platform and the performance of individual sponsors.
3. Crowdfunding provides many benefits to investors, including access to real estate or private equity deals, lower minimum investment requirements, passive income generation, greater portfolio diversification, the potential for higher nominal returns, and greater transparency and due diligence with respect to private offerings.
4. Crowdfunding has many risk factors, reflecting the underlying private asset classes being marketed. These risks include illiquidity, limited information around offerings, higher potential for fraud, dilution, and regulatory risks. Do not assume that the platform has done any degree of due diligence on any offering.
5. Growth and changes occurring in the crowdfunding markets are allowing for greater access to capital for startup companies, more jobs, and more opportunities for investors. Consolidation, coupled with the fundamental value proposition of quality commercial real estate and private equity funds, should further democratize access to private assets over the next decade.

Chapter 10 - The Capital Stack

Private investments involve the purchase of real estate or a Main Street business, and the composition and relationship of the various sources of funds necessary to acquire these assets is referred to as the capital stack. Because the capital stack provides various options for investors in commercial real estate, our focus will start with this asset class. Investors can really "dial in" on the appropriate risk/return profile that meets their overall objectives by analyzing and selecting between debt, preferred equity, and common equity positions in the capital stack. The private-passive investor framework is expanded to include this dimension, as illustrated in Figures 23 and 24 for commercial real estate and private equity, respectively.

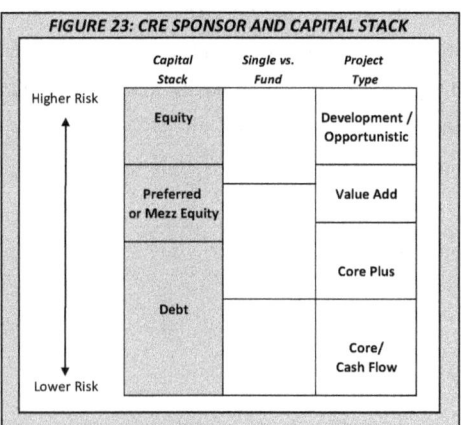
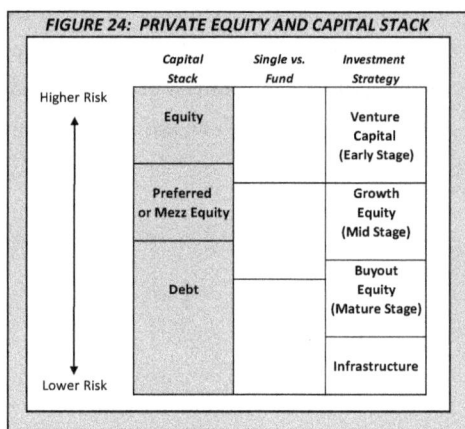

This chapter is extremely important for investors, and in the process of writing, it has changed my perspective regarding investing in safer debt instruments or more risky common equity positions in the capital structure. It is March 2023, and Silicon Valley Bank just failed. Even before the high-profile bank failures of 2023, I realized my risk appetite was transitioning to a more risk-averse stance. Investment policy and strategy is an ever-moving target. This topic quickly became my favorite topic for the private-passive investor to consider.

First, let us break down the capital stack for commercial real estate. Figure 25 below illustrates a typical capital stack for a commercial real estate project.

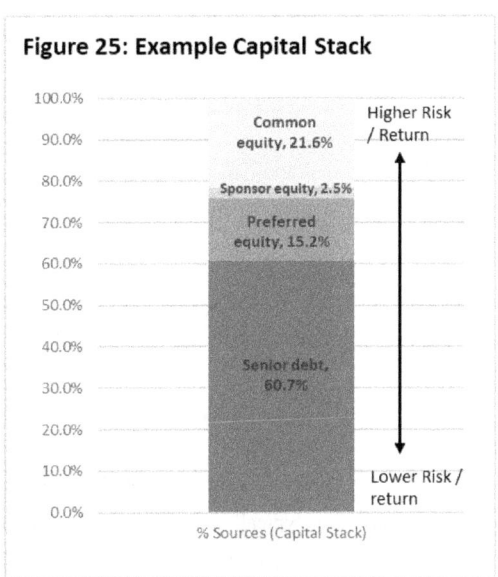

Figure 25: Example Capital Stack

Debt Investments in Commercial Real Estate

A variety of conservative debt options exist for private-passive investors in the commercial real estate asset class, enabling investors to earn predictable monthly or quarterly income. Looking at the capital stack diagram in Figure 25, the risk and expected returns for investors increase as one moves up the stack from debt to preferred equity to common equity. In the case of a foreclosure, the claims of the debt holders are addressed first, then the preferred equity holders, and last, the common equity holders. In the interests of completeness, there is also a level called mezzanine debt that sits between the senior debt and the preferred equity. For single-asset investments, investors will have the opportunity to invest in a specific component of the capital stack. Funds also tend to specialize, but they may provide access to more than one component of the capital stack, for example, senior debt and preferred equity.

Investors in private real estate debt are attracted by the higher yields and lack of correlation with public fixed-income alternatives. Even after the rapid increase in nominal interest rates during 2022, traditional fixed-income investments still represent a fraction of the current rate of inflation. Investors should expect a return on private real estate debt in the range of 8-12% in the recent market environment (2021-22), although the return over time would likely be measured as a spread over a short-term credit index such as one- or two-year treasuries to match the duration of loans in private debt. Figure 26 shows the relative yield of sectors of the credit markets over the recent 15-year history.[36]

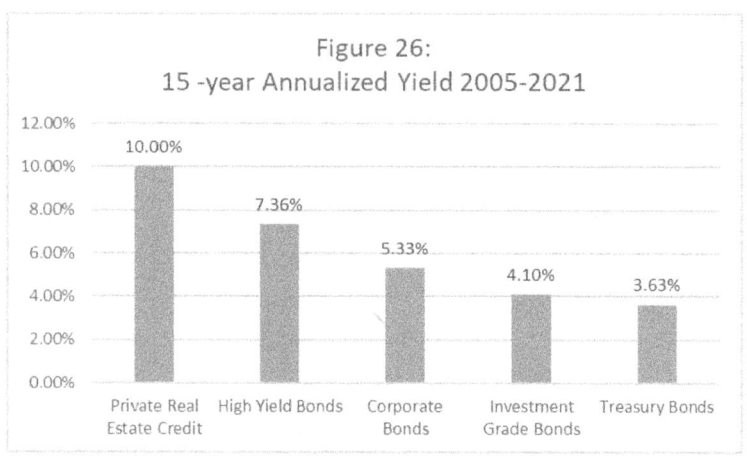

Figure 26: 15-year Annualized Yield 2005-2021

- Private Real Estate Credit: 10.00%
- High Yield Bonds: 7.36%
- Corporate Bonds: 5.33%
- Investment Grade Bonds: 4.10%
- Treasury Bonds: 3.63%

The term "loan-to-value ratio" (LTV) is important to understand. It represents the loan principal divided by the value or purchase price of the asset. The typical range for senior debt would be 55%-75%. The LTV quantifies the percentage of leverage in a project, and that leverage is paramount to generating the double-digit returns that the equity investors expect. In difficult economic environments such as 2022, LTV ratios declined to 50-65% as traditional financing sources tightened their lending standards. In good economic times, the ratios tend to drift higher. The higher the LTV, the higher the risk and potential returns for all participants in the capital stack, but particularly for the preferred and common equity holders in the capital stack.

Investors in real estate debt appreciate the margin of safety measured by the LTV. Assuming an LTV of 65%, the value of the property would have to fall by over 35% before the senior debt investors would suffer a loss in investment principal. Lower LTV ratios increase the odds of full recovery of principal by the lender, mitigating the risk of principal loss.

Mortgages and security agreements are the documents that provide the lender with a security interest in specific properties that the borrower pledges as collateral. Collateral is a consideration that is not as critical for investors in the preferred equity or common equity position of the capital stack. For debt investors, these agreements provide important protections for the investor. For investors looking to invest in real estate debt for a single property or a real estate debt fund, it is important to understand the structure of the collateral and developer/sponsor guarantees that support the debt.

Traditionally, banks and commercial lenders are the main sources of real estate debt, similar to how such institutions would fund a personal mortgage. Another major source is agency debt, which is backed by either Fannie Mae or Freddie Mac. Bridge loan providers provide financing for acquiring properties that have a value-add strategy. Increasingly, modern digital platforms or "crowdfunding" are bringing to market offerings focusing on the debt component of the capital stack, typically in the form of funds. Funds will specialize in a known niche or niches of the market, for example, single-family homes (fix and flip), small apartment buildings, small office buildings, and self-storage.

Investors benefit from debt because it offers a safer position in the capital stack, reducing the risk of a loss of principal. Protection from loss is fortified by using the property as collateral for the loan and the equity cushion as represented by the inverse of the LTV ratio. Although an investor's return on investment is less than that of preferred or common equity, it is still higher than the returns offered by public fixed-income investment alternatives. Borrowers benefit from the debt because it is usually the largest piece of the capital stack, making it mandatory in funding a project; plus, it is the cheapest form of capital for a real estate sponsor/project. Most importantly, investing in the debt component of the capital stack provides investors with the resilience to withstand adverse turns in markets or geopolitical events. Preserving investment principles should be the primary goal. In private-passive investing, one does not need to take excessive risks to thrive.

Incorporating Private Real Estate Debt into a Private Portfolio

As with many pockets of the private markets, it is difficult for accredited investors to get access to the large institutional sources of real estate debt. Debt in the large real estate syndication business is really the province of the banking institutions and government agencies. However, many creative solutions have entered the market over the past decade due to commercial banks reducing their exposure to commercial real estate lending due to the Global Financial Crisis of 2008-9, and private sources of funding have filled this void fittingly.

Boutique real estate debt funds are a very attractive alternative for private investors. These funds comprise a pool of private capital investing in loans that are collateralized by real estate. Fund sponsors focus on a single strategy in terms of position in the capital stack, asset type and profile, and geography. The level of diversification inherent in a debt fund provides a shield against defaults from any single asset in the fund. Funds can diversify in a variety of ways, including diversification of individual borrowers, asset type, and geography.

Common Features Real Estate Debt Fund

Listed below are the common features of a real estate debt fund:

1. **Term of Underlying Loans**: Up to one year with a range of 3-36 months. The short duration allows for continuous redeployment of capital, maintaining an overall portfolio that is highly reflective of current interest rate conditions.
2. **Target IRR**: Returns in the range of 10-12% with continuous distributions around 8% in today's market. Distributions are either monthly or quarterly, providing an excellent stream of predictable cash flow for investors.
3. **Leverage**: Funds may have multiple sources of institutional, efficient capital that increases a fund's buying power while reducing funding risk. It is important to understand where a fund gets its sources of capital from. For the fund's loans, LTV up to 85% and Loan; Loan-to-After-Repaired-Value (LTARV) of 75%, relevant with value-add projects.
4. **Fund Sponsor Quality**: Understanding the strategy of the fund, its track record, and how it fits with an investor's personal objectives are important activities, no different than the due diligence performed on

real estate sponsors. The key employees tend to have gained experience in the fixed-income groups of major investment banks.
5. **Borrower Quality**: The borrowers are typically real estate developers, and the funds are used for acquisition, value-add renovations, ground-up development, and refinancings. How the debt fund filters and qualifies their borrower pool is an important activity to understand. What due diligence processes does the lender perform, such as background checks, FICO scores, and review of the borrower's relevant local experience and track record?
6. **Risk Protection**: Collateral from property and borrowing entities and personal guarantees provide necessary protection against loss. If borrowers are on the hook personally, they will be motivated to execute a successful value-add project.
7. **Minimum Investment Requirements**: Minimum investments are in the range of $50,000 to $250,000.
8. **Redemptions**: Private investors know that lack of liquidity is a price they pay for higher returns. Typical terms include a 1-year lock up (no redemptions), 90-day notice of redemption, and limited to once per every calendar quarter.

Another method of incorporating private real estate into a portfolio is through digital platforms that allow smaller investors to build their own portfolios. Diversified fund offerings may be difficult to find, but the minimum investment requirements are attractive. For example, occasionally, private debt fund offerings will show up on Crowdstreet with lower minimums.

Realty Mogul's digital platform has provided offerings in various positions of the capital stack. From their website, they have over 140 realized investments related to residential loans and fixed income, which includes both debt and preferred equity structures, with realized returns on average in the 9-10% range. Many of their offerings currently have a $35,000 minimum investment requirement.

Groundfloor is a digital platform that allows investors to invest in fix-and-flip residential projects. There are products for both accredited and non-accredited investors. Due to the low minimum investment requirements, $10 in many cases, an investor can build a highly diversified portfolio. As you might imagine, there is a lot of inherent risk in these projects, and Groundfloor is quite transparent in how they rate the underlying borrowers. They will report your achieved IRR based on realized investments, typically about a 10% return. However, many unrealized projects can wind up in default status. Managing foreclosure processes is a part of their business model. It is scary, but I have not lost principal on a foreclosure (yet), but it extends the term dramatically. Having a small investment in Groundfloor is a great way to keep tabs on the local markets in a portfolio. Local markets that are shaky result in higher percentages of loans in extended or default status. When economic times are improving, timely repayments will start improving.

FundThatFlip is similar to Groundfloor, offering fix and flip projects and fund products (of multiple fix and flip) projects to accredited investors only with $5,000 minimum investment requirements. Their business model seems a bit less hectic than Groundfloor. Loans are secured by the properties and borrower guarantees. My experience is that yields of 10-11% can be expected, but like always, try to diversify with multiple offerings on the platform.

Fundrise is another innovative platform that aims to match investor risk/return profiles with unique fund offerings, including fixed-income investments for conservative investors. The access points are very attractive, with minimum requirements as low as $1,000 ranging up to $100,000 with higher return potential. Since this chapter deals with private debt, there is a supplemental income fund profile that allocates 70-80% of the portfolio to fixed income and 20-30% to growth-focused assets.

The average accredited investor will likely have to rely on third-party digital platforms or crowdfunding sites to get access to diversified debt funds. New digital platforms are rapidly filling the niche of affordability, but then you run the risk of a platform-specific issue such as bankruptcy due to business model deficiencies or management failures.

Preferred Equity Investments in Commercial Real Estate

Preferred equity is used by real estate sponsors/developers as a source of financing to acquire significant commercial real estate investments. In addition, this use of preferred equity is commonly used when additional funds are needed to advance an existing project. This tool is highly prioritized in the capital stack and ranks senior to the common equity, sitting right behind senior debt or mezzanine debt. When profit comes in, or in the event of default, the senior debtholder receives payments first, followed by preferred equity holders and, lastly, common equity holders.

The expected returns from investing in preferred stock naturally fall in between the yield earned by the bank or other senior lenders and the expected return to be earned by the common equity holders. A common benchmark for the expected return on preferred stock in real estate is 10%, but this will vary depending on the LTV for the senior debt, the amount of common equity, and the overall risk profile of the project, as well as other variables. Typically, there is an added sweetener or "paid in kind" (PIK) that is paid upon a liquidity event such as a sale. The PIK would add another 2-3% to the IRR if the project is successful. In short, your downside is protected with preferred stock in exchange for giving up most of the upside. Investors receive priority for both cashflow payments and the return of capital, and this should result in an IRR in the 9-12% range. The term of preferred stock investments generally mirrors that of the common equity, from 5 to 10 years for real estate projects.

Preferred equity is offered primarily by sponsors who are funded by institutional-grade capital providers. These firms aggregate large funds and prefer large minimum investments from investors in order to maximize their operational efficiency. It is generally much more difficult for small- to middle-market real estate sponsors to get access to preferred equity, and it is difficult for the average accredited investor to invest in this part of the capital stack as well.

Preferred stock might constitute 15% of the capital stack, sitting between the debt and common equity. Assuming the debt is 60%, and the common equity is 25%, the value of the property being financed would have to decline by more than 25% for the preferred equity investors to lose principal. Preferred equity is less risky than common equity. It is an attractive place in the capital stack for investors during difficult economic times and during periods of rapid inflation. Also, real estate investors may find it easier to find preferred stock investments than private debt investments since the bank or agency debt typically occupies the debt component of the capital stack.

Preferred equity generates predictable cash flow to investors, as preferred equity investments typically pay distributions on a monthly or quarterly basis. Funds of preferred equity offer additional diversification benefits to the investors. Commercial real estate sponsors like preferred equity as it may make it easier to raise the necessary funding, and it could reduce their overall cost of capital on a project or fund. Common equity investors might appreciate an offering with a preferred equity tranche, as this can boost their returns relative to the same project that is funded with only common equity.

Incorporating Preferred Equity into a Private Portfolio

Use of funds is preferred. Did you see that play on words? Boutique funds exist that focus mainly on multi-family housing, but I would expect there are offerings in other property types as well. A typical preferred real estate credit fund would offer a 9% preferred return paid on a quarterly basis and a target IRR of 10-12%. The fund can be either evergreen, meaning it goes on indefinitely, or a fixed-term fund invested in a definite portfolio of properties. The fees on the fund would be approximately 1% management fee plus 20% of the profits. The minimum investment required starts at a healthy $100,000.

Occasionally, an investor will find real estate syndications on Crowdstreet and similar digital platforms that offer preferred equity. These offerings have all the inherent pros and cons of preferred equity investments and returns in the 10-13% range, but with the disadvantage being a lack of diversification. That is unless you can find multiple offerings that can help to diversify your own portfolio. The advantage of the crowdfunding offerings is a much lower minimum investment requirement of approximately $25,000.

Preferred equity is not a mandatory component of the private-passive portfolio, but it does have some attractive features. An investor can achieve the same aggregate risk/return profile with either conservative core common equity investments coupled with private real estate debt. If you happen to come across a preferred equity offering or fund, it is worth analyzing and discussing with the sponsor of the offering.

Capital Stack Considerations for Private Equity

Debt offerings for accredited investors are difficult to find in the private equity or venture capital world. Preferred equity is certainly difficult for an investor to discover, but the basic tenets involved with preferred equity are the same for private equity as they would be for commercial real estate. Fortunately, the private debt sector within private equity is extremely interesting for private-passive investors looking to build a diversified income portfolio or to balance the risk involved with investing in private equity. The innovation is definitely trickling down to individual investors.

According to Preqin, during the period 2009-2018, private debt funds had a median net IRR of 9.4%, and a standard deviation of 12.8%. These returns are clearly less favorable compared to private equity returns of 17.7% and venture capital returns of 22% over the same period since private debt carries significantly less risk.[37]

Private Credit (Debt)

Private debt includes any debt held by or extended to privately held companies. The lenders consist of different types, including traditional banks, private equity firms, institutional sources such as pension plans and insurance companies, crowdfunding platforms, and even venture capital firms. With private debt, the borrowing company retains ownership but must sign debt and security agreements that require repayment of the loans, plus interest and associated fees over a defined term.

How substantial are private credit markets? Private debt accounts for a substantial piece of the private markets—about 10%-15% of total assets under management.[38] Private debt is the third largest asset class in the alternative private markets, behind private equity and real estate.[39] Accordingly, this is a substantial asset class for inclusion in your private portfolio. Private debt is large and growing, as this sector has grown from $320 billion in 2009 to $875 billion at the end of 2020 and is expected to demonstrate 11.4% compound annual growth after 2020.[40] This rapid growth has been fueled by the regulatory response to the 2008-9 Global Financial Crisis when banks were forced to retreat from direct private lending while adhering to the Basel III capital requirements, cultivated demand for financing opportunities from non-bank lenders.

The rise of non-bank lenders of private debt has benefitted institutional investors, and the benefits are slowly trickling down to individuals through family offices, feeder funds, and new digital crowdfunding platforms. The demand side of the equation has also ballooned as the Federal Reserve moved interest rates to near zero, creating demand for any debt instruments that held an attractive yield. Private debt can be further broken down into specific variations or strategies.

Direct Lending: Senior or junior loans are made to mid-market companies without an intermediary. Loans include revolving credit lines term loans. The lenders often choose to specialize in certain sectors of the economy and/or geographic regions. Target annual returns of 4-7% as it sits in the safest location in terms of liquidation preference at the top of the capital stack.

Specialty Lending: Debt or structured equity investments made with the intent of gaining control of a company—generally, one in special circumstances or limited distress. Target returns of 6-12%, as this form of lending can be senior debt or subordinated debt, depending on the strength of the borrower.

Mezzanine: Subordinated debt, with features such as warrants, which increase the potential return on the debt. Mezzanine debt is often used in leveraged buyouts. Target return is in the range of 8-13%.

Distressed: Differs from specialty lending in that it generally involves the purchase of securities in the secondary market rather than new origination of debt or structured equity. The target rate of return is higher in the range of 12-20%.

Real Estate: The most common real estate debt strategy is direct lending for real estate acquisitions but may include the buying and selling of real estate loans in the secondary market. Risk profiles vary based on the underlying assets, with target return in the range of 8-12%.

Infrastructure Debt: Debt is used for infrastructure development and investment in existing assets (for example, a toll road), generally with longer terms (30+ years) due to the extended useful life of the assets and the predictability of the cash flows associated with the infrastructure project.

Venture Debt: Venture debt is a type of short- to medium-term debt financing provided to venture-backed companies by specialized banks or non-bank lenders to fund growth. Borrowers are attracted to venture debt, up to 20% of the capital stack, since it lowers their overall cost of capital since debt is cheaper than equity and is less dilutive to the common equity holders. For lenders, venture debt has the highest liquidation preference. Placing debt into the capital stack of an early-stage venture may seem unusual, but the model has been successfully developed and deployed. The result is "venture debt" funds in which you are investing alongside reputable venture capital firms in the region of investment. The equity capital is provided by traditional venture capital firms, and the debt part of the capital stack is provided by a specialized venture debt firm.

As an example, a venture debt fund would collect a diversified group of debt instruments with the following typical provisions or characteristics:

- 36 month-loans, with regular amortization over the loan term so it gets paid off as a venture progresses through its progressive venture equity funding rounds.
- Target companies are Series A-D, between seed capital and pre-IPO stage, where growth debt options replace the extensive venture debt funding.
- Up to 20% LTV percentage (i.e., equity is 80% of the capital stack)
- Loan to Cash ratio less than 1. Nothing better than loans protected by cash balances on the target entity.
- Senior secured.
- The target interest return is 12%, with a range of 10-15%.

- Upfront fees of approximately 2%.

- Warrants add a kicker to the return. Equal to about 10-15% of the loan amount at issuance. The target is 20-30% IRR. 7-10 years. The warrants provide the necessary return to reflect the added risk of investing in early-stage ventures.

- Warrants give investors the right to buy a specific stock or equity instrument at a certain price level (strike price) before a certain date (expiration date). Warrants are good for a fixed period of time, but they are not worth anything when they expire. Accordingly, venture debt funds participate in successive "up-rounds" and the eventual exit of a venture, potentially a unicorn.

- Funds tend to be regionally focused.

Having the ability to invest more in private debt is a very exciting development for accredited investors. Naturally, the main benefits are creating a reliable source of income while reducing the volatility in your overall private-passive portfolio. Because of its conservative position in the capital stack, private debt can avoid collateral damage from economic downturns relative to public equity investments. At its core, private credit instruments are contractual bilateral documents that provide stable income over time and tend to smooth returns over time. Of course, since private debt is in most respects illiquid, an investor cannot choose to sell at a market bottom even if it was so desired.

If you can stomach the lack of liquidity, private credit funds can diversify and add yield to a portfolio relative to public fixed-income markets, which have experienced very low nominal yields and sometimes negative returns in real terms over the past decade. The elevated risk-adjusted returns of private debt should be measured versus the public fixed-income markets, not the returns on private equity. Private debt investment also serves as an effective inflation hedge. Private debt is typically floating rate notes, or they have a relatively short maturity, allowing for reinvestment at higher interest rates during periods of rapidly rising interest rates. For illustrative purposes, Figure 27 provides a representation of the yield advantage of private debt vs. the public markets primarily due to the illiquidity premium of the private markets for various periods of time ending December 31, 2021. The bottom line is 10% for private vs. approximately 6% for public fixed income, an annual premium of 4%, and this was during periods of falling interest rates when floating private credit loans are generally disadvantaged compared to public fixed income. It seems a reasonable expectation that investors could earn a predictable return of 8-10% each year from a carefully constructed portfolio of private credit funds (including real estate debt). This caught my eye, and such a result would have large ramifications with regard to retirement planning and social security strategy. I will expand on this topic in the planning considerations in Chapter 12.

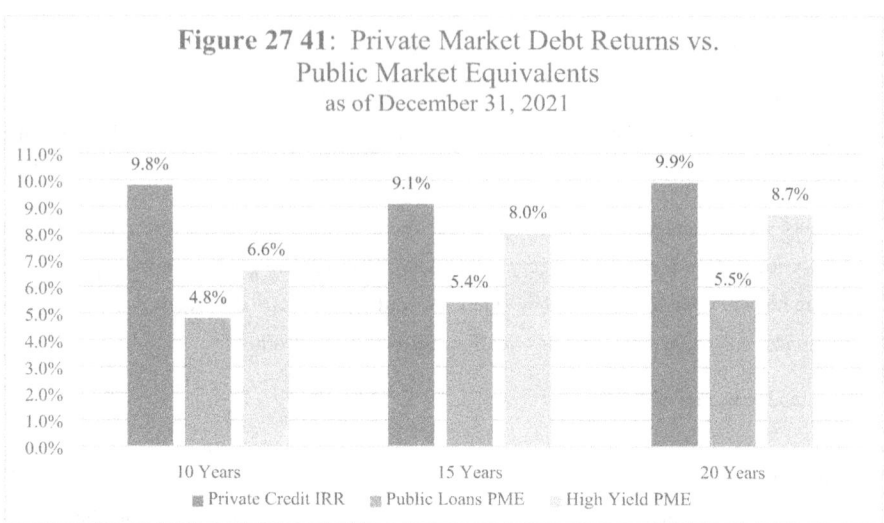

Figure 27 41: Private Market Debt Returns vs. Public Market Equivalents as of December 31, 2021

Incorporating Private Debt into a Private Portfolio

Just as with the 60/40 (equity/fixed income) public market portfolio, private debt deserves a place in a private-passive portfolio due to its diversification benefits, income generation properties, and downside protection offered by the nature of the capital stack.

The way to access private debt is directly or indirectly through the private debt fund managers themselves. Passive investors will not be working directly with the target borrowers. Fund managers have well-established lending criteria securitization standards and have systematized due diligence processes in their respective niches. They are true specialists, so be careful of private debt fund managers who pretend to be all things to everyone. Similar to evaluating the pedigree of a private equity fund, you will need to become equally satisfied with the abilities and experience of a private debt fund's management.

If you have a pension fund, it is very likely you already indirectly invested in private debt. State pension systems are traditionally near the top of the investor ranks in private credit. Financial advisors or wealth managers may be able to provide access, assuming one has sufficient assets under management.

The most promising and developing method of getting access to private credit is through (relatively new) innovative independent digital platforms. On these crowdfunding platforms, an investor can discover private debt offerings that are more localized geographically, more nimble, able to find off-market deals, and at the same time have a long-established track record and experience working with large global debt funds such as Goldman Sachs and Oaktree. These niche global debt fund platforms are also taking advantage of inefficiencies in their local market banking systems that provide the opportunity for private funders to step in and provide credit. The niche may also be sector-based, focusing on specialty niches such as technology that can generate excess spreads. Funds typically are hybrid funds, focusing on multiple strategies, including distressed situations or venture debt, with different weights. Similar to private equity funds, look for sponsors that have proven prior vintages with performance that corroborate their strategy.

Fund sponsors/managers should co-invest in the fund, so ask about the level or percentage of co-investment. A co-investment of 10% or greater is not unusual, demonstrating conviction in the fund and alignment of interests. The targeted IRR for these offerings is likely in the 12-13% range, and distributions are typically on an annual basis, creating a great source of passive income for investors. The fees will be similar to the 2 and 20 model for private equity: 1.5-2% annual management fee and 20% of the profits. Minimum investments typically start at $50,000.

Examples of platforms where a private passive investor can find private debt include OurCrowd and Moonfare. Excellent digital platforms will do an excellent job with due diligence, only presenting the best opportunities for investors. For the average accredited investor, finding opportunities on digital platforms will be the only reliable method of finding consistent deal flow in private debt markets. The trend is for more innovation and opportunities to invest in private credit.

There is also an emerging group of digital platforms that create their own private debt opportunities for investors, marketed as alternative investments. Yieldstreet is an example of a company that provides financing and structured debt products, as well as commercial real estate equity offerings. Many others exist that focus mainly on private real estate. Alternative platforms have lower minimum investment requirements, which is good news. When evaluating alternative platforms, I think to ask three questions that are fundamental to the principles of this book related to private debt:

1. Is the offering a diversified fund, or is it reliant on one borrower or a small group of borrowers?

2. What is the historical loss rate for this type of offering?

3. Is the private debt offering underpinned by real Main Street businesses requiring capital for their operations? Or is this debt underpinned by derivatives of Wall Street? Main Street is what private markets are all about.

Like private equity, it may be difficult to locate affordable offerings in private debt funds. One diversified fund may have to suffice if you have a limited portfolio size.

Quick Summary

1. Selecting the optimal location in the capital stack to invest in is one of the critical decisions in designing your optimal private-passive portfolio. Debt is the safest position, followed by preferred equity and then common equity. Expected returns run in the opposite direction.

2. Every private real estate investor should consider the inclusion of debt and preferred equity to some degree into their portfolios.

3. Debt fund products are offered directly by sponsors or offerings on digital platforms.

4. Private debt fund offerings for accredited investors are an exciting area of growth, complementing nicely investments in private equity funds. Investors need to rely on fund products offered through third-party digital platforms that serve as feeders for funds that were traditionally the domain of institutional investors only.

Chapter 11 - Single Asset versus Funds

Investors face a dilemma as to whether to invest in single assets, fund products, or a combination. For example, in the venture capital market, an investor could try to select the next YouTube or invest in a venture capital portfolio that holds 20-25 investments in startup companies. In the commercial real estate market, a private-passive investor can invest in a specific industrial property in Chicago or a portfolio of industrial properties across the Southwest region of the USA. A critical element underpinning this decision will be sufficient diversification within a private-passive portfolio. Do you have enough capital to build your own diversified portfolio of private placements? The answer will likely be a negative unless you have over $2 million to invest. In many cases, the minimum investment for a single investment is $50,000. Therefore, the case is to seek out a fund product.

In private equity, excluding venture capital, investing in single assets is off the table. It is hard enough to find a private equity fund to invest in, regardless of your level of wealth. A fund is the only vehicle that can spread your risks. Venture capital, unfortunately, allows accredited investors to select single ventures to invest in, typically located on crowdfunding sites. Unless you have a $10 million net worth and seriously want to donate your hard-earned money, do not do it. Venture capital funds are the best vehicle for investing in this private asset class. Finding the best sponsors of private equity and venture capital funds is the challenge!

I strongly encourage investors to focus on fund products, which I am defining as one private investment vehicle or "envelop" that holds investments in multiple businesses or properties. This advice is simply applying lessons from the public markets to private markets. The accepted wisdom is that stock pickers in public equities underperform mutual funds, and furthermore, investors in actively managed mutual funds underperform investing in the S&P 500 Index. Just 26% of all actively managed funds beat the returns of their index-fund rivals over the decade through December 2021, according to Morningstar.[42] It is illogical to assume that individuals can beat investment professionals with asset selection and that investment professionals can beat the over-market. The same applies in private-passive markets. Since there is not yet an official index for private markets, the best approach is to cast a wide net and achieve as much coverage of an asset class as possible, given the constraints of the portfolio size. Funds are the best vehicle for achieving high-risk adjusted returns.

Moving to the private market side of the ledger, do you think you can pick single assets better than a seasoned venture capitalist or real estate syndicator with a long track record with given property types and geographical regions? As we dive deeper into the options that provide instant diversification for private markets in this chapter, this question will be repeated.

Utilizing funds effectively delegates the deal due diligence process for single assets to the fund sponsor, which is a positive thing if you do not enjoy that activity. As long as the sponsor is vetted and trusted, utilization of funds can free your time to focus on portfolio allocation and what your next move should be for your private-passive portfolio. Figures 28 and 29 contain a further extension to the private-passive investment framework, specifically related to funds vs. single assets for commercial real estate and private equity, respectively.

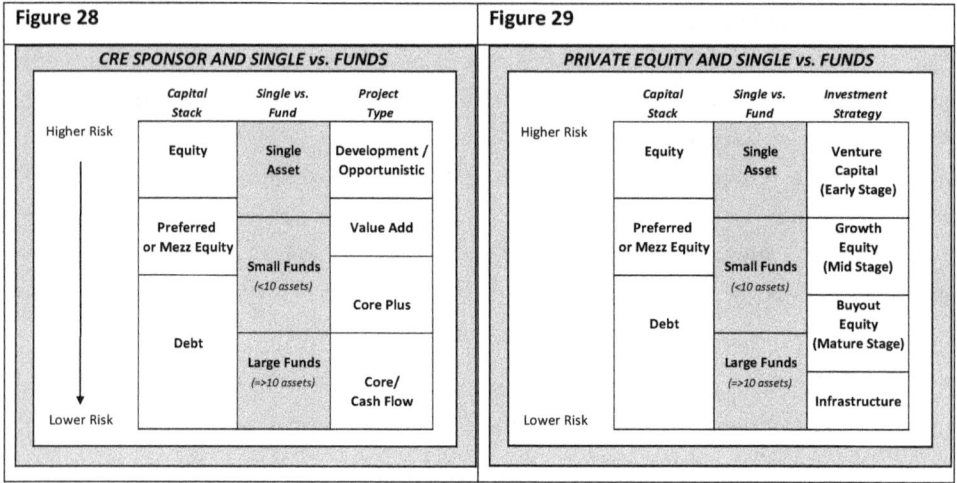

These categories are where investors should focus their attention with regard to investing in funds vs. single assets for private-passive markets. From the bottom up, large funds would contain ten or more properties or businesses. Is ten or more arbitrary, yes. In private market funds, we are not dealing with traditional mutual funds that may hold hundreds of stock positions. Private markets are very unique, customized, and deal-dependent. This box would cover most vintage private equity funds that seek to hold 20-25 companies. The small funds designation is from 2-9 properties or companies. This middle layer applies to most private commercial real estate funds. Even private REITs can hold fewer than ten properties in the portfolio. There are some purchased real estate portfolios that package 2-3 properties in one portfolio. But even two properties are better than one with regard to diversification benefits. Single-asset investments are riskier, more so with companies or ventures than commercial real estate properties. Accordingly, investing in single business ventures is the most risky and speculative action you can take that will impact your overall portfolio performance and volatility. Of course, how an investor defines risk tolerance will factor into each investment decision, which we will consider in the next chapter.

I have participated in multifamily syndication over the last three years, a fund that was initially invested in six properties from Arizona through Florida to Georgia. I would classify this fund as a "small fund" and very typical of multifamily funds. Overall, I estimate this fund will ultimately close out with an IRR in the range of 15-20% despite an amazing variation of events impacting the portfolio. The period from 2019-2021 was very good for multifamily properties due to declining interest rates, which pushed exit cap rates to record-low levels. One property was sold within two years since it achieved its five-year targeted sale price in only two years. A second property was sold, and then the buyer backed out due to their inability to obtain financing. Three of the properties were nailed in a record-breaking freeze event in the South that broke water and fire system pipes. There is a lot going on in this portfolio, but as is typical, the positive and negative tend to balance each other out. Looking at it from another angle, I have invested in three single properties via syndications, and each such experience was nerve-wracking. Single real estate investments do not increase in a linear fashion, but they are a very forgiving asset class. I have decided that the fund approach works better for me and that the syndications are smarter than I am with regard to which properties to invest in. A good night's sleep is a valuable commodity.

Types of Funds

There are three primary structures that fall into this overarching label of funds.[43]

- **Multi-asset Syndication**: Investors invest in an already identified group of properties offered by a sponsor. The fund could be purchasing two properties; it could be twenty. This type of structure is common for commercial real estate properties but not for private equity.
- **Blind Pool**: Investors invest in a single fund that pools the investors' money and subsequently purchases multiple properties in time, and the properties to be purchased are not known at the time the investment is made. This is common in commercial real estate syndications and private equity/venture capital. Again, this does not bother me since experienced sponsors are better positioned to underwrite a property or company.
- **Semi-blind Pool**: Similar to the blind pool, but there are parameters or boundaries defined by the agreement that ringfence what the sponsor can investor in, such as startups in the digital health industry. This is more common than blind pools, per se. Funds of all types describe parameters and boundaries that restrict where they will invest funds raised. Private equity funds will highlight sectors, geographies, and strategies to be utilized by the fund and associated limits.

Single Asset Investing - Pros and Cons

There are benefits to single-asset investing on the condition that you are a very sophisticated accredited investors. Foremost, an investor gets to identify the property or business that best fits in with their investment plan objectives or convictions. Investors will have visibility to detailed business plans, projections, and the entire pitch deck associated with the offering when making an investment. The sponsor will provide clarity around the assumptions used, as well as pro forma financials, which is quite useful for commercial real estate investments but near worthless for a startup business. Post-investment, an investor may never see another set of financials for the next five years, especially for an early-stage venture investment, but that is the reality. There is a good chance the early-stage business will also perform a pivot (major shift in strategy) in the near future. So, what you thought you invested in, you really did not. Also, let's say you are on a crowdfunding site and see five potential technology-related startups to fund. Do you have the experience of picking the best one? Is there anyone smarter than you, such as a team of venture capitalists in Silicon Valley?

Regarding disadvantages from the sponsor's perspective, a sponsor has to raise capital for each property under contract. Some deals will be harder to raise capital than others. Essentially, creating new offerings for every property to be acquired is more work for a sponsor. In addition, sponsors can usually increase their odds of acquiring a property if they can demonstrate to the sellers that they have the capital already raised, which a fund structure enables since funding is raised in advance and subject to mandatory capital calls.

The main disadvantage from a typical investor's perspective is that the investor becomes the de facto fund manager, selecting each deal that will slot into the portfolio. I hope you are qualified. With early-stage ventures, the higher the risk, the higher the reward. Unfortunately, a large percentage of startup businesses will not survive. Nine out of ten startups will fail, and a majority of venture-funded investments will not survive.[44] With commercial real estate projects, the success rate will be much better for the most part, but I still prefer funds.

Multi-Asset Funds – Pros and Cons

Diversification is a major advantage for investors. Investors are delegating the decision on specific asset acquisitions to an experienced real estate or private equity sponsor. As long as investor and sponsor interests are aligned, fund structures make sense. Due diligence is still required around items such as co-investment amounts and carried interest (or promote), and investors should be confident that if the fund manager wins, the investors win as well. Underlying the decision to invest in a fund is a strong measure of investor trust in the sponsor. Sponsors that have successfully progressed through a series of vintage funds provide a key clue to new investors that they have built this level of trust with their investors to date. Again, it comes down to whether you are smarter at picking investments than a proven syndicator or private equity firm. Choose the jockey, not the horse.

Fund products can provide investors with access to exposure to investment profiles or parts of the capital stack that they cannot with single-asset investments. Fund sponsors like to specialize in one type of asset type or sector, geographical region, investment strategy or profile, and place in the capital stack. They become experts in their niche or strategy. As investors contemplate various options, it is pertinent to examine the competitive advantages of each fund and how these may impact their risk/return profile.

The primary disadvantage for an investor is not having a say in which properties are acquired for the fund. An exception with commercial real estate is a pure multi-property syndication offer, where a sponsor identifies a portfolio of properties to acquire simultaneously or very close to each other. In this case, each property being purchased can be analyzed by prospective investors in the offering documents.

Private Equity / Venture Capital Fund Example

Funds are widely available for investing in private equity and venture capital. Expected returns in this arena are healthy because they supply more than just a check to purchase a target. The investment team remains on the deal to work with the management team to unlock the value and improve the business. If you think that, as an individual investor, you can select a single business to invest in passively and make money, you are deceiving yourself. It is not that easy. If you invest in a single startup and the business subsequently fails, the entrepreneur will have mainly lost other people's money. Such entrepreneurs will move on with raising funds for a new business. If, on the other hand, you partner with a proven fund that has a track record and clout, the same entrepreneur will be receiving assistance from the venture capital firm in terms of strategic counsel and industry contacts, thus increasing the odds of success. If, ultimately, that business still fails, at least there are still a dozen or so other investments in the fund.

I have invested in three private equity funds, all through crowdfunding platforms, after a series of failures investing in single startups. All three funds are mid-way through their ten-year initial term and have double-digit IRRs to date. I will highlight a VC fund of the type I am advocating for passive-private investors in this book, a fund of a very experienced California-based firm I will call VC Capital Partners.

The salient points regarding VCCP and the fund are as follows:

- 40+ years' experience, with investments in over 500 companies.
- Focus on key sectors of healthcare, enterprise software, and cybersecurity.
- Fund vintage XII focused on early-stage companies.
- Fund size $325 million
- No leverage was employed.
- $100k minimum investment in 2018; (My) expected return 20%+ IRR.
- Portfolio of twenty companies built up (to date) over 5 years.
- One company has gone public, two sold in the first four years.
- IRR of 40%; TVPI 1.63x (to date)
- Cash returns to investors in the first four years of 15.4% of invested capital, with one exit proceeds pending. VC investments should not be viewed as a cash flow strategy, but it can be with some early exits.
- Challenges navigated with Covid-29 and subsequent risk in interest rates.

It may be more boring investing in funds, but personally, I don't find these results boring. Based on my journey, my mindset is to invest in this sponsor through future vintages and perhaps find a similar private equity sponsor that operates with a buyout strategy with more geographical (Europe and Asia) reach to complement the venture capital fund. It is also nice that one investment commitment can last 10+ years. Committing $200,000 to the above-described two-sponsor strategy and earning 20% net IRRs to investments would result in a $1.2 million nest egg in ten years.

Commercial Real Estate Fund Example

I have invested in three multifamily funds directly with proven sponsors. I have not had any failures with single asset syndications yet, although a hotel property is still trying to recover from the COVID-19 shutdown. My comfort level is much higher with funds, and I can sleep better at night. I have also invested in the Crowdstreet Private REIT because it provides a higher degree of diversification with a 15% target IRR. I will highlight a multifamily, multi-asset syndication organized by a top-tier real estate sponsor. Twenty apartment complexes were under contract and batched in one syndication offering. I will call it Multifamily Fund 21.

To provide a good flavor of what this type of offering looks like, here are the high-level features of Multifamily Fund 21:

- The firm has over 40 years of experience with multiple well-defined segments, including multifamily value add.
- September 2021 closing, expected term of 5 years with multiple exit options (piecemeal sales or bulk-sale of the portfolio to a large REIT)
- Multifamily 21 funds consisted of 21 units across 4,000+ doors, over seven states, simultaneously acquired.
- Fund size $100 million
- 74% debt leverage, fixed rate agency debt at 2.7% interest, 10-year term
- $100k minimum investment in 2019; (My) expected return 30%+ IRR.
- It's too early to discuss the experience with cash distributions and exits. Renovations are currently proceeding on all properties.

My mindset with regards to commercial real estate is to have core holdings of multifamily funds, plus diversification into other asset types such as office, storage, and industrial through private REITs. For multifamily, there is a mixture of multi-asset syndications (described above) and semi-blind pool funds, semi with respect to a focus on multifamily in defined states in the Sunbelt region. Also, I define multifamily broadly to include mobile home parks or student housing. I have in-depth relationships with three excellent sponsors and intend to invest in each vintage fund offered. As a rule, commercial real estate is less risky than venture capital, so the return expectation I have for this asset class is 13-15% net. Committing $300,000 to these sponsors, earning 15% net IRRs, and reinvesting proceeds of exits would generate a $1.2 million nest egg in ten years.

Fund of Funds

The fund of funds, one investment with multiple sponsors, is not common or necessary in commercial real estate. Sponsors with funds are abundant, and it is not difficult to assemble your own portfolio of funds. With private equity, as previously discussed, it is not as easy to locate fund offerings directly. Crowdfunding or digital platforms must be relied upon to a large extent, and fund of funds offerings are finding traction in this environment. Examples include OurCrowd, Moonfare, and NewVest.

Quick Summary

1. Funds provide you with the ultimate tool for portfolio construction, leveraging the experience of managers who are experts.
2. Trust the syndicator. Bet on the jockey, not the horse. This is subject to performing proper due diligence on the sponsor prior to committing to funds.

3. Every asset will have problems. Even a small portfolio can reduce the volatility of returns and smooth out the really big problems.
4. Funds are better for the psyche, resulting in a better investor experience, lifetime learning, and the ability to stick with a private-passive strategy for the long term.

Section III, Planning Private-Passive Strategy & Asset Allocation

Chapter 12 - The Private-Passive Plan

The moment has arrived, and you now qualify as an accredited investor. You have a firm understanding of the building blocks for private market investing as presented in Section II, registered with crowdfunding platforms, initiated your Google searches for sponsors, and perhaps reacted to an interesting multifamily syndication advertisement on Instagram. What do you do? Firstly, forget the Instagram advertisement. Next, develop an investment plan to guide the activities that will lead to success as a private-passive investor. In short, you first define the game that you want to play and then select the players that will help you achieve your goals. You need a plan.

This chapter is not primarily about spreadsheets. It begins with the equally important topics of private market investor mindset and principles. The unique nature of private markets, and in particular the lack of liquidity of investments, requires a customized approach to developing an investment plan and the systems that will be necessary to achieve success as a private-passive investor. This chapter introduces a simple system that can be used or customized to investors' particular needs.

Private-Passive Investor Mindset

If private markets do not feel right in your gut, or if you do not understand the underlying assets, please stay in the public markets and avoid the private markets. A private-passive approach is not for everyone.

Private-passive investors are aware of the importance of developing productive habits, simple systems, and the discipline to adhere to them. In the public equity markets, an example would be investing 10% of your income regularly in an index fund, not deviating. This is good advice, certainly for younger investors in building their financial freedom. What percentage of investors have the discipline to follow this simple system? Too few. It is difficult to replicate this level of simplicity in private markets due to the large menu of alternative assets. However, systems have been developed outside of public markets that are simple, but still require discipline and, of course, education. In private-active investing, the BRRRR method is a popular real estate investment strategy used by investors to acquire and finance rental properties. The acronym stands for Buy, Rehab, Rent, Refinance, and Repeat. If interested, look it up online or with Bigger Pockets.

This chapter delves into developing an investment plan or framework for private-passive investors. Hopefully, it can serve as the starting point for investors in developing their own simple systems that can guide their activities and as a foundation for positive habit formation. If a plan is too complicated, investors are unlikely to maintain their confidence or discipline during periods when the broader financial markets become less stable. James Clear, in his book *Atomic Habits*, knowingly states, **"You do not rise to the level of your goals. You fall to the level of your systems."**

It is absolutely critical for investors to embrace the lack of liquidity inherent in private markets. They are perfectly happy to tie up capital for five years or more if they can generate 10-20% IRRs with steady cash flow generation each year. This mindset has implications for other aspects of your financial life. Sufficient emergency funds should be established outside of the private-passive portfolio. A lack of understanding and acceptance of this lack of liquidity will result in high stress levels for investors in private markets.

In reality, a positive mindset around liquidity should apply to public equity markets as well. Most legendary investors acquire stocks with a long-term perspective, a period of time necessary for an undervalued stock to become fully valued. Investors such as Warren Buffett, Charlie Munger, and Sir John Templeton have this long-term horizon mindset. Smaller investors in the public markets should follow their lead and view their holdings as untouchable for as long as necessary, despite the reality that they can sell anytime. Lack of liquidity is real for an accredited investor. Accredited investors who react emotionally and make mistakes (relative to goals) must live with these decisions for years. Successful investing as an accredited investor requires you to know yourself, your mindset, goals, and risk tolerance.

Private-passive investors relish their passive mindset. The public markets are a barometer of human emotion. In contrast, managing a private portfolio does not subject one to the daily gyrations inherent in the public markets. Turn off the news and the financial channel. The mindset of a private-passive investor is always to be mindful of the next investment, to bring the portfolio into balance, or to utilize the cash for other purposes in life. An investor should perform a quarterly review of each position in the private portfolio in conjunction with the distribution of quarterly reports by the sponsor. Reports are usually available within 60 days of the end of each calendar quarter. It is helpful to review the commentary, the financials, and the distributions received and understand why the cash received might be different from expectations. Take up some new hobbies if you are used to watching financial news and overtrading your account. As Alexander Green says in The Gone Fishin Portfolio, **"Time, not money, is your most precious resource. It is the most valuable thing you have. It is perishable, irreplaceable, and, unlike money, cannot be saved."**

Private-passive investors have the constant awareness to avoid chasing higher returns than the investment plan requires. Joel Greenblatt, renowned value investor at Gotham Asset Management, once said, **"I don't buy more of the ones I can make the most money on. I buy more of the ones I can't lose money on."** There is no need to be heroic. Certainly, in private markets, one must be satisfied with achieving a portfolio's expected returns. This contradicts many an investor's human nature, but remember that the average returns in the private markets are already expected to exceed those in the public markets due to the illiquidity premium. There can be a strong pull towards deals with outsized internal rates of return (on paper), but chasing returns in the private markets is as big a mistake as it is in public markets. Envy is an emotion that needs to be kept in check. Be content with your own strategy, and don't get caught up in the investing success of others.

Investors who are optimistic by nature tend to have a blind spot with regard to the risks. Pessimistic investors miss out on opportunities to create generational wealth. I tended to fall into the former camp, and so much of my efforts have been in developing a plan for private market investing that I can maintain. An investment system is crucial for keeping an investor on the correct path and minimizing a tendency to be overconfident with investment decisions. The importance of good decisions is amplified, as there are fewer, larger investment decisions to make with a private-passive portfolio.

Each investment decision should have embedded a good margin of error. Sponsors should be doing their part in building offerings with a decent margin of error; however, I always ask myself how I can make the investment a little safer before hitting the "send" button. Possible ways are to reduce the committed amount if there are doubts or, if available, select a safer option within the capital stack, such as a preferred or debt option rather than common equity. Prior to developing my own plan and system, I spent too many nights worrying about my initial private placements. During this period, I heard author and fund manager James Altucher as a guest on a podcast, and he commented that if you cannot sleep at night, it could mean that the investment positions in the portfolio are too large. This may seem obvious, but at that moment, it was like a revelation to me. The appropriate mindset is to start small, increase "bet size" over time as familiarity with the private markets and sponsors increases, and be satisfied with the expected return, which is a function of your asset allocation.

Investors in private markets have a patient mindset. This is a close cousin to having a passive mindset, which I equate more with the mental adjustment of moving from public financial markets to private markets. It is about quieting down the mind. With a patient mindset, I am referring to how an investor operates within the private markets. An alternative private portfolio has to be managed in a different way. Once the target asset allocation is determined, the success of the private-passive investor is a direct function of the purchase decisions that are made. There is no trading or exit until the general manager says there is an exit. One must possess a long-term mindset in generating attractive returns as measured by IRR. You will make your money each day that you hold investments, not trading investments.

Patience is not only required during the holding period; it is essential in deciding when and how to deploy capital. Successful private investing requires that investors resist the internal and external forces that cause investors to make impulsive purchase decisions. Every dollar invested has an opportunity cost, which is all of the other deals foregone. There is always another deal coming to market, and it will likely be more appealing and a better fit for an investment plan. I have never regretted an offering that I passed on. **"The public equity market is a no-called-strike game. You don't have to swing at everything – you can wait for your pitch. The problem when you're a money manager is that your fans keep yelling, 'Swing, you bum!"** as quoted from the 1999 Berkshire Hathaway Annual Meeting. This is equally applicable to private markets, where the purchase decision is the most important part of the process.

Private-passive investors have a curious mindset and understand the business or assets in which they invest. This is the mindset of being curious, educating yourself thoroughly about a sponsor and their offering before handing the money over. Warren Buffett and others espouse this mindset in the public markets, and it applies as well in the public markets. The problem with investors in the public market is that they refuse to accept this mindset, possibly because of the ease and lack of friction required for a public market investor to purchase a stock. In private offerings, the transaction sizes are much larger, the stakes are higher, and there is no quick and easy exit. It is a long-term marriage, placing a premium on ensuring that your upfront research and due diligence process results in a complete understanding of what you are investing in. **"Know what you own, and know why you own it,"** famed money manager Peter Lynch advised in the book *One Up On Wall*.

Private-Passive Plan Principles

Proven principles that apply to investing in the public equity markets also apply to investing in funds available to accredited investors.

Asset allocation is the most important determinant of your portfolio's return, absent stupid behavior. This is true in public markets and should also be true in private markets. In fact, investors in private markets may have an advantage since they will be able to change their allocation less frequently than public investors, who face ever-present temptations to change their minds and trade excessively. Also, the more diversified a portfolio is, the truer that asset allocation is a prime determining factor of portfolio returns.

Diversification is a free lunch. Part of the value proposition for private-passive investing is that you can earn equal or greater returns with fewer units of risk than in public equity markets. The liquidity of public markets, by definition, increases volatility in public asset returns. Private market investors must find smart and creative ways to diversify, and fund investing is the primary tool that can be utilized. Diversification in all variables of the private-passive investing framework is important, mainly geography, sponsor, strategy, property type, and placement in the capital stack.

Buy, hold, and be patient. Conversely, excessive trading hurts long-term returns. Again, this is much less of a problem with a private-passive portfolio due to the long-term nature of the underlying projects. Once a private asset or fund is acquired, let nature take its course. There is nothing an investor can do except wait and continue the learning process as each investment proceeds down the path toward exit or liquidation.

The power of compounding returns is magical. It is common wisdom for all markets that the power of compounding is what creates generational wealth, and the earlier an investor begins a program of systematic investing, the more amazing the end result. With regards to private markets, they can be even more powerful if executed properly. Assuming a small 2% illiquidity premium for private markets versus public markets, an upfront investment of $100,000 grows over time, as exhibited in Figure 30.

Figure 30

	Investment	IRR	10 years	20 years	30 years
Private	$100,000	12%	$310,585	$964,629	$2,995,992
Public	$100,000	10%	$259,374	$672,750	$1,744,940

Dollar-cost-averaging can protect an investor from investing too much at the wrong time of a business or real estate cycle. This principle or technique smooths out the entry points for investing sums of money.

While more difficult to accomplish with the large minimum investment requirements inherent with private offerings, investing in sequential fund vintages of a proven fund sponsor can smooth out or normalize returns over time. This is a great advantage of utilizing funds, as to some extent, you will be delegating the timing of investments to an experienced sponsor. It is unlikely that an individual investor is more astute at market timing in a particular niche of the commercial real estate asset class than a sponsor who has been through decades of real estate cycles.

Excessive leverage (margin) can sabotage any type of investment. Higher returns in real estate syndications and private equity are predicated on the use of leverage. Investors in private markets must understand how an investment intends to utilize leverage. The large, most established private equity firms and real estate sponsors have likely institutionalized an aversion to excessive leverage, but an investor should be able to recite exactly how much leverage (in terms of LTV or loans to total cost) a strategy intends to deploy. This importance is amplified if the nature of lending in a particular market is floating-rate debt. Why is there a banking crisis every ten years or so? Because of the fractional reserve nature of banks – they are one of the most highly leveraged sectors of the market.

Investors need to maintain sufficient cash reserves. This serves two primary purposes. First, maintaining a healthy cash balance will help investors avoid becoming impatient with an illiquid portfolio of private investments. Second, it allows investors to take advantage of opportunistic opportunities in the private markets that will inevitably present themselves in challenging times.

Investors should invest passively in index funds and own the market. This principle is difficult for investors to replicate in private markets. This principle supports the strategy of utilizing funds and diversifying across as many private markets as possible.

Developing a Private Markets Investment Plan (PACER)

Investors in private markets need a systematic procedure in order to achieve success as uniquely defined by an individual's needs. Systems will also keep you out of trouble. There is no one-size-fits-all all system, but I have developed the PACER system to guide my actions.

- Define a general investor **profile or persona (P)** based on investment goals and risk tolerance.
- Decide on the private market **asset allocation (A)**.
- Memorialize **constraints (C)** on the portfolio.
- **Execute (E)** the private portfolio plan.
- **Reinvest and rebalance (R)** the portfolio continuously.

Determine the General Investor Profile (PACER)

The first step of this system is to categorize investors into one of four profiles or personas. Every investor has different objectives, which can change over time. The profiles include growth, growth and income, and income plus the additional intriguing category of conservative income. Undoubtedly, there exist formal scientific tests to categorize investors into these buckets, but for now, the process is to review the categories and characteristics posed in Figure 31 to see which profile best describes your situation. The characteristics are rough measures of risk tolerance, the need for regular income, the percentage of investable assets devoted to private markets, and the level of education and comfort with private markets. These criteria need to be viewed as a bundle, as one outlier should not disqualify an investor from a particular profile.

Figure 31	
Investor Profile	**Characteristics**
Growth investor	• Risk taker. Temporary drop in asset values of 50% or more does not shake confidence; • Regular portfolio income is not necessary, generational wealth creation more important; • Percentage of investable assets in private markets is low or investor with very high net worth; • Education or experience level in private markets high.
Growth and income investor	• Moderate risk taker; • Regular portfolio income needed, but some upside in form of capital appreciation is desired; • Percentage of investable assets in private markets is moderate; • Education or experience level in private markets moderate.
Income investor	• Risk averse. Even a 10% drop in asset is alarming; • Regular portfolio income is necessary to replace paycheck or live-off in retirement; • Percentage of investable assets in private markets is high; • Education or experience level in private markets may be low-moderate.
Conservative income investor	• Very risk averse. Wants a very high-yielding portfolio that acts similar but not as safe as a money market fund; • Regular portfolio income is necessary to live; • Percentage of investable assets in private markets is secondary to the other criteria in this category; • Education or experience level in private markets is anywhere on the continuum.

The writing of this or any book is an educational process, not simply a process of placing concepts that you think you know on paper. What I have learned during this process has had the effect of moving me down to the income profile. It has even piqued my interest in the conservative income profile for reasons that will be explained in the later chapter on retirement issues.

Private market portfolio design is a different beast, and in my case, it requires a specific tool to keep my asset selection consistent with my investor profile or persona. I created the IP Scoring Matrix, as shown in Figure 32.

Over time, I would expect this to evolve. In the past, my lack of a systematic approach to asset selection has caused a lot of post-investment regrets, not due to the asset itself but the general feeling that my portfolio had become too aggressive for my investment objectives and mental health. Before investing in a new syndication, I will calculate the IP Score for the new investment, and I will also calculate how the new investment impacts my overall portfolio IP Score to ensure I am always moving in the correct direction.

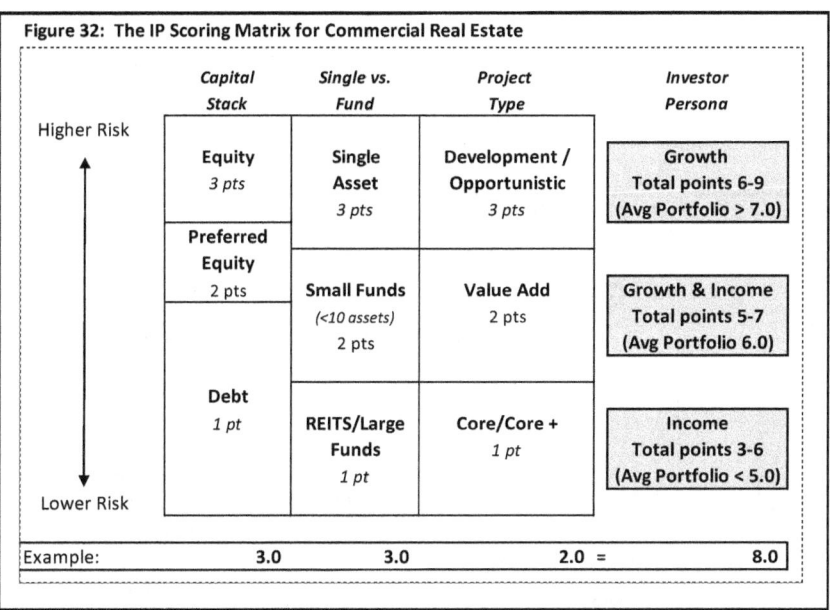

The above example represents a syndication offering for a single multifamily property with a value-added business plan. A score of 3.0 is provided due to the offering being common equity (capital stack), a score of 3.0 is provided since it is a single asset (single vs. fund), and a score of 2.0 is provided for the value-add (project type). The grand total is 8.0, and this would be an appropriate investment for the growth and growth and income investor personas. It is important to note that this project may be acceptable for the income persona, assuming that adding this project to the overall portfolio results in a portfolio average score between 3.0-7.0. Note that the conservative income persona is not represented in Figure 32, and the desired range for this persona would be 3.0-5.0. This system has the main purpose of ensuring you stay honest with yourself and your primary objectives.

The IP Scoring Matrix for private equity is similar, with the project type being replaced by investment strategy. Otherwise, it is the same as illustrated in Figure 33. In this example, we have an equity investment opportunity (score 3.0) in a large fund (score 1.0) of private equity investments with a buyout-equity investment strategy (score 2.0, total offering score of 6.0). This offering could potentially fit in all investor personas, but most likely the growth or growth and income persona.

Another example not shown would be investing in a single company's new venture on some crowdfunding site, which would result in a maximum score of 9.0, placing it squarely in the growth persona. At the risk of being repetitive, this speculative approach is not recommended for a private passive investor. If insistent on creating a portfolio of, say, 10 single ventures with equal-sized small investments, a variation would be to score this as a "large fund," reducing the total score of each item in this portfolio to 7.0. By building your own portfolio of ventures, you are making the statement that you can do a better job of assembling a venture portfolio than a proven venture capital firm that has been doing this for decades.

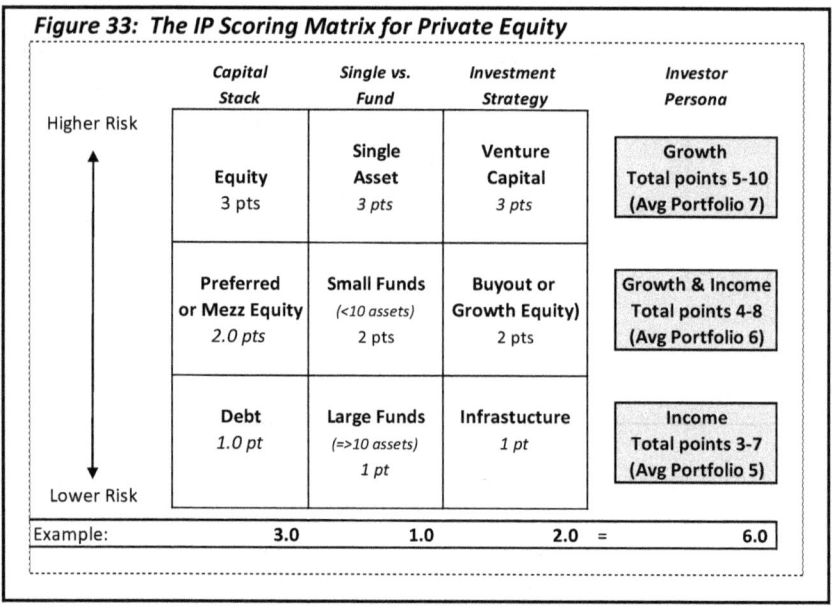

Define the Private Market Asset Allocation (PACER)

Asset allocation is the singular most important variable in determining long-term investment returns. The proper asset allocation is based on the investor's profile for risk and return expectations.

Stepping back to the public markets, classical wisdom is to have 60% in equities and 40% in fixed income or bonds. This prescription is based on the capital stack dimension, riskier equity vs. safer debt. Fundamental to this allocation is a historical lack of correlation between stocks and bonds, meaning when one goes up, the other goes down. Going one step further, the equities portion of this asset allocation is further broken down into one-third international equities and two-thirds USA equities. This is not a capital stack delineation but a geographical definition that is again based on a free lunch created by a historic lack of correlation between domestic and foreign equity markets. So, asset allocation is really an optimization technique, trying to squeeze out equal or higher returns with fewer units of risk. And the capital stack is the foundational element of asset allocation dogmas. As you might imagine, this optimization could quickly become overly complex for the average individual to implement, so target allocations are rightly expressed in these simple terms. As we have seen previously with the Yale Model, the next step to added complexity is to add other non-correlated asset classes such as real estate, commodities, and private equity.

How should we translate this conventional wisdom to a private market portfolio? Consistent with the concept of starting with asset classes, designing a proper asset allocation for private markets would start at the level of the following three asset classes:

- Commercial Real Estate (CRE)
- Private Equity (PE)
- Venture Capital (VC)

As each investor will have a different comfort zone around these asset classes, there must be flexibility around assigning percentages for asset allocation at this level. CRE is the most readily understood asset class for most investors, so allocating 100% to CRE is perfectly fine. Private equity is about real Main Street businesses, which most investors can relate to as well. Venture capital is essentially private equity in the very early stages of development, clearly the riskiest of these asset classes. Would it be more optimal to include all three asset classes in this primary level of asset allocation? Theoretically, the answer is yes. However, this determination has to also consider (1) an investor's degree of knowledge or understanding of these asset classes and (2) the availability of suitable investments for less wealthy investors in the private equity and venture capital markets. Therefore, it is very difficult to prescribe that investors aim for a particular target, such as 70%, 20%, and 10%, to commercial real estate, private equity, and venture capital, respectively. To keep this simple, aim to have all three classes represented but remain flexible with regards to allocation percentages to each asset class. A private passive investor can be reasonably diversified within commercial real estate, and the same goes for private equity/venture capital.

At the next level within each asset class, therein lies the opportunity to develop a properly allocated or diversified portfolio. The IP (Investor Persona) Scoring Matrix is a tool that attempts to match investments with an investor's unique risk/return appetite, much like the public equivalent of a 60/40 portfolio. More aggressive or younger investors may choose a public market allocation of 80/20, and more conservative or older investors may opt for a 40/60 portfolio. Fittingly, the IP Scoring Matrix incorporates the equity vs. debt variable (capital stack). It goes a bit further by incorporating a measure of diversification (single asset vs. fund) and the riskiness of investment strategy. The overall average score of a private portfolio will place an investor in either the growth, growth and, income, or income persona, similar to how a public investor's portfolio translates into an equity/fixed income ratio allocation. Accordingly, the IP Scoring Matrix Tool is sufficient for guiding asset allocation as well. As an added check, we will add a capitalization ratio to the IP Scoring Matrix, defined as total debt plus preferred equity divided by total capitalization, as illustrated in Figure 34.

Figure 34

Investor Persona	(Debt + Preferred) /Total Capitalization
Growth investor	20%
Growth and income investor	40%
Income investor	60%
Conservative income investor	80%

So, how do sub-asset classes factor into asset allocation? Asset allocation guidelines in public markets are general; again, consider the 60/40 portfolio. There is a presumption of a solidly diversified portfolio supporting this target, but there is really no further breakdown into industry sectors such as technology or healthcare, for example. Inside private commercial real estate, sub-asset classes include multifamily, industrial, hospitality, office, retail, and mixed-use properties. Some subcategories of commercial real estate are simpler to understand. Everyone understands what a single-family home or an apartment building is. They understand the asset, its utility, and how revenues are generated. In the private equity class, this could be further broken down into investment strategies, assuming that an investor wishes to participate materially in private equity. For this purpose, in order to simplify the concepts, I feel no need to break down private equity and venture capital any further. For these subclasses, the ideal way to deal with this added measure of diversification is through portfolio constraint rules, the subject of the next section.

Summing up, in the interests of simplicity, I have integrated asset allocation into the IP Scoring Matrix Tool, where we align investor goals with portfolio construction. The portfolio's IP Score and the debt-to-capitalization ratio are the ultimate metrics that indicate if an investor is properly allocated. A simple system is important, as investors will give up on something overly complex. Figure 35 presents the final integrated IP Scoring Matrix for a growth investor that holds ten separate investments.

FIGURE 35: GROWTH PORTFOLIO EXAMPLE

	Capital Stack	Single vs. Fund	CRE Strategy (PE Strategy)	Investor Persona	Debt/Pref To Total Cap
Higher Risk	Equity 3 pts	Single Asset 3 pts	Development (PE = Venture) 3 pts	Growth Total points 6-9 (Avg Portfolio > 7.0)	20.0%
	Preferred Equity 2 pts	Small Funds (<10 assets) 2 pts	Value Add (PE = Buyout, or Growth Equity) 2 pts	Growth & Income Total points 5-7 (Avg Portfolio 6.0)	40.0%
Lower Risk	Debt 1 pt	REITS/Large Funds 1 pt	Core/Core + (PE = Infrastucture) 1 pt	Income Total points 3-6 (Avg Portfolio < 5.0)	60.0%

	Principal	Score	Score	Score		Total Score	Weighted Total Score	Debt or Preferred
PE - VENTURE FUND	$100,000	3.0	1.0	3.0	=	7.0	0.88	$ -
PE - BUYOUT FUND	$100,000	3.0	1.0	2.0	=	6.0	0.75	$ -
CRE - HOTEL DEVEL	$100,000	3.0	3.0	3.0	=	9.0	1.13	$ -
CRE - MULTIFAM DEV	$ 50,000	3.0	3.0	3.0	=	9.0	0.56	$ -
CRE - MULTIFAM FUND	$100,000	3.0	2.0	2.0	=	7.0	0.88	$ -
CRE - MULTIFAM FUND	$100,000	3.0	2.0	2.0	=	7.0	0.88	$ -
PRIVATE REIT	$ 50,000	3.0	1.0	2.0	=	6.0	0.38	$ -
CRE-OFFICE V-A	$ 50,000	3.0	3.0	2.0	=	8.0	0.50	$ -
CRE - DEBT FUND	$ 50,000	1.0	1.0	2.0	=	4.0	0.25	$ 50,000
CRE - PREF FUND	$100,000	2.0	1.0	2.0	=	5.0	0.63	$100,000
	$800,000						6.81	$150,000
				(Debt and Preferred Equity) / Total Capitalization				19%

In the above example, this growth investor has a portfolio with a weighted average IP Score of 6.81 vs a target of 7.0. The debt-to-capitalization ratio is 19%, which is consistent with the target of 20%. The only inputs to the tool are located in the table at the bottom. These fields of data include asset description, investment amount, and the scorings for the three dimensions (capital stack, single vs. fund, investment strategy). A private investor would always be striving to steer the portfolio towards the target scores with subsequent investments. To ensure proper diversification, an investor should aim to hold at least five positions in the portfolio. Without a system or similar tool, it is very easy for an investor in private markets to stray from their ultimate goals and comfort zone.

Memorialize Constraints on the Portfolio (PACER)

The concept of portfolio constraints is well-engrained in the operation of mutual funds and private equity funds to ensure consistency with investment objectives and to ensure proper diversification. Examples of constraints or rules that you might place on a private-passive portfolio include the following:

- For stubborn investors that invest in single ventures or properties, a rule that any single investment will not exceed 10% (suggestion only) of the total private portfolio value.

- For CRE, a limit on what percentage of the portfolio can be invested in development projects tends to be the riskiest.
- For CRE investors that prefer a certain sub-asset class, such as multifamily, a rule is that at least 50% of the portfolio will be invested in multifamily properties.
- A limit on total venture capital investments as a percentage of the total portfolio.
- Foreign investments cannot exceed a certain percentage of the total portfolio (generally only a factor with private equity or venture capital)

Constraints should be viewed as guardrails that are completely customizable to an investor's situation and preferences. These rules should be viewed through a lens of risk avoidance. What areas of concentration in my private portfolio might cause me loss of sleep at night? Too many constraints are not advisable either, as investors should allow ample flexibility to achieve their objectives.

Execute the Private Portfolio Plan (PACER)

The topic of daily execution of a private-passive portfolio goes back to the building blocks of private markets, finding great sponsors and then connecting with their deal flow. This step encompasses the identification of offerings, performing due diligence on sponsors and specific offerings, understanding an investment's IP score and its impact on your portfolio's IP score, the portfolio constraints, and being attuned to your need for cash flow at the present moment. Execution requires selectivity – every deal will look good at first since that is how sponsors want them to appear. In the end, it is only a good deal if it meets your investment objectives and survives your due diligence process. Once you locate the right investment, commit and move on. There is no need to ruminate on these all-important investment decisions and no room for regrets.

Reinvest and Rebalance Continuously (PACER)

Exits will occur regularly once the plan has been in effect for a couple of years. A simple cash forecast spreadsheet is a useful tool for anticipating future cash flows generated from the passive portfolio. It would appear similar to Figure 36.

Figure 36 – Cash Forecast from Private Portfolio

	Invested	Est. Cash on Cash	Exit Multiple	2023	2024	2025	2026	2027
Asset #1	$ 100,000	3.0%	1.6	$ 3,000	$ 163,000			
Asset #2	$ 100,000	0.0%	2.0	$ -	$ -	$ 200,000		
Asset #3	$ 100,000	8.0%	1.5	$ 8,000	$ 8,000	$ 8,000	$ 8,000	$ 158,000
Totals	$ 300,000			$ 11,000	$ 171,000	$ 208,000	$ 8,000	$ 158,000

This allows investors to visualize the anticipated cash inflows in order to plan and decide how to redeploy capital. Options might include:

1. Pocket the cash for daily living expenses;
2. Reinvest in private-passive portfolio; or
3. Move the capital to a brokerage account to invest in traditional public market investments.

As sponsors provide quarterly updates, an investor should review the cash forecast and alter these estimates as warranted. Another great tactic is to look for gaps in future cash inflows and plan the next investment to fill the gap. For example, an investor might look for new syndications with a planned 2026 exit to attempt to have a continuous flow of annual returns for time diversification purposes. It is difficult to estimate when liquidity events or exits in private markets will occur, as the life of a private investment rarely goes exactly as planned. The spirit is to always be anticipating the cash flows and rebalancing the portfolio regularly.

A Plan for Continuous Improvement and Education

A formal plan for succeeding in private market investing would not be complete without a plan for continuing education and improvement. Of paramount importance is to continue to build a network of sponsors and fellow investors in order to advance your understanding of the field. Attending at least one conference a year is a worthwhile goal. In addition, leverage your relationship with existing sponsors to advance your learning through regular conversations with investor relations and carefully reading all periodic investor reports.

Experience is the best teacher. If I have a bad experience with a new sponsor, the reasons for the underperformance will be reviewed and stored in my memory bank. Were the issues self-inflicted on the part of the sponsor or the result of unavoidable problems in the macroenvironment? Was the underwriting simply poor, was execution lacking, poor investor relations, or a combination thereof? Or did the COVID-19 crisis arrive at a time when you just happened to be an equity holder in a hotel in a gateway market? It is hard to blame a sponsor for that one.

Investors need to have a continuous dialogue externally and internally to better understand these unique markets and their aptitude for dealing with these challenges. At the end of the day, an investor needs to have a natural interest in these asset classes to make the effort worthwhile.

These are the main components for establishing a plan for investing in private markets. Chapter Thirteen applies these principles and provides examples for portfolios of various sizes and for different investor personas.

Quick Summary

1. It takes a particular mindset to succeed in the private investment markets. The important variables are the importance of developing systems, embracing the lack of liquidity in these markets, enjoying the passivity and patience required, the avoidance of chasing higher returns, and a natural curiosity for how private market investments operate. Investors should maintain a reasonable emergency fund of 10-20% of the portfolio size to embrace the lack of liquidity inside the private portfolio and to take advantage of market downturns.

2. The proven principles of investing in public markets also apply to private markets. Investors need to be mindful of the need for proper asset allocation and a well-diversified portfolio. In addition, investors should use dollar-cost-average in order to reduce the risk of poor market timing and allowing the magic of compounding returns to work over a long-term horizon.
3. Investors in private offerings need to fully understand how leverage is being utilized in a project or fund. Excessive leverage is the enemy of consistent success in any market.
4. A systematic approach is recommended to managing a private portfolio in a manner that is consistent with an investor's goals and risk tolerance. The PACER system is an example of such a system. The IP (investor profile) Scoring Matrix is a tool that allows investors to manage their asset allocation in a manner consistent with their investing profile. Determining your investor profile or persona is a key step in defining how to construct a private-passive portfolio.

Chapter 13 - Applied Plan Designs for Various Investor Profiles

This is the spreadsheet chapter, where the IP Scoring Matrix asset allocation system is applied for various investor profiles. Example portfolios of $5 million and $500,000 will be provided for the following investor profiles: growth, growth and income, income, and conservative income. For each model portfolio, the IP Score and Debt/Preferred to Total Capitalization ratio will be illustrated, as will the expected internal rate of return for the portfolio. In addition, for newly accredited investors, I will present a "Starter Portfolio" of $250,000. Can an investor start in private markets with less than $250,000? Certainly, these investors should place a premium on fund products and crowdfunding platforms. Note that positions that begin with "PE" represent private equity. Otherwise, all positions represent commercial real estate.

These portfolios are for illustration only and are not sponsor-specific. Investors may be more comfortable or knowledgeable about hospitality, RV parks, storage facilities, or diversified real estate products. The portfolios I have crafted tend to favor multifamily investments. It is important to note that the expected IRRs and the expected cash yields from portfolios are relative to the interest rate environment existing in early 2023. The returns on private assets will change as the risk-free rate of interest changes over time.

FIGURE 37: GROWTH PORTFOLIO - $5 MILLION (IPS SCORE TARGET 7.0, DEBT/CAP RATIO 20%)

	IP SCORING MATRIX			Principal	% Cap	Est IRR
	Cap Stack	Fund	Strategy IP Score			
Common Equity						
Industrial Development Asset	3	3	3 9.0	$ 400,000		20.0%
Multifamily Development Asset	3	3	3 9.0	$ 400,000		14.0%
Multifamily Value-add Fund	3	2	2 7.0	$ 500,000		14.0%
Multifamily Value-add Fund	3	1	2 6.0	$ 500,000		14.0%
Multifamily Core Fund	3	2	1 6.0	$ 300,000		10.0%
Private REIT	3	1	2 6.0	$ 250,000		15.0%
Mixed-use Development Asset	3	3	3 9.0	$ 300,000		20.0%
Medical Office Value-add Fund	3	2	2 7.0	$ 250,000		14.0%
PE - Venture Capital Fund	3	1	3 7.0	$ 300,000		22.0%
PE - Growth Equity Fund	3	1	2 6.0	$ 300,000		20.0%
PE - Buyout Fund	3	1	2 6.0	$ 250,000		20.0%
PE - Co-investment Fund	3	2	2 7.0	$ 250,000		20.0%
Total Common				$ 4,000,000	80%	16.6%
Pref Equity and Debt						
Preferred Funds	2	1	2 5.0	$ 300,000		11.0%
Debt Funds	1	1	2 4.0	$ 250,000		9.0%
Real Estate Note Platforms	1	1	2 4.0	$ 250,000		10.0%
PE - Venture Debt Fund	1	2	3 6.0	$ 200,000		15.0%
Total Pref and Debt				$ 1,000,000	20%	11.1%
Total Portfolio			6.7	$ 5,000,000	100%	15.5%

In Figure 37, a portfolio example is presented for a $5 million private portfolio with a growth profile. This investor is interested in maximum capital gains and generational wealth creation. Investors with this size portfolio can invest in all asset classes, including private equity and its venture capital subclass. The IP Score of this portfolio is 6.7, which is slightly below the target of 7.0 for a growth investor. The debt + preferred equity / total capitalization ratio is 20%, equivalent to the 20% benchmark for a growth investor. I do not recommend exceeding 80% common equity, as debt and preferred stock can be very useful in balancing any portfolio. An important constraint would be to define the maximum percentage of any position to the entire portfolio; in this case, no position represents more than $500,000, or 10% of the portfolio. Clearly, this portfolio will not generate much regular income and instead will generate returns in the form of capital gains from periodic exits of individual positions. The expected IRR of this portfolio is 15.5%, which, given the diversification and number of fund products, is achievable.

FIGURE 38: GROWTH PORTFOLIO - $500,000 (IPS SCORE TARGET 7.0, DEBT/CAP RATIO 20%)

	IP SCORING MATRIX				Principal	% Cap	Est IRR
	Cap Stack	Fund	Strategy	IP Score			
Common Equity							
Industrial Development Asset	3	3	3	9.0	$ 50,000		20.0%
Multifamily Value-add Fund	3	2	2	7.0	$ 75,000		14.0%
Multifamily Value-add Fund	3	1	2	6.0	$ 100,000		14.0%
Private REIT	3	1	2	6.0	$ 50,000		15.0%
PE - Venture Capital Fund	3	1	3	7.0	$ 100,000		22.0%
Total Common					$ 375,000	75%	17.1%
Pref Equity and Debt							
Preferred Fund	2	1	2	5.0	$ 100,000		11.0%
Debt Fund	1	1	2	4.0	$ 25,000		9.0%
Total Pref and Debt					$ 125,000	25%	10.6%
Total Portfolio				6.4	$ 500,000	100%	15.5%

In Figure 38, a portfolio example is presented for a $500,000 private portfolio with a growth profile. This investor is interested in maximum capital gains and generational wealth creation. Investors with this size portfolio can invest in all asset classes, including private equity and its venture capital subclass. The IP Score of this portfolio is 6.4, which is within a reasonable range of the target of 7.0 for a growth investor. The debt + preferred equity / total capitalization ratio is 25%, slightly higher than the 20% benchmark for a growth investor. I do not recommend exceeding 80% common equity, as debt and preferred stock can be very useful in balancing any portfolio. An important constraint would be to define the maximum percentage of any position to the entire portfolio. In this case, no position represents more than $100,000, or 20% of the portfolio, as it is more difficult for investors with smaller portfolios to diversify. Clearly, this portfolio will not generate much regular income and instead will generate returns in the form of capital gains from periodic exits of individual positions. The expected IRR of this portfolio is 15.5%, which, given the diversification and number of fund products, is achievable.

FIGURE 39: GROWTH & INCOME PORTFOLIO - $5 MILLION (IPS SCORE TARGET 6.0, DEBT/CAP RATIO 40%)

	IP SCORING MATRIX			Principal	% Cap	Est IRR
	Cap Stack	Fund	Strategy IP Score			
Common Equity						
Industrial Development Asset	3	3	3	9.0	$ 200,000		20.0%
Multifamily Development Asset	3	3	3	9.0	$ 200,000		14.0%
Multifamily Value-add Fund	3	2	2	7.0	$ 500,000		14.0%
Multifamily Value-add Fund	3	1	2	6.0	$ 350,000		14.0%
Multifamily Core Fund	3	2	1	6.0	$ 300,000		10.0%
Private REIT	3	1	2	6.0	$ 250,000		15.0%
Mixed-use Development Asset	3	3	3	9.0	$ 250,000		20.0%
Medical Office Value-add Fund	3	2	2	7.0	$ 200,000		14.0%
PE - Venture Capital Fund	3	1	3	7.0	$ 200,000		22.0%
PE - Growth Equity Fund	3	1	2	6.0	$ 200,000		20.0%
PE - Buyout Fund	3	1	2	6.0	$ 200,000		20.0%
PE - Co-investment Fund	3	2	2	7.0	$ 200,000		20.0%
Total Common					$ 3,050,000	61%	16.3%
Pref Equity and Debt							
Preferred Funds	2	1	2	5.0	$ 500,000		11.0%
Debt Funds	1	1	2	4.0	$ 750,000		9.0%
Real Estate Note Platforms	1	1	2	4.0	$ 500,000		10.0%
PE - Venture Debt Fund	1	2	3	6.0	$ 200,000		15.0%
Total Pref and Debt					$ 1,950,000	39%	10.4%
Total Portfolio				6.0	$ 5,000,000	100%	14.0%

In Figure 39, a portfolio example is presented for a $5 million private portfolio with a growth and income profile. This investor is interested in a blend of capital appreciation and the generation of a regular income stream. Investors with this size portfolio can invest in all asset classes, including private equity and its venture capital subclass. The IP Score of this portfolio is 6.0, which is equal to the target of 6.0 for a growth and income investor. The debt + preferred equity / total capitalization ratio is 39%, essentially equivalent to the 40% benchmark for a growth and income portfolio. An important constraint would be to define the maximum percentage of any position to the entire portfolio; in this case, no position represents more than $500,000, or 10% of the portfolio. This portfolio would conservatively generate an annual income of $203,000, or a 4.1% yield. Adding in the income from multifamily funds, the yield might be around 5%. As the portfolio ages, there will also be substantial capital gains realized from periodic exits of individual positions. The expected IRR of this portfolio is 14.0 (versus 15.5% for the same-sized growth portfolio).

FIGURE 40: GROWTH & INCOME PORTFOLIO - $500,000 (IPS SCORE TARGET 6.0, DEBT/CAP RATIO 40%)

	IP SCORING MATRIX						
	Cap Stack	Fund	Strategy	IP Score	Principal	% Cap	Est IRR
Common Equity							
Industrial Value-add Fund	3	2	2	7.0	$ 50,000		14.0%
Multifamily Value-add Fund	3	2	2	7.0	$ 50,000		14.0%
Multifamily Value-add Fund	3	1	2	6.0	$ 50,000		14.0%
Private REIT	3	1	2	6.0	$ 50,000		15.0%
PE - Venture Capital Fund	3	1	3	7.0	$ 100,000		22.0%
Total Common					$ 300,000	60%	16.8%
Pref Equity and Debt							
Preferred Fund	2	1	2	5.0	$ 100,000		11.0%
Debt Fund	1	1	2	4.0	$ 100,000		9.0%
Total Pref and Debt					$ 200,000	40%	10.0%
Total Portfolio				5.8	$ 500,000	100%	14.1%

Figure 40 contains a portfolio model for a $500,000 private portfolio with a growth and income profile. This investor is interested in a blend of capital appreciation and the generation of a regular income stream. Investors with this size portfolio can invest in all asset classes, including private equity and its venture capital subclass, although the number of positions will obviously be constrained. The IP Score of this portfolio is 5.8, roughly equal to the target of 6.0 for a growth and income investor. The debt + preferred equity / total capitalization ratio is 40%, equal to the 40% benchmark for a growth and income portfolio. An important constraint would be to define the maximum percentage of any position to the entire portfolio; in this case, no position represents more than $100,000, or 20% of the portfolio, as it is more difficult for investors with smaller portfolios to diversify. This portfolio would conservatively generate an annual income of $20,000, or a 4.0% yield. Adding in the income from multifamily funds, the yield might be around 5%. As the portfolio ages, there will also be substantial capital gains realized from periodic exits of individual positions. The expected IRR of this portfolio is 14.1 (versus 15.5% for the same-sized growth portfolio).

FIGURE 41: INCOME PORTFOLIO - $5 MILLION (IPS SCORE TARGET 5.0, DEBT/CAP RATIO 60%)

	IP SCORING MATRIX				Principal	% Cap	Est IRR
	Cap Stack	Fund	Strategy	IP Score			
Common Equity							
Industrial Development Asset	3	3	3	9.0	$ 100,000		20.0%
Multifamily Development Asset	3	3	3	9.0	$ 200,000		14.0%
Multifamily Value-add Fund	3	2	2	7.0	$ 400,000		14.0%
Multifamily Value-add Fund	3	1	2	6.0	$ 300,000		14.0%
Multifamily Core Fund	3	2	1	6.0	$ 300,000		10.0%
Private REIT	3	1	2	6.0	$ 200,000		15.0%
Distressed Real Estate Fund	3	2	3	8.0	$ 100,000		14.0%
PE - Venture Capital Fund	3	1	3	7.0	$ 100,000		22.0%
PE - Growth Equity Fund	3	1	2	6.0	$ 150,000		20.0%
PE - Buyout Fund	3	1	2	6.0	$ 200,000		20.0%
Total Common					$ 2,050,000	41%	15.2%
Pref Equity and Debt							
Preferred Fund	2	1	2	5.0	$ 500,000		11.0%
Debt Fund	1	1	2	4.0	$ 750,000		9.0%
Real Estate Note Platform 1	1	1	2	4.0	$ 500,000		10.0%
Real Estate Note Platform 2	1	1	2	4.0	$ 500,000		10.0%
Storage Facility Debt	1	1	2	4.0	$ 500,000		9.0%
PE - Venture Debt Fund	1	2	3	6.0	$ 200,000		15.0%
Total Pref and Debt					$ 2,950,000	59%	10.1%
Total Portfolio				5.3	$ 5,000,000	100%	12.2%

Figure 41 contains a portfolio model for a $5 million private portfolio with an income profile. This investor is interested in creating an alternative income stream to supplement regular wages or for retirement. Investors with this size portfolio can still invest in limited amounts in all asset classes including private equity and its venture capital subclass. The IP Score of this portfolio is 5.3 versus the target of 5.0 for an income investor. The debt + preferred equity / total capitalization ratio is 59%, essentially equivalent to the 60% benchmark for an income portfolio. An important constraint would be to define the maximum percentage of any position to the entire portfolio; in this case, no position represents more than $750,000, or 15% of the portfolio. It is a little more difficult to find top-quality debt funds than equity funds. This portfolio would conservatively generate an annual income of $300,000, or a 6.0% yield. As the portfolio ages, there will also be some supplemental capital gains realized from periodic exits of individual positions. The expected IRR of this portfolio is 12.2% (versus 14.0% for the same-sized growth and income portfolio).

FIGURE 42: INCOME PORTFOLIO - $500,000 (IPS SCORE TARGET 5.0, DEBT/CAP RATIO 60%)

	IP SCORING MATRIX				Principal	% Cap	Est IRR
	Cap Stack	Fund	Strategy	IP Score			
Common Equity							
Industrial Value-add Fund	3	2	2	7.0	$ 50,000		14.0%
Multifamily Value-add Fund	3	2	2	7.0	$ 50,000		14.0%
Multifamily Value-add Fund	3	1	2	6.0	$ 50,000		14.0%
Private REIT	3	1	2	6.0	$ 50,000		15.0%
Total Common					$ 200,000	40%	14.3%
Pref Equity and Debt							
Preferred Fund	2	1	2	5.0	$ 100,000		11.0%
Debt Fund	1	1	2	4.0	$ 100,000		9.0%
Real Estate Note Platform 1	1	1	2	4.0	$ 50,000		10.0%
Real Estate Note Platform 2	1	1	2	4.0	$ 50,000		10.0%
Total Pref and Debt					$ 300,000	60%	10.0%
Total Portfolio				5.2	$ 500,000	100%	11.7%

Figure 42 contains a portfolio model for a $500,000 private portfolio with an income profile. This investor is interested in creating an alternative income stream to supplement regular wages or for retirement. Investors with this size portfolio can still invest in all asset classes, including private equity and its venture capital subclass, in limited amounts. The IP Score of this portfolio is 5.2, roughly equal to the target of 5.0 for an income investor. The debt + preferred equity / total capitalization ratio is 60%, equal to the 60% benchmark for an income portfolio. An important constraint would be to define the maximum percentage of any position to the entire portfolio, in this case, no position represents more than $100,000, or 20% of the portfolio, as it is more difficult for investors with smaller portfolios to diversify. This portfolio would conservatively generate an annual income of $30,000 or a 6.0% yield. Adding in the income from multifamily funds, the yield might be around 7%. As the portfolio ages, some capital gains realized from periodic exits of individual positions will add to the total return. The expected IRR of this portfolio is 11.7% (versus 14.1% for the same-sized growth and income portfolio).

FIGURE 43: CONSERVATIVE INCOME - $5 MILLION (IPS SCORE TARGET 4.0, DEBT/CAP RATIO 80%)

	IP SCORING MATRIX				Principal	% Cap	Est IRR
	Cap Stack	Fund	Strategy	IP Score			
Common Equity							
Multifamily Value-add Fund	3	2	2	7.0	$ 200,000		14.0%
Multifamily Value-add Fund	3	1	2	6.0	$ 200,000		14.0%
Multifamily Core Asset	3	3	1	7.0	$ 150,000		10.0%
Private REIT	3	1	2	6.0	$ 200,000		15.0%
Total Common					$ 750,000	15%	13.5%
Pref Equity and Debt							
Preferred Fund	2	1	2	5.0	$ 750,000		11.0%
Debt Fund #1	1	1	2	4.0	$ 650,000		9.0%
Debt Fund #1	1	1	2	4.0	$ 650,000		9.0%
Real Estate Note Platform 1	1	1	2	4.0	$ 500,000		10.0%
Real Estate Note Platform 2	1	1	2	4.0	$ 500,000		10.0%
Real Estate Note Platform 3 - Core	1	1	1	3.0	$ 600,000		9.0%
Storage Facility Debt	1	1	2	4.0	$ 250,000		9.0%
REIT Income Fund 1	1	1	2	4.0	$ 250,000		9.0%
REIT Income Fund 2	1	1	2	4.0	$ 100,000		15.0%
Total Pref and Debt					$ 4,250,000	85%	9.7%
Total Portfolio				4.4	$ 5,000,000	100%	10.3%

Figure 43 contains a portfolio model for a $5 million private portfolio with a conservative income profile. This investor is interested in the generation of income only. Investors with this size portfolio will focus on preferred equity and debt primarily. There may be room for a common equity position in a conservative real estate fund. The IP Score of this portfolio is 4.4 versus the target of 4.0 for a conservative income investor. The debt + preferred equity / total capitalization ratio is 85%, slightly greater than the 80% benchmark for a conservative income portfolio. Investors will need to dig to find the quantity of debt funds necessary to avoid having more than 15% of assets in one position. This portfolio would conservatively generate an annual income of $413,000, or a 9.7% yield. As the portfolio ages, there should be minor supplemental capital gains realized from periodic exits of individual positions. The expected IRR of this portfolio is 10.3% (versus 12.2% for the same-sized income portfolio).

The interesting question with the conservative income portfolio is, how conservative is it? Can a private investor create a reliable income stream of around 9%? There is not a lot of duration risk, as most private loans typically mature within one year. A portfolio of these loans is continuously repriced to reflect current interest rate conditions. A major macro credit event, such as 2008-9, would likely be this portfolio's kryptonite.

FIGURE 44: CONSERVATIVE INCOME - $500,000 (IPS SCORE TARGET 4.0, DEBT/CAP RATIO 80%)

	IP SCORING MATRIX			Principal	% Cap	Est IRR
	Cap Stack	Fund Strategy	IP Score			
Common Equity						
Private REIT	3	1	2 6.0	$ 50,000		15.0%
Total Common				$ 50,000	10%	15.0%
Pref Equity and Debt						
Preferred Fund	2	1	2 5.0	$ 100,000		11.0%
Debt Fund #1	1	1	2 4.0	$ 100,000		9.0%
Debt Fund #2	1	1	2 4.0	$ 100,000		9.0%
Real Estate Note Platform 1	1	1	2 4.0	$ 100,000		10.0%
REIT Income Fund	1	1	1 3.0	$ 50,000		9.0%
Total Pref and Debt				$ 450,000	90%	9.7%
Total Portfolio			4.3	$ 500,000	100%	10.2%

Figure 44 contains a portfolio model for a $500,000 private portfolio with a conservative income profile. This investor is interested in the generation of income only. Investors with this size portfolio will focus on preferred equity and debt primarily. There may be room for a common equity position in a conservative real estate fund. The IP Score of this portfolio is 4.3, roughly equal to the target of 4.0 for a conservative income investor. The debt + preferred equity / total capitalization ratio is 90%, greater than the 80% benchmark for a conservative income portfolio. Investors will need to dig to find the quantity of debt funds necessary to avoid having more than 20% of assets in one position. This portfolio would conservatively generate an annual income of $47,000, or a 9.7% yield. Adding in the income from multifamily funds, the yield might be around 10.2%. As the portfolio ages, some minor capital gains realized from periodic exits of individual positions will add to the total return. The expected IRR of this portfolio is 10.2% (versus 11.7% for the same-sized income portfolio).

Starter Portfolio, $250,000

Investing in private markets requires a good chunk of capital over and above an emergency fund. An accredited investor can start to invest with $50,000, but to classify it as a diversified portfolio, a sum of $250,000 is suggested. In Figure 45, I have illustrated an example starter fund of $250,000 with some investments identified by the sponsor. These are not specific investment recommendations but rather indications of the type of platform to utilize. Note that each position is a fund-type product with seven positions within the starter portfolio. Diversification by the real estate sector and the sponsor is an absolute must in any portfolio of any size. Private equity is typically limited to $100,000 investment tranches, although occasionally, a crowdfunding site will post an offering from a great sponsor for $50,000. Private equity may be added earlier in the process for growth investors.

This fund is 100% invested in various commercial real estate options and, accordingly will be subject to economic cycles that impact this sector. By reinvesting distributions and adding additional new positions each year, the impact of economic cycles should be mitigated, and investors can earn these types of returns over the long term.

FIGURE 45: STARTER PRIVATE PORTFOLIO - $250,000

	IP SCORING MATRIX							
	Cap Stack	Fund	Strategy	IP Score	Principal	% Cap	Est IRR
Common Equity							
Multifamily Value-add Fund	3	2	2	7.0	$ 50,000		14.0%
Crowdstreet C-REIT	3	1	2	6.0	$ 50,000		15.0%
Industrial Blend Fund	3	2	2	7.0	$ 25,000		17.0%
Realty Mogul Income REIT	3	2	2	7.0	$ 25,000		10.0%
Total Common					$ 150,000	60%	14.2%
Pref Equity and Debt							
Fund that Flip Notes	1	1	2	4.0	$ 25,000		10.0%
Fundrise Balanced	1	1	2	4.0	$ 25,000		9.0%
PPR Note Fund	1	1	2	4.0	$ 50,000		10.0%
Total Pref and Debt					$ 100,000	**40%**	9.8%
Total Portfolio				**5.6**	$ 250,000	100%	12.4%

Chapter 14 - Private Market Risk Factors

In 2016, my daughter and I flew to Panama to kick the tires on a new beachfront condominium investment in Punta Chame, Panama. The project was and continues to be an aggressive project along a beautiful, untouched stretch of beach. In the USA, finding anything with sweeping views of the Pacific Ocean from your apartment would cost an investor a fortune, but not at this time in Panama. The project executives drove us to the beach location with another gentleman who was a real estate professional from Florida. As we toured one of the model units, the real estate professional asked the Panamanians, what is the black swan event that could impact the value of this (condo) investment? Per Britannica, a black swan event is an unexpected and, therefore difficult to prepare for event but is often rationalized with the benefit of hindsight as having been unavoidable. By definition, there was no answer to this question because black swans are only known in hindsight. The question made an immediate impression on me as interesting, but it was useful to try and draw out further information from our hosts. Naturally, there was no specific answer to this question. The Panama Canal drying up would be the first risk that came to mind, but that would be too obvious.

I mention this because when an investor reviews a private placement memorandum, there will always be a long list of risks that are drafted by the lawyers to protect the project sponsor. The list will be the standard litany but nonetheless written in inglorious detail. Black swans are not listed, but the reality is that these are the risks that will take an investor down. Finishing the story, the black swan became known in 2020 when COVID-19 shut down the world. The Panama condominium project, fortunately, survived Covid just fine; in fact, digital nomads fled the city to the beach, and the rental income associated with these condos soared. Investors in hotel syndications around the same time would not have been so lucky. There were no specific risk factors in private property memorandums at the time regarding a worldwide pandemic that could shut down the world for multiple years.

I am not suggesting that investors in private placements ignore the risk factors in a private placement memorandum. In fact, investors should review each and every risk factor. Over time, these risk factors will all seem familiar to experienced accredited investors, and that is a good thing. Risk factor disclosures are simply a way that a sponsor protects themselves against future legal action, less formally known as "CYA." However, it is important for investors to at least ponder potential black swans, as these will be the risks that derail a private investment. Stuff happens in private markets as it does in public markets. The Cases are Russia's war with Ukraine, Covid-19, Silicon Valley Bank's failure, Enron, and the Global Financial Crisis of 2008-9. I do want to make a strong impression on readers that the risk is real and that deploying capital in private markets is not an impulsive activity. This chapter will reinforce the seriousness of these risks with a series of examples of unexpected events. The goal is for investors to understand the difference between risk factors that they should be able to recognize and those that are beyond their ability to control or comprehend.

As this chapter is being put together, the Silicon Valley Bank Crisis of March 2023 was unfolding. Was this outcome for SVB foreseeable or preventable by the public equity stockholders of SVB? Investors getting in at the high of October 2021, just seventeen months earlier, paid $717 per share for the company. Investors entering the stock as recently as March 1, 2023, paid around $283 per share. Less than one month later, the stock was worthless. The earlier the stage of a company, the more uncertainties with future prospects abound. SVB was a well-established and successful bank. There were no disclosures in the most recent quarterly reports that a risk factor was insolvency due to poor risk management practices or a cell phone-induced run on the bank at any moment. I put this more in the Enron category, a management failure. Also, when the Federal Reserve increases short-term interest rates by 450 basis points in less than one year (from zero), there will be damage inflicted on the frail. This same risk is omnipresent in the private markets as well. Combinations of poor management and unforeseen events will bring new ventures down and fast. The particular case SVB was directly germane to the venture equity asset class being addressed herein. Many early-stage ventures were banked at SVB, and can you imagine doing all your due diligence on a single venture? The round is funded, the venture deposits all funds in SVB in advance of deploying it, and SVB goes insolvent. This would be quite unfair and likely not a risk disclosed in the private placement memorandum.

Because crowdfunding is an important component of the private investing ecosystem, the risks extend to these platforms as well if your money happens to be there even temporarily. Jon Medved, the CEO of OurCrowd, responded to his customers following the SVB Crisis, "We want to reassure you that OurCrowd took proactive measures to mitigate any potential impact of this crisis by transferring almost all our funds, including capital in OurCrowd managed funds and deal related SPVs, to other financial institutions by the end of the day on Thursday. The remaining funds were held in fully FDIC-insured accounts with low balances at the time of the bank failure on Friday. Consequently, our exposure to SVB's collapse was minimal. Please be assured that we have ample cash reserves at other institutions to continue our operations without any disruption."

Yieldstreet is a prominent alternative (private) investing platform that offers a variety of investment types, including real estate and other structured financing products. Some are fairly esoteric. In 2022, investors filed a class-action lawsuit over the loss of over $100 million. The lawsuit filed focused on false and misleading statements Yieldstreet made to investors to induce them to purchase certain Yieldstreet investment products, including vessel deconstruction funds, oil & gas wells, commercial real estate, and modern art. Yieldstreet has said the investors were not defrauded, and no fraud was committed. The outcome of this case is still pending.[45] According to WSJ.com, the investigation revolved around non-traditional offerings pertaining to loans linked to "shipbreaking." This has to do with extracting metal and harvesting parts of value from older ships. The report claims approximately $90 million in loans were sold to investors for shipbreaking. It was determined that "roughly a dozen" ships that were collateral for some of these loans have disappeared. The crux of the case is that the loans were not a diversified pool but instead provided to one creditor, Dubai Trading Agency. The average accredited investor probably is not conversant with ship-breaking investments. Even if Yieldstreet tracks down the borrowers at the root of the fraud and/or the collateral, investors will have to wait for a recovery net of any legal expenses incurred for their trouble.

This may be a bit of a field, but the BlockFi story amalgamates so many unknown risk factors that it is almost comical, if not so sad. BlockFi was an alternative platform that was mainly a cryptocurrency exchange and wallet service, and they also had a popular Visa credit card program in which one could earn cryptocurrency rewards based on purchasing volume. BlockFi was known for offering high rates of interest (8-9%) on stablecoin holdings such as USDC and the Gemini Dollar. Stablecoins are meant to trade on par with the US Dollar through (over)collateralization with USD or other cryptocurrencies. It sounded very appealing, and it was. Interest flowed into investors' accounts religiously each month. Credit card rewards are racked up every month as a function of users' credit card spending.

Investors should have been asking how secure the collateral behind these stablecoins was (i.e., know what you own). They should have also had a better idea of the lack of regulation of BlockFi (not alone) and where the cryptocurrency actually was. Once a string of failures occurred in the sector, most notably FTX, everything tumbled down from there. BlockFi ended up in bankruptcy, and all deposits were frozen. Crypto investors knew how much Bitcoin or other currencies they owned; it just was nowhere to be found. Fortunately, I was out before this happened. Adding insult to injury, even the credit card rewards that were earned (and not moved out prior) and paid out in the form of cryptocurrency were frozen. It is true, as I have $400 worth of Bitcoin rewards that are tied up in bankruptcy. It should be indisputable that I own this Bitcoin, as a permanent record of ownership and transactions was supposed to be the awesomeness behind blockchain technology. I cannot wait to learn the outcome of this matter. As icing on the cake, The Wall Street Journal reported that the bankrupt BlockFi had $227 million of deposit exposure with Silicon Valley Bank when it failed in March 2023. This exemplifies the dangers of investing in non-traditional assets to the extreme. Private investors need to be skeptical and should understand what they own and where the assets are located in the event of bankruptcy.

Risk factors are everywhere, and they are many times unavoidable. When public markets fall 20% in a year, you can be confident private markets have followed suit. It is just not plastered on the news every day, and private investors would do well to shrug it off. The important takeaway is to be able to identify risk factors that should be identified prior to investing in a private offering. Mostly, this comes down to knowing what assets you are purchasing and how they operate, if there is a concentration of credit risk, and whether excessive leverage is being deployed to generate the target internal rates of return.

Commercial Real Estate Risks

The more traditional risk factors related to commercial real estate investments or funds are plentiful. The known risks disclosed in a private placement memorandum include:

Economic Downturns: Commercial real estate funds are vulnerable to economic downturns that can impact the demand for office, retail, and industrial spaces. This can lead to lower occupancy rates, lower rental rates, and lower returns for investors. These risks are uncontrollable, although predictable, and result in lower operating revenues and net operating income.

Market Risk: The value of commercial real estate can fluctuate based on market conditions, such as changes in interest rates, supply and demand, and economic conditions. This can affect the value of a real estate property or fund and lead to losses. Increased levels of construction activity in a market area can adversely impact occupancy rates and rental income. Population migration from heavily taxed and regulated states to states that are less taxed can impact the demand for commercial real estate in certain markets. Commercial real estate funds often invest in a specific geographic region or property type, which can increase concentration risk if the market experiences a downturn or if the property type becomes less popular.

Interest Rate Risk: Commercial real estate funds typically use debt to finance their investments, which exposes these vehicles to interest rate risk. If interest rates rise, the cost of any floating rate debt increases, which can lower the net operating income, the exit cap rate, and the overall valuation of a property or group of properties. Changes in interest rates and bank lending standards can also directly impact a sponsor's ability to refinance portfolio properties, which can impact the bottom line, and the timing of distributions to investors and may result in the loss of principal for investors.

Risk of Uninsured Losses: Investors could lose some or all of their investment if a property suffered an uninsured or underinsured loss. Sponsors should carry reasonable amounts of comprehensive insurance, including casualty, liability, and extended coverage insurance, but there are certain risks that may be uninsurable or not insurable on terms that are economical. Earthquakes and floods are two examples.

Operational Risk: Commercial real estate projects require excellence in property management. Conversely, poorly managed properties can lead to operational risk if they make poor decisions or fail to execute their strategy effectively. This will depend on the property manager's skills in setting rents, identifying prospective tenants, screening tenants, and selecting and performing improvements (value-add), which will have a direct impact on occupancy rates, rental revenues, and net operating income.

Environmental Risk: Investors could lose some or all of their investment if, as the result of the discovery of hazardous substances on a property, the project would become required under environmental protection laws to pay cleanup or other remediation costs.

Dilution Risk: Ownership interests in a partnership could be disproportionately diluted or impaired if a sponsor were forced to sell additional equity interests.

Liquidity Risk: Commercial real estate properties may not be easily tradable or sold, making it difficult for investors to exit their investments at certain times. Interest rate and bank lending conditions are prime examples of conditions that can delay property sales, and even if a property were sold in a bad economic environment, some of the sale price may be in the form of seller financing, further delaying the return on investment.

Lack of liquidity is the main drawback of investing in real estate projects or syndications. As long as one of your primary objectives as an accredited investor is to create a new stream of income, this should not be a deal breaker. People buy a primary residence for shelter and potential income from capital appreciation in the future, and they understand that the asset is illiquid in the short term. In order to generate a capital gain in the future, individuals understand that a holding period of over five years is typically required. Investing in projects as an accredited investor is even more restrictive because, as a limited partner of minority shareholders, we have no control over when the exit will occur. If nothing else, remember that these investments are illiquid and may extend far beyond the advertised holding period for reasons that can be positive or negative. Therefore, investors need to maintain a strong emergency fund prior to committing capital to a private placement.

With traditional equities and fixed-income investments, including ETFs and mutual funds, liquidity can be achieved instantaneously. Investors growing up with these investments have been conditioned to expect instant gratification with buying and selling positions. Liquidity itself is a benefit, all else being equal. However, the counterpoint is that this right is commonly misused, allowing investors to enter and exit positions excessively based on talking heads on television, lack of discipline, and proper long-term mindset, or any reason. The lack of liquidity in private markets can be positive since there is no alternative other than to buy and hold. Accordingly, the decision to invest in a project as an accredited investor is the most critical moment. Do you have the right sponsor, in the right segment, in the right project, at the right time? Pull the trigger, and your work is done, and the consequences will result over the term of the business plan.

Accordingly, a complete assessment of the risk profile of a private investment must be understood prior to making the investment, and the project sponsor can provide some additional clues through their marketing efforts. I have developed the following list of things a commercial real estate sponsor might say that could potentially be a warning signal:

- We take a tech-driven approach to achieve higher IRRs. (Really?)
- This project will allow you to create generational wealth! (Hearing this a lot.)
- We have this incentive if you agree to commit your investment early (A sign of weak market conditions or a new sponsor.)
- On average, we have returned a 55% IRR to investors as a multifamily sponsor. (Too good to be true, or the sponsor has not been around very long and has experienced some luck.)

I like stories that can reinforce the topic of risk, and here is another one related to commercial real estate. It was February 2019, and I discovered a value-added hospitality asset in a region of the Rocky Mountains that I am very familiar with. It offered a cash-on-cash return of 9-10%, an IRR of 16%, and a five-to-seven-year hold. The asset was in a strong area of growth, an economy-class hotel with lots of vacationing and drive-through customers. Monthly distributions were paid at an annualized rate of 9% for the first year. What happened next was obvious: Covid-19. Occupancy, average daily rate, and resultant revenue per available room cratered for an extended period of time. This is an example of how external factors can impact the value and operations of any single property. A true black swan. But unlike other markets such as New York, Washington DC, San Francisco, and gateway markets that relied a lot on large events, this asset fortunately did not fall as hard as other markets. The investment has not yet resulted in a realized loss of investor principal as of 2023, but the hold period will be very long. Fortunately, the sponsor has a strong incentive to keep the property due to a large co-investment. I thought it would be a conservative long-term play, and that saved me. There were major mistakes that I learned that I would not have made today. Falling in love with an asset in an area you know, for no other material reason, is not a good approach. Also, there was evidence that the sponsor had significant problems getting the deal funded and issuing supplemental PPMs before closing. If a deal is not funded properly or in a timely manner, and the terms have to change materially before closing, such as more preferred equity, you should, in most cases, find another investment if not too late.

Commercial real estate risks extend to crowdfunding and fintech solutions as well. Per their website, "Groundfloor is an award-winning fintech company that makes real estate investing easy for everyone, whether you're a beginner or a pro. Known for its regulatory prowess and development of completely new financial products for individual investors, the company was the very first to be qualified by the U.S. Securities & Exchange Commission to offer real estate debt investments for both accredited and non-accredited audiences alike. The company has won numerous awards for its product innovation and growth, including three years in a row of being on the Inc. 5000 List. Since it launched in 2013, Groundfloor's investors have consistently seen 10% annualized returns across its short-term investment offerings."

Investors may invest as little as $10 per fix-and-flip housing project and are encouraged to build a large, diversified portfolio of these loans, termed LROs (limited recourse obligations). Since these are debt investments, there is a margin of error for investors as quantified by the Loan to ARV ratio (After Repaired Value) that ranges between 60-70% for these LROs. This implies that investors would not suffer a loss of principal unless the after-repair value of properties decreased by 30-40% versus the ARV estimate. Groundfloor provides monthly asset management reports, which focus mostly on the volume of composition of repayments to investors. As of November 2022, Groundfloor claims a small loss ratio related to actual repayments of a small - .15%. It does not disclose the composition of the existing portfolio in terms of its three categories of loans: performing, extended, and default. The percentage of loans in their current portfolio (not yet repaid) that are in default status would be a better indication of the risk inherent in a portfolio of LROs. I have test-driven the Groundfloor platform, and as of March 2023, I have 91 LROs with a total value of only $3,000 in my portfolio, of which twenty-three are in default status (a whopping 25%). I can vouch for the 10% IRR on loans repaid, but it is the unpaid loans that are worrisome. Granted, 2022 was a year of dramatic increases in interest rates, making refinancing extremely difficult for fix-it projects. However, there is a significant disconnect in the reporting that will have to be resolved one way or another over the coming year. Groundfloor needs to disclose more metrics around their "inventory" in their periodic asset management reports to improve investors' understanding of the risks involved and what to expect.

Private Equity Risks

Private equity funds can be an attractive investment opportunity for accredited investors. However, they also carry several risks that investors should be aware of. Some of these risks include:

Reliance on the General Partner/Sponsor: Investors are betting that the sponsoring private equity firm knows what they are doing. Limited partners have no voice in decision-making, which is fine with me.

Competition for Investments: The sponsor will be attempting to build a strong portfolio of approximately twenty companies using well-defined strategies. In executing this mandate, the private equity firm will be competing with many other strong private equity firms and investors. In certain environments, this will drive up prices and reduce investor returns.

Lack of Liquidity: Private equity investments are illiquid, and sponsors (and, therefore, investors) may not be able to sell their stakes easily. They may have to wait many years before they can exit their investment, which can be risky if they need the money urgently. Enough said on the lack of liquidity.

Blind Pools: Investors entrust the capital to the private equity firms upfront and typically do not know what companies will be invested in. Accordingly, an investor in such a fund must rely upon the ability of the general partner in making investments consistent with the stated investment objectives and policies.

High Leverage: Private equity firms often use a significant amount of debt to finance their investments, which can increase the risk of default. If a company defaults on its debt, the private equity fund may lose its investment.

Lack of Transparency: Private equity funds are not required to disclose as much information as publicly traded companies, which can make it difficult for investors to fully understand the risks associated with their investments. That being said, the funds I have experienced provide excellent quarterly reporting with transparency that exceeds expectations.

Economic Interest of General Partner: This is a good risk to be aware of, but not much a limited partner can do anything about. Because the profits of a private equity fund are allocated using different methodologies (including the carried interest paid to the general partner), the general partner may have an incentive to make investments that are riskier or more speculative than if the general partner received allocations on a basis identical to that of the limited partners.

Concentration Risk: Private equity funds typically invest in a small number of companies, which can increase the risk of losses if one of the investments performs poorly.

Operational Risk: Private equity firms often take an active role in managing their portfolio companies, which can lead to operational risk if they make poor business decisions or fail to execute their strategy effectively.

Regulatory Risk: Private equity funds may be subject to changes in regulations that could affect their investments or their ability to raise funds in the future.

On top of all of this, there are all the risks inherent in each portfolio company in the fund as well.

One of my first limited partner SAFE investments was in a startup named Acre Designs, a graduate of the Y Combinator program for new innovative concepts. They say experience is the best teacher, so this was a key part of my private market MBA. The company was planning to build zero-energy homes in California and expand from there. They had proprietary designs and technology. Two years later, many homes were delivered, and the business was scaling. One morning in January 2020, I visited their website, which was down. It remained down a week later. What had happened was the entrepreneurs picked up and disappeared – they were a husband-and-wife team. Employees were unpaid, customers had large security deposits in their future homes, and investors were left with nothing. Employees and home buyers eventually sued, but to my knowledge, the fugitive executives were never located. Investors understand that 100% of principals in risky startups may be lost, but imagine how employees and customers feel. Referring back to the offering documents, there was no risk factor for the proprietors of the business pillaging the business and disappearing in basic cases of fraud and theft. Private investors need to understand that this happens, but it would be highly unlikely if the investor is a legendary private equity fund.

Ways for Accredited Investors to Control Risk

Accredited investors can attempt to minimize or control risk by utilizing the following techniques:

- Select high-quality, experienced sponsors.
- Review the sponsor's track record before investing.
- Invest the minimum required investment with new sponsors.
- Repeat invest with sponsors that treat you well in terms of service and return on investment.
- Invest in funds only.
- Do not invest in single ventures or properties (unless using money that one can afford to gamble with outside the private-passive portfolio)
- Invest in multiple funds that invest in different geographies, property types, and strategies.
- Network continuously and adopt a lifetime learning mentality related to private markets. Develop personal relationships with sponsors.

Quick Summary

1. Private investors should understand the difference between risk factors that are controllable and those that are beyond their ability to control or comprehend.
2. Credit risk and overleverage are two of the most common risks private investors face. For debt investments, understand how diversified the borrower base is and the general types of borrowers. Investments that are highly leveraged have less margin of error.

3. Investors in private equity offerings and real estate syndications must read the risk factors sector of the private placement memorandum to fully understand how principal may be lost.
4. Investors have certain tools at their disposal to reduce risk, including choosing which sponsors to do business with, determining the size of investments, utilizing fund products for diversification, and using multiple funds for additional diversification.
5. Investments will rarely go perfectly. Be prepared for setbacks, and do not let them shake your long-term resolve to succeed as a private-passive investor.

Section IV, Advanced Topics in Passive-Private Investing

Chapter 15 - Retirement Issues and SDIRAs

A fundamental disconnect between these abundant private investment opportunities and individual investors is the likelihood that most of their investable money is housed in retirement plans such as 401K plans or IRAs. Certain pundits say "ditch the 401k" for this very reason, as these plans are captive to the public financial markets, limiting access to more attractive private investments that investors may understand better. Regardless of where an investor's funds are located, the accredited investor regulations apply since these are directed at the issuer or sponsor of investments, not the investor. Issuers must play a role in protecting investors. But once we enter the world of retirement assets, additional regulatory hurdles apply, including the topic of self-directed IRAs or Roth IRAs. Traditional retirement plan vehicles do not provide investors with direct access to private market investments.

Self-directed IRA (SDIRA) accounts were first legalized in 1974 by the Employee Retirement Income Security Act (ERISA). This law established the legal framework for several types of retirement accounts, including traditional IRAs, Roth IRAs, and self-directed IRAs. The idea behind a SDIRA is to allow individuals to have more control over their retirement savings by giving them the ability to invest in a wider range of assets, such as real estate, private equity, and other non-traditional investments. And as one might imagine, the rules governing SDIRA investing are extremely complex and fraught with hidden risks for unsophisticated investors.

This chapter limits the discussion to two primary retirement issues that are related to or a consequence of private market investing. The first is the topic of utilizing a SDIRA, the headline issues that investors must be aware of and navigate. The second area is how private market investing can impact retirement planning at the highest level, such as how large a portfolio needs to be for a "safe" retirement and how the expected returns from a conservative private market portfolio can impact decisions for claiming Social Security benefits. These are two technical and meaty topics. Accordingly, my goal is to introduce the types of issues a private investor should consider for enabling individuals to retire on their timetable and with dignity. It is not meant to be specific tax or legal advice because you will see that there are a lot of tricks and traps involved with this subject matter. A myriad of resources are available for a more in-depth review of any of these topics. In short, this is a practical consideration based on personal experience.

Self-Directed IRAs – An Account for Private Investing

One thing I had to learn from listening to financial podcasts is that there are no "one-sized fits all" solutions for any financial topic. Podcasters are espousing their ideas, but they never really tell listeners exactly to whom they are speaking in order to maximize the size of their audience. Some of the advice is tailored to high-net-worth individuals, while other advice is targeted to individuals with an average net worth or those just trying to get out of debt. It takes some experience to differentiate between the various lines of advice. It took me a long time to understand the nuance. The use of a SDIRA is definitely one of these topics. Based on experience, a SDIRA is best suited for a high-net-worth individual with access to a full team of accounting, tax, valuation, and legal professionals supporting them. They are not as attractive for an investor looking to place a single $50,000 investment in a commercial real estate syndication. The primary reason is that managing a SDIRA can be costly and extremely complex. Another attractive use case for a SDIRA is for investors that have "inside access" to or deep experience with certain alternative asset classes, for example, stock options in a private enterprise, coupled with the use of a Roth SDIRA, resulting in the future appreciation being shielded from income taxes permanently. Again, this requires advanced legal structuring and the fixed legal costs of setting this up make more sense for wealthier investors and larger-sized investments.

The bottom line is that I am not a huge fan of utilizing a SDIRA for private investing. Being a successful private investor is complex enough without layering in more risk and potential trouble with tax authorities. Unfortunately, the use of a SDIRA is the primary way for accredited investors to access private market offerings using retirement funds. They are unavoidable until the SEC, Department of Labor, and the US Congress figure out a more elegant solution that the big-box brokerage houses buy into. But given that, let us start with the headline benefits of utilizing a SDIRA.

The benefits of a SDIRA are significant for private-passive investors. For most investors, the majority of investable capital is tied up in Traditional or Roth IRAs or 401k employer plans. Inside these plans, there is no way for investors to participate in private investments unless and until the target date funds begin to include private equity investments within their overall allocation. A SDIRA can be set up as a Traditional, Roth, or SEP IRAs, and they are different than regular IRAs because of the types of investments they allow. SDIRAs may invest in real estate, private companies, precious metals, Crypto, private debt, and other alternative asset classes. Accordingly, SDIRAs are the primary vessel for individuals to have direct control of private investments with their retirement funds. For experienced private investors, this is paradise. For the rest of us, it is intimidating. To invest in private markets inside a SDIRA, one is still subject to the same accredited investor rules that apply when investing from taxable accounts. More choice for investors means that SDIRAs effectively allow investors to be even more diversified within their retirement funds, moving closer to a "mini-Yale Model" that was previously highlighted. An additional obvious benefit is the potential higher ROI offered from alternative private investments. This higher level of control over retirement funds should translate into more investment success, assuming investors leverage their specialized knowledge, experience, and interests in specific private alternatives. Stated another way, do not invest in a Molybdenum mining operation if you know nothing about it. It is even possible for an individual to acquire their own commercial real estate, such as a multifamily building, through an LLC that is owned by the SDIRA.

Getting to the details of how an SDIRA works, a SDIRA is administered by a specialized custodian. SDIRA custodians are firms that are specialized in the legalities and documentation required to operate these accounts. The Vanguards and Fidelity Investments of the world are not in this business because of the burdensome requirements and the reality that private investments would interfere with their legacy commission-generating business models. The primary tax benefits of both Roth IRA and Traditional IRA accounts apply to their SDIRA counterparts. Opening a SDIRA is straightforward, similar to traditional retirement accounts. Figure 46 illustrates potential pathways for getting funds into SDIRA accounts. The commentary below is based on the tax rules in existence in 2023.

Figure 46: Funding a Self-Directed IRA

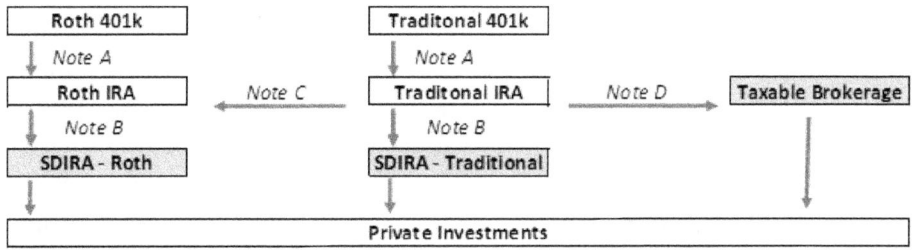

Shaded Boxes - Accounts that can be used to fund private investments.

Note A: Transfers are allowable when you leave the employer, for limited hardships, and upon reaching 59.5 years of age if still in service with the employer. Check with your 401k plan administrator, the IRA custodian, and, if necessary, your financial adviser. Roth 401k transfers to Roth IRA, and Traditional 401k transfers to Traditional IRA only.

Note B: Roth IRA funds are transferred to a self-directed Roth IRA account. Traditional IRA funds are transferred to a self-directed Traditional IRA account. To avoid mishaps, work with your IRA custodian (i.e., Fidelity) and your self-directed IRA custodian to directly transfer the funds between accounts.

Note C: This transaction is a Roth Conversion. Performing this at your large brokerage mitigates risk and simplifies the transaction. A Roth Conversion is a separate decision and based on many variables, which a financial planner or consultant can assist with a Roth Conversion Plan. Getting funds into a Roth SDIRA account is a desirable outcome, as future investment returns would be tax-free. The high rates of return that private-passive investors can expect can impact the math surrounding a Roth conversion plan since this model is extremely sensitive to the expected IRR that an investor expects to earn inside a Roth IRA.

Note D: This transaction is a taxable distribution to be claimed on the personal tax return. In addition, if done prior to age 59.5 years of age, a 10% penalty would apply in most cases. Again, work with your tax advisor and financial planner to understand the consequences.

Figure 46 is also a nice visualization of how difficult it can be to get investable funds into an account that can purchase private investments. My prioritization for the preferred account to be used by the majority of investors to invest in private investments is as follows:

1. Taxable brokerage account, then
2. Roth SDIRA, and last
3. Traditional SDIRA

To reiterate, the funding of SDIRA accounts should be done using a **direct transfer of funds** from a same-type IRA account to the new SDIRA account. For example, if you have a Traditional IRA account at Fidelity, investors wishing to fund a Traditional SDIRA would work very closely with Fidelity and the new SDIRA custodian to execute a proper direct transfer. More on this in the tips and tricks discussion that follows. Alternatively, investors can contribute directly to SDIRA accounts up to the annual limits authorized by the IRS.

Once a SDIRA is opened and funded, the owner can make investments in alternative assets. The documentation required will vary depending on the asset being purchased. However, the documentation required will be the same as if you were purchasing the asset in your non-retirement account. The only thing to keep in mind is that the SDIRA is the entity that is making the investment and not you personally. You are merely directing the custodian to invest on your behalf, and in most cases, the IRA custodian will ask the owner to sign the contract as "read and approved" to document the owner's consent. In all cases, the account owner manages the SDIRA investments inside the account. Since the custodian is responsible for handling these transactions, SDIRA clients can occasionally experience delays in buying and selling their investments. The bottom line is that the SDIRA custodian must sign all contracts affecting the SDIRA and must receive and pay all funds related to the investments held in the SDIRA account.

Once you have acquired private assets inside of a SDIRA, another unique (and painful) compliance feature is the requirement to report the fair market value (FMV) of each asset at least annually. The onus is on the SDIRA account owner to generate the necessary documentation and perform this function. If the custodian does not receive updated FMV reports, the last known value of the assets in your account will be reported to the IRS. The IRS uses this information to set minimum required minimum distributions for those account holders over the age of seventy-two with traditional IRAs and for taxable events. Examples of taxable events include the following:

- Converting a traditional IRA to a Roth (or a specific investment in the account), which would be a taxable event or
- Taking an in-kind asset distribution (transferring an asset out of the SDIRA and into your personal name).

Required valuation documentation for assets in an SDIRA varies based on the type of asset held. Investments with a readily available market price, such as certain precious metals, do not require annual valuations. As a general rule, the fair market value assessment for each asset needs to be provided and signed off by one of the following qualified, independent sources:

- Managing Partner in the case of an LLC, LP, or Entity
- Certified Appraiser
- Licensed Real Estate Professional (such as a broker/real estate agent)

In short, these are knowledgeable parties such as a CPA, attorney, or financial planner who is strictly at "arm's length" from both you and the investment. If there are costs associated with valuation services, the

SDIRA must pay these costs directly; otherwise, a distribution from your IRA will have taken place, creating a taxable event and potential penalties. The hits just keep on coming.

Private investors need to consider what happens if an investment fails and becomes worthless. Most investors spend little time pondering this scenario upfront. It is not in our nature to consider failure. With a SDIRA, to change the status and value of a worthless asset in an LLC, entity, or private placement, you must provide the necessary documentation that will support this. You will not need a qualified, independent third party to perform the valuation. Some acceptable examples of documentation for a worthless asset include bankruptcy or receivership paperwork or a cease-and-desist order from an entity such as the SEC or a similar state agency. Especially with new ventures that go bankrupt, providing either of these types of evidence can be problematic in the absence of a formal bankruptcy and/or the lack of cooperation by the entrepreneur to provide any assistance.

More Risks and Complexity of a Self-Directed IRA

Utilizing a SDIRA creates a 3-way relationship for all administrative activities surrounding an investment: the sponsor, the investor, and the SDIRA custodian. Let us say the SDIRA custodian changes their primary bank and sends you the investor new banking details for future distributions. As an investor, you have done nothing, but now you have to go back to the general partner of your investment and make sure these banking changes get implemented. Investing in private markets is difficult enough with just you and the sponsor, but now there is a third party involved in the background in all matters. The annual valuation requirement for each asset that was just described is another administrative burden and may contain additional costs that must be funded by the SDIRA itself. For these reasons, SDIRAs are not an elegant solution for investors to invest in private markets using retirement money. Investors will need a team of legal and tax experts to invest effectively using an SDIRA and to prevent trouble with the IRS.

The risks and complexity of a SDIRA expand far beyond its administrative burdens. Knowing what transactions are legally prohibited is vital to self-directing investments with an SDIRA. IRS Publication 590 defines a prohibited transaction as any improper use of your SDIRA by you, your beneficiary, or any disqualified person (defined below). Per the IRS, "prohibited transactions are certain transactions between a retirement plan and a disqualified person." These rules are not unique to the self-directed variant of IRAs; they also apply to the more typical IRA accounts at large brokerages. It is just that self-directed accounts are more susceptible to violations of these rules. Types of prohibited transactions include:

- The sale, exchange, or leasing of a property between an IRA and a disqualified person. Example: You sell a home your IRA owns to your spouse.
- Extension of credit or cash loan between an IRA and a disqualified person. Example: Using IRA funds to invest in your son's bakery.
- Furnishing goods, services, or facilities between an IRA and a disqualified person. Example: Hiring your son-in-law to paint the walls of a condominium owned by your IRA.

- Transfer of IRA income or assets to, or use by, or for the benefit of, a disqualified person. Example: Renting a property owned by your IRA to your father.

There is much to consider, depending on the type of asset you wish to have inside a SDIRA. The definition of "Disqualified Persons" includes yourself, your spouse, lineal descendants and their spouses, and your lineal ascendants, a beneficiary of the IRA, investment advisers and managers, any corporation, partnership, or estate that you (or any disqualified person) have at least a 50% stake in, and your trustee, custodian, or anyone providing services to the IRA. If you are using a SDIRA to invest in a top private equity fund or a large commercial real estate syndication deal, these provisions should not be a worry. If you plan to purchase a 4-plex in your hometown and manage it yourself, there is significant potential for running into prohibited transaction issues. These rules apply equally to Roth and Traditional SDIRAs.

As an account holder, you will want to avoid any self-dealing transactions. If a transaction benefits you beyond the scope of your retirement account, you may want to consult a CPA or tax advisor. Violating prohibited transaction rules can jeopardize your IRA's tax-free or tax-deferred status. If not cured in a certain time period, the entire account may be deemed distributed, and income taxes and 10% penalties may apply. In addition, the IRA will no longer receive preferred tax treatment in the future.

The next unfortunate reality of SDIRAs is the fees. To this point, we have justified the fees that a private-passive investor pays as a cost of doing business, sponsors doing real work to create value with property, or real businesses. Crowdfunding platform fees are baked into the cake as well. The fees and expenses involved with using SDIRA accounts can also add up. There are fixed costs for entering into investments, an annual asset management charge, and charges for sending and receiving funds. Figures 47 and 48 show the internal rate of return for investments of $50,000 made outside and inside a SDIRA, respectively. For this simple example, the SDIRA fees are defined as $299 per year for the asset management charge (per asset) and a $30 transaction fee for incoming receipts (distributions from the sponsor to the SDIRA). These examples assume a 7% annual cash-on-cash return, received monthly, a five-year term with an exit at a two times multiple. Figure 47 shows the investment using a taxable account, and the resulting IRR is 20.3%. Figure 48 is the investment made using a SDIRA, and the resulting IRR is 19.3%. In this case, the SDIRA custodian shaves 1% of the total IRR.

Figure 47

Investment Amount	$ 50,000					
Annual Yield, Frequency	7.0% Monthly					
Exit Multiple	2.0 X					
Annual Custodian Fee:	$ 299					
Transaction Fee:	$ 30					

WITHOUT FEES	Year 0	Year 1	Year 2	Year 3	Year 4	Year 5
Investment	$ (50,000)					
Annual cash flow		$ 3,500	$ 3,500	$ 3,500	$ 3,500	$ 3,500
Exit cash flow						$ 100,000
Net cash flow	$ (50,000)	$ 3,500	$ 3,500	$ 3,500	$ 3,500	$ 103,500
IRR	20.3%					

Figure 48

Investment Amount	$ 50,000					
Annual Yield, Frequency	7.0% Monthly					
Exit Multiple	2.0 X					
Annual Custodian Fee:	$ 299					
Transaction Fee:	$ 30					

WITHOUT FEES	Year 0	Year 1	Year 2	Year 3	Year 4	Year 5
Investment	$ (50,000)					
Annual cash flow		$ 3,500	$ 3,500	$ 3,500	$ 3,500	$ 3,500
Exit cash flow						$ 100,000
Custodian Annual Fees		$ (299)	$ (299)	$ (299)	$ (299)	$ (299)
Custodian Transaction Fees		$ (360)	$ (360)	$ (360)	$ (360)	$ (360)
Net cash flow	$ (50,000)	$ 2,841	$ 2,841	$ 2,841	$ 2,841	$ 102,841
IRR	19.3%					

What happens if the size of the investment increases to $500,000? The IRR for the non-SDIRA investment is the same as in Figure 46, 20.3%. The IRR for this investment inside of a SDIRA is 20.2%, a difference of only .1%, as shown in Figure 49. The impact is much less in this case because the fees are fixed in nature. Size does matter when using an SDIRA for private market investing. Another reason I dislike the SDIRA vehicle is because the fees impact the small investor more. This is a significant barrier to democratizing private investing for an average accredited investor.

Figure 49

Investment Amount	$ 500,000						
Annual Yield, Frequency	7.0% Monthly						
Exit Multiple	2.0 X						
Annual Custodian Fee:	$ 299						
Transaction Fee:	$ 30						
WITHOUT FEES	**Year 0**	**Year 1**	**Year 2**	**Year 3**	**Year 4**	**Year 5**	
Investment	$ (500,000)						
Annual cash flow		$ 35,000	$ 35,000	$ 35,000	$ 35,000	$ 35,000	
Exit cash flow						$ 1,000,000	
Custodian Annual Fees		$ (299)	$ (299)	$ (299)	$ (299)	$ (299)	
Custodian Transaction Fees		$ (360)	$ (360)	$ (360)	$ (360)	$ (360)	
Net cash flow	$ (500,000)	$ 34,341	$ 34,341	$ 34,341	$ 34,341	$ 1,034,341	
IRR	**20.2%**						

We have already discussed the additional expenses the investor may incur for experts to assist with the annual valuation of the investment. Also, if used incorrectly, an SDIRA can result in additional income taxes and penalties due to the IRS, such as when you sell a property in your SDIRA to your sister for an inflated amount.

Unrelated Business Income Tax (UBIT)

Unfortunately, the complexity of SDIRAs does not end there. Another issue for private-passive investors to be aware of relates to Unrelated Business Taxable Income (UBTI). If the private investment generates UBTI, then the IRA may owe taxes on a portion of its share of the investment's income. UBTI arises when an IRA invests in a business that generates income from an activity that is considered to be unrelated to the IRA's tax-exempt purpose. So, what type of investments, you might ask? Would not index funds in a Traditional IRA account generate UBTI? The key distinction is that UBTI is generated by partnerships that pass through earnings to their limited partners, publicly traded partnerships (PTPs), master limited partnerships (MLPs), private equity partnerships, and hedge fund partnerships. In addition, Limited Liability Companies (LLCs) are taxed as partnerships and can generate UBTI. Essentially, most of the private investing offerings covered in this book would be subject to UBTI. An investment in a C corporation would not be subject to UBIT since they pay tax at the corporate level.

The UBTI rules were created by Congress in 1950 and started applying to IRAs upon their creation in 1975. UBTI rules pre-date the existence of IRAs and were originally developed so that charitable organizations did not have a competitive advantage over taxable organizations and businesses. For example, if a tax-exempt entity were to buy a gas station, the profits would not be subject to tax. So, the gas station could choose to sell gas at a lower cost than its competitors, causing customers to flock to this gas station to purchase lower-cost gas. This would give the gas station unfairly high profits, and this unfair advantage could potentially drive competitors out of business. As a result, tax law dictates that the income generated by the gas station would be considered UBTI and, therefore, would be taxable to the tax-exempt entity.[46]

The good news is that even if the SDIRA is investing in a company that is a pass-through entity, such as an LLC, there are the following exceptions to UBIT:

Passive Investments. Passive income is earnings derived from a rental property, limited partnership, or other enterprises in which a person is not actively involved.

Rental Income. Rental income and real estate capital gains are also exempt from UBIT if the real estate was held for longer than 1 year. Shorter-term fixes and flips are subject to UBIT, as are property development projects.

Interest Income, such as loan payments.

Dividend Income from C-Corp stock or properly structured REIT dividends.

Capital Gains Income, except property or assets sold in under one year. This is an important exception for real estate syndication investors, and as long as the property is held for more than one year, then the UBIT tax is avoided.

Royalty Income, intellectual property rights, land rights, oil, and gas rights.

C-Corps will pay a corporate tax, so C-Corps do not trigger UBIT.

The SDIRA account owner is tasked with preparing the annual tax Form 990-T to calculate the tax based on inputs, which are typically Form K-1s from sponsors, to account for UBIT and UDFI issues. The filing is not for the individual owner; it is the self-directed IRA entity that must file. As one might imagine, this is additional complexity for your tax preparer, including the requirement for estimated tax payments related to Form 990-T, resulting in yet more compliance fees. The tax preparer needs to be someone with experience in preparing Form 990-T, not TurboTax, and not your primary Form 1040 tax preparer. The custodian will sign the tax return and help with making the annual tax payment. To emphasize, Form 990-T must be paid for by the SDIRA, not with personal funds. These tax requirements apply to Traditional and Roth SDIRA accounts. Yes, it is possible to pay income taxes related to income earned in a Roth account! Finally, the tax rates on Form 990-T may be higher than the typical corporate tax rates. In 2022, the rate of tax for trusts and estates starts at 10% and quickly reaches a 37% marginal bracket at a $13,450 level of taxable income.

As an example, if you invest in a new food-tech startup that is an LLC that does not pay corporate income tax, then the net income from that business that is paid to the SDIRA will be subject to UBIT. On the other hand, a similar investment in a company organized as a C corporation will result in no UBIT tax owed on the dividends paid to the SDIRA since that corporation was subject to corporate income tax prior to issuing the dividend.

So, what is the bottom line for private-passive investors? The good news is that most of the asset classes presented in this book can be exempt from UBIT. However, there are many gray areas. The main items that may trigger UBIT are as follows:

- Income from ordinary businesses, when organized as a flow-through company, does not pay corporate tax.
- Real estate development, construction, and, or property fix-and-flip businesses (intent to hold less than one year). Does this include the value-added business model for multi-family syndication? It all depends on the facts and circumstances, which leads to some discomfort for private investors. Longer hold periods, in terms of years, argue in favor of this being an investment activity. The fact that the ultimate exit will be to another professional real estate sponsor helps as well.

You should assume it is necessary to enlist professional tax assistance for compliance when using SDIRA accounts for private investments and have your tax preparer identified to assist. The taxation consequences related to SDIRAs is one of the most significant impediments to investing in private markets with your retirement accounts, where likely a lot of your investible capital resides. On the other hand, it is certainly possible that an investment opportunity is well worth the additional administrative and tax compliance headaches. Also, large investment opportunities are more likely to be worth the effort of building your support team since compliance processes and associated costs are the same regardless of the size of the SDIRA account.

Unrelated Debt-Financed Income (UDFI)

UDFI is a tax concept that can come into play with SDIRAs that use leverage or debt to acquire an asset. It is a subset of the UBIT tax. SDIRAs may use non-recourse debt to leverage their investment (i.e., real estate), but the debt cannot be secured or, guaranteed or extended from the personal assets of the IRA owner since that would constitute a prohibited transaction. Non-recourse debt may be used inside a SDIRA, and the SDIRA account is the legal borrower on the contract. It may be helpful to seek lenders who are very experienced in providing non-recourse loans to self-directed IRA accounts since this is a niche market.

When an IRA uses a permitted, non-recourse loan or other debt to purchase an asset, such as a rental property, a portion of the income or gains generated from that asset may be subject to UDFI. The UDFI issue with SDIRAs arises because the IRA itself is a tax-exempt entity, but the use of debt to purchase an asset may trigger UDFI, resulting in the IRA owing taxes on a portion of its income that is debt-financed. What about the case when there is debt utilized by the sponsor inside of their legal structure, which is typically the case for real estate syndications and private equity funds? This applies equally to commercial real estate syndications in which the sponsor's LLC indirectly holds the debt. It would apply to private equity fund investments since leverage is a part of this strategy to generate higher returns. Venture capital is less susceptible since the use of debt is not as prevalent.

In short, SDIRA investors may find exceptions to the UBIT rules for private funds but, in most cases, cannot avoid the UDFI tax since leverage is a key factor in how private offerings deliver attractive returns. It is a hassle, requires the filing of Form 990-T annually, more tax preparation fees, and will "ding" your investment IRR further.

Checkbook Self-Directed IRAs

A Checkbook IRA, sometimes referred to as an IRA/LLC, is a variation of the SDIRA that can eliminate delays in funding new investments and administering payments related to these investments. Checkbook IRAs are different from regular SDIRAs in that the custodian only handles account setup; after that, the account holder writes checks to make investments on behalf of the IRA. Self-Directed IRAs with checkbook control are a good fit for clients who want the flexibility to manage their own investments, prefer to branch out into less traditional investments, and who like being able to make investments on their own time. As can be expected, a Checkbook IRA includes additional setup and recurring fees. Checkbook IRAs are also still subject to all of the regulatory and tax rules the SDIRAs are subject to.

Tips and Tricks of a Self-Directed IRA

- Use a direct transfer from a Traditional IRA to a self-directed Traditional IRA (or from a Roth IRA to a self-directed Roth IRA) rather than a rollover. Rollovers are limited to one for every twelve months, and the consequence of multiple rollovers is a deemed distribution and a potential 10% penalty.
- If you have a "sure thing" investment to place in a SDIRA, try to utilize a Roth Self-directed IRA to avoid future income taxes as the asset appreciates.
- Know who will provide the annual valuation report for an asset or how it will be valued. A sponsor accepting SDIRA investments should provide the report, but make sure before investing.
- To access private markets, an investor can use a taxable account, a Roth SDIRA, or a Traditional SDIRA. What is best depends on individual circumstances, which include financial considerations and non-financial considerations, including a desire to keep things simple. SDIRAs are not simple. I avoid SDIRAs due to the complexity and risks. Investing in private markets with taxable funds is much more pleasurable.
- Have a tax advisor onboard who knows Form 990-T compliance prior to setting up and utilizing a SDIRA.
- SDIRAs favor the wealthy, those with lots of investable cash, due to the large team of experts needed to successfully navigate this world. This framework has not democratized investing.
- If you have vast amounts of investable assets in an IRA, are in a high tax bracket, and expect to remain there, a self-directed Roth IRA may be beneficial, especially if you have special expertise around the asset classes you wish to invest in.

The 4% percent Rule in Retirement Planning

The 4% rule is a general guideline used for retirement planning that posits that retirees can safely withdraw 4% of their retirement savings each year, adjusting for inflation, without running out of money during their retirement years. This rule assumes that retirement savings are invested in a diversified portfolio of stocks, bonds, and other assets, with an average rate of return of around 7% per year. The 4% withdrawal rate is based on historical market data and the assumption that retirees will need their savings to last for 30 years or more. The 4% rule is not a fixed rule but rather a starting point for retirement planning.

For example, if you have a retirement portfolio of $1 million, then a 4% withdrawal rate would equate to annual distributions of $40,000 for living expenses. Another way to tackle this is using the inverse of 4%, or twenty-five times, to answer the question of how large a portfolio is required to generate $100,000 of annual income. The answer would be twenty-five times $100,000, or $2.5 million of invested assets.

To avoid backlash, I do advocate the 4% rule as a reasonable benchmark, and I plan to abide by it. However, not everyone can or will be able to. There is a retirement crisis in America with the exiting of defined benefit pension plans and Social Security benefits under threat from the simple fact that it is mostly smoke and mirrors. The target retirement age for Social Security will continue to climb either directly or indirectly. Because this is the reality we have to embrace, a long-term "hack" is needed for most families to save enough for retirement. As we have learned, the growing ranks of accredited investors are a trend that will continue, placing private investment alternatives on the menu for many households. What if the 4% rule could become the 6% rule? The 6% target would translate to an average rate of return of around 9% per year to cover inflation, the target returns for the conservative income portfolio described in Chapter 13. One could argue that events similar to the Global Financial Crisis of 2008-9 might make it difficult to earn 9% over the long term. A valid risk, but a similar argument could be made for achieving a consistent 7% return in public markets. A 9% average return reflects the 2% (or so) illiquidity premium that investors in private markets can expect, so therein rests the symmetry in this argument. With a 6% rule, investors needing $100,000 per year would require an investable asset of $1.66 million to retire versus the $2.5 million required with the 4% rule. This difference is significant and may provide a realistic path for the millions of households that are struggling to save enough for retirement in 401K and IRA plans.

Private Investments and Social Security

Recently, I have been thinking about when to start taking Social Security benefits – age 62, age 65, age 67? Even if you are not in the 55-60 age range, retirement planning is a topic that needs to be on the radar early in your career. A recent study from a group called United Income estimated that retirees collectively lose $3.4 trillion because they claim Social Security "at a financially sub-optimal time."[47] That works out to $111,000 per household. Most U.S. adults claim Social Security by the time they turn 63, even though their monthly Social Security income would be higher if they waited to claim it later.[48] A 2019 release from the Social Security Administration revealed that age 62 remains the most common age for Americans, with nearly 35% of men and 40% of women jumping into the program then.[49]

There are many reasons Americans are taking the money as early as possible, one of which is a lack of public education about the trade-offs of early versus delayed claiming of benefits. There is actually a lack of public education about most financial topics really. During my career, the only training on this topic has been presented as a service to employees by my employer and the administrator of our 401k plan. A second reason is likely that Americans need the money to survive since retirement benefits in the form of traditional pension plans have all but disappeared from the benefits packages of corporations. However, a significant reason that Americans are interested in getting money as early as possible may also have to do with the uncertain future of the Social Security program, as it does with any lack of education. A recent U.S. government report found that, with no action from Congress, Social Security only has the funds to continue paying out 100% of benefits through 2034.

The commonly espoused wisdom and the conclusions of the United Income report referenced earlier is that most Americans should wait as long as possible to claim Social Security benefits in order to maximize the lifetime benefits from the program. Naturally, this is not true for 100% of Americans, as other factors such as general health and expected lifetime need to be considered on a case-by-case basis.

This is one of those topics that only complete books can cover. Recognizing everyone's situation is unique, consultation with a financial adviser is highly recommended. Accordingly, I will not offer advice and instead will focus on the math. I can say that when I entered the workforce as a post-graduate in 1984, I entered this "contract" with Social Security in a material way as they commenced taking 6.2% of each paycheck in order to provide full benefits when I turned sixty-five. The terms of this contract have been amended a few times, but not by me and never in my favor. But back to the math. If you have not registered for the Social Security Administration website, I highly recommend that you monitor your account. From their website, I know what my monthly benefit will be (as of March 2023) at ages 62 and 67. The age 67 benefit is about 44% higher than the age 62 benefit.

The key assumption for determining which is better is the rate of return that you can effectively earn in the future on your monthly benefits from Social Security. For example, as of March 2023, an investor could earn 4.5% in a government money market account for all investable assets. Let us call this the risk-free IRR. Next, there is the 7% return for a typical public portfolio that we mentioned above in the 4% Rule discussion. Let us call that the 60/40 IRR. Finally, there is the 9% return bogie on a private conservative income portfolio, which we will refer to as the private conservative income IRR. Figure 50 takes these IRR benchmarks and calculates the future value of a portfolio "Built by Social Security benefits" alone to determine the break-even age for the decision to take benefits.

Figure 50

	Future Value of SSI Benefits - Age 62	Future Value of SSI Benefits - Age 67	Break-Even Age
Risk Free IRR (4.5%)	$ 1,285,000	$ 1,285,000	85.67
Public 40/40 IRR (7%)	$ 5,712,000	$ 5,631,000	Values are age 100
Private Conservative IRR (9%)	$ 9,832,000	$ 8,887,000	Values are age 100

Granted, nobody is going to take all their SSI benefits, place them in a fund, and never touch the principal. If you did, given today's Risk-Free IRR, an individual would come out ahead by taking distributions at age 62 until the ripe age of 85.67 years. After that, you should have waited until age 67 to start taking benefits. Granted, if you lived to one hundred, then taking SSI benefits at 62 was a mistake. Using the 7% IRR, the classic 60/40 portfolio, the break-even age is north of one hundred years of age. This is the same with the private conservative portfolio, which shows that at age one hundred, your decision to take benefits at age 62 was worth about $1 million in your favor. This is why education is so important. When studies are performed that say that Americans should hold off as long as possible to take benefits, there is an embedded assumption called the internal rate of return that implies that the average American does not know how to invest their funds to achieve even slightly more than a risk-free rate of return. Do you want to prove them wrong? This topic is much larger than the issue of a private investment return premium. And there are many wrinkles to Social Security that can impact this analysis. My point is to be aware and question studies and conventional wisdom. The government has a personal stake in its citizens deferring their claims on Social Security. It is my hope that by learning how to navigate private markets and building wealth during your productive years, your decision as to when to claim SSI benefits is a minor decision in your life.

Quick Summary:

1. Self-directed IRAs, Roth or Traditional, are a vehicle for investing in private markets with retirement funds. It may be the only material source of investable assets available for individuals. However, they come with a heavy administrative burden and cost.
2. Map out carefully, with the assistance of a financial planner, your strategy regarding what type of account or accounts will be the source of funds – a taxable brokerage account, a Roth SDIRA, or a Traditional SDIRA. A separate decision or strategy with regards to a Roth conversion plan will impact on the latter two choices.
3. SDIRA investing regulations prohibit transactions that are not at arms-length or involve disqualified persons such as the IRA owner and other close relatives.
4. UBIT and UDFI taxes need to be evaluated prior to making an investment. If UBIT or UDFI tax is due, then the owner of the IRA must file a Form 990-T tax return to the IRS, and the SDIRA is responsible for paying the tax (or estimated tax throughout the year).
5. An allocation of investable funds to private markets can enable individual investors to achieve their retirement goals faster and with less volatility.
6. The expected rate of return on a portfolio can be higher with an allocation to private offerings – even very conservative private offerings. This rate of return can have a favorable effect on a variety of retirement decisions, such as when to retire and when to draw Social Security benefits.

Chapter 16 - Private Investing and Income Taxes

In the previous chapter's discussion of self-directed IRAs, we entered a world where private investing and income taxes intersect. Investing inside a self-directed IRA is fundamentally a tax decision since there is always the option of paying the tax and distributing the retirement funds to a taxable account. Accordingly, that is a perfect segue to the natural income tax benefits associated with the private asset classes where the source of funds is a previously taxed brokerage account. This is clearly the simplest way to invest in alternative assets, as the investor can focus completely on the merits of an offering rather than all the potential traps of using a self-directed IRA account. This discussion will again be an introduction to the types of issues a private-passive investor will confront, and a deeper dive into any of these topics is warranted. This is not tax advice. It is important to consult with a tax professional to fully understand the implications of this provision for your specific situation.

Private asset classes have attractive income tax benefits, but I am careful never to invest primarily for the tax benefits of any particular offering. The economics of the investment come first; the tax implications will follow. Investors will eventually pay taxes; it is simply a question of how long the taxes can be deferred (unless investing with a Roth IRA). It is more important to stick with the investment plan that you have defined, knowing there are likely significant tax deferral benefits inherent in such a plan as compared to an income stream entirely reliant on a W-2 salary.

One specific example relates to Opportunity Zone investing. I have nothing against the concept of Opportunity Zones and am supportive of the objectives of this program. An Opportunity Zone is a designated economically distressed community where new investments may be eligible for preferential tax treatment. Opportunity Zones were created under the Tax Cuts and Jobs Act of 2017 in order to encourage private investment in low-income urban and rural areas that need economic development. The goal of Opportunity Zones is to stimulate economic growth and job creation in distressed communities while providing tax benefits to investors who support these efforts.

Investing in Opportunity Zones can offer several tax benefits to investors. The first is the deferral of capital gains taxes. Investors can defer paying taxes on capital gains from the sale of any asset, such as stocks or real estate, by investing those gains in a Qualified Opportunity Fund (QOF) within 180 days of the sale. The deferred gain must be recognized no later than December 31, 2026, or when the investment is sold, whichever comes first. Also, if the Opportunity Zone investment is held for at least five years, the investor can reduce the deferred capital gains taxes owed by 10%. If the investment is held for at least seven years, the reduction increases to 15%. Finally, if the Opportunity Zone investment is held for at least ten years, any capital gains realized from the investment are tax-free.

By their nature, Opportunity Zone investments have a longer projected term of ten years or more, which some investors prefer in their investment plans as it reduces the number of future reinvestment decisions that a commercial real estate investor has to make. The main point is that the Opportunity Zone investment still has to pass all of the due diligence and economic hurdles necessary to qualify for inclusion in your private portfolio. If the sponsor is unproven or known to be shaky, all the tax benefits in the world will not ease your regret from investing in such a project.

The second observation with regards to income taxes is the general difference in how Main Street versus Wall Street businesses are taxed. The majority of the time, public investors own a share of C Corporations, and these corporations are taxed on their taxable income. Dividends are then paid to investors out of the "after-tax" net income. In contrast, a structural difference is that private equity investments usually provide pass-through taxation. Private alternatives, including real estate, are typically structured as partnerships or limited liability companies (LLCs), which means that income and losses are passed through to investors. This allows investors to potentially deduct any losses against other income on their tax returns, reducing their overall tax liability. The tax document associated with partnerships or LLCs is Schedule K-1, which is an input to the Form 1040. Public security activities are reported by a brokerage on a consolidated Form-1099.

Private investments will add some complexity to an investor's 1040 income tax return. Most private asset class investments report their annual activities on Schedule K-1, which will have to be input into Form 1040. Schedule K-1s can be quite intimidating and can include up to forty pages for real estate equity fund investments. The K-1 includes information such as the partner or shareholder's share of the business or rental income, deductions, and credits, as well as any distributions or dividends they received from the business. The information on the K-1 is divided into distinct categories, such as ordinary income, rental income, capital gains, and foreign transactions. For investors with many K-1s, you can expect your tax preparer to raise the cost of your tax return preparation by a few hundred dollars. On a positive front, at least investors have to file a Form 1040 anyway; there are no additional tax returns required to be filed which was not the case with self-directed IRAs.

Regardless of how income is earned, the basic tax rate schedules illustrated in Figures 51 (ordinary income) and 52 (capital gains) apply.

Figure 51 *(source: Internal Revenue Service website)*

2023 Tax Brackets – Ordinary Income

Tax Rate	For Single Filers	For Married Individuals Filing Joint Returns
10%	$0 to $11,000	$0 to $22,000
12%	$11,000 to $44,725	$22,000 to $89,450
22%	$44,725 to $95,375	$89,450 to $190,750
24%	$95,375 to $182,100	$190,750 to $364,200
32%	$182,100 to $231,250	$364,200 to $462,500
35%	$231,250 to $578,125	$462,500 to $693,750
37%	$578,125 or more	$693,750 or more

Figure 52 *(source: Internal Revenue Service website)*

2023 Tax Brackets – Capital Gains

Tax Rate	For Unmarried Individuals, Taxable Income Over	For Married Individuals Filing Joint Returns, Taxable Income Over
0%	$0	$0
15%	$44,625	$89,250
20%	$492,300	$553,850

It is important for investors to maintain a knowledge of these brackets and which marginal income tax bracket they currently fall into and may fall into in the future. All things being equal, it is better to pay taxes later rather than today unless there is an obvious case in which a taxpayer currently is temporarily in an extremely low tax bracket. Notice the differences between the ordinary income tax rates and the capital gains tax rates. Capital gains tax rates are preferential in most cases. Ordinary rates apply unless the taxpayer has a capital gain. The basic rules for capital gains are as follows:

1. **Short-Term Capital Gains**: These are gains from the sale of assets held for one year or less. Short-term capital gains are taxed using ordinary income tax rates, which range from 10% to 37%, as shown in Figure 51.
2. **Long-Term Capital Gains**: These are gains from the sale of assets held for more than one year. Long-term capital gains are taxed at lower rates than short-term capital gains, ranging from 0% to 20%, as shown in Figure 52.

3. **Capital Losses**: These are losses from the sale of assets held for investment purposes. Capital losses can be used to offset capital gains, reducing the overall tax liability. If capital losses exceed capital gains, up to $3,000 of the excess losses can be used to offset other income in the current tax year. Any remaining excess losses can be carried forward to future tax years. Public investors who panic and take an elevated level of losses in any particular bear market lament this $3,000 loss limitation. Private investors cannot act on that emotion. However, private market investors can incur large losses when a private investment becomes worthless. In either case, it may take years to fully deduct significant capital losses. Although a small benefit, the ability to offset ordinary income with some level of capital loss activity is a benefit to taxpayers.

The next hurdle for investment taxation is the 3.8% Net Investment Income Tax (NIIT), which applies to individuals, estates, and trusts with net investment income above applicable threshold amounts. The Net Investment Income Tax (NIIT) was introduced as part of the Affordable Care Act (ACA), which was signed into law by President Barack Obama on March 23, 2010. The NIIT was a revenue-raising provision included in the ACA to help fund the expansion of health care coverage. In the case of an individual as of 2023, the NIIT is 3.8 percent on the lesser of:

1. the net investment income or
2. the excess of modified adjusted gross income over the following threshold amounts:
   a. $250,000 for married filing jointly
   b. $125,000 for married filing separately
   c. $200,000 for single or head of household

Net investment income includes but is not limited to, interest, dividends, capital gains, rental and royalty income, and passive income from businesses. However, it does not include income from wages, self-employment income, or income from retirement accounts like traditional IRAs or 401(k)s. Even including the NIIT, capital gains rates are preferable versus ordinary income tax rates.

Given these taxation fundamentals, individual investors and workers should strive to adhere to a set of principles, when possible, to continually minimize income taxes:

- Deferring income taxes is preferred versus paying taxes now.
- Earning income in the form of capital gains/losses is preferred versus earning ordinary income.
- Tax-exempt income is preferred over taxable income. In public markets, one can invest in municipal bonds as a form of tax-exempt income. Private real estate, other than Opportunity Zones, does not have any material tax-exempt features.
- Accelerated expenses (depreciation) are preferred over expense deferrals.
- Active business income is preferred over passive activities, in which case losses from activity investment activities can be used to reduce income from other active earnings such as salaries.

Figure 53 summarizes methods of earning income and how the tax code incentivizes or disincentivizes these methods. This figure is illustrative of the primary income tax features – I suspect there may be minor exceptions to each of these methods and features. For example, private real estate may allow an investor to deduct losses from rental activities against wage income, discussed in more depth later in this chapter, an advantage that may not be available to public equity investors.

Figure 53

	Salary Income	Public Market - Brokerage	Private Real Estate	Opportunity Zones	Private Equity
Can produce tax-exempt income	☐	✔	☐	✔	☐
Income deferral abilities	☐	✔	✔	✔	✔
Can generate capital gains income	☐	✔	✔	✔	✔
Accelerated depreciation expense	☐	☐	✔	✔	☐
Potential for write-off of losses	☐	✔	✔	✔	✔

The bottom line is that a salaried worker is in the worst position with regards to income taxes. Investors in equities, public or private, are in a preferential position with regard to income taxes. Investors in commercial real estate are in the optimal position to defer income taxes for extended periods of time. Private equity and public equity assets are similar in terms of taxation. Public equities are more susceptible to negative tax benefits since investors have more opportunities to "over-trade" their accounts, which can produce suboptimal income tax consequences for any given tax year. If that is all you need, you can move on to the next chapter. If you want to understand more of the details, continue on.

Private Debt Taxation

Generally, income from real estate or business debt investments is considered Form 1099-dividend income and subject to ordinary income tax rates. This includes interest earned from loans made to real estate developers, mortgages, and mortgage-backed securities, and other secured or unsecured debt investments. As such, there is no material beneficial tax treatment as compared to public debt instruments. Private investors will sometimes find funds structured as partnerships for debt and preferred equity that report investors' taxable activities on Schedule K-1. In the case of real estate, the benefits of accelerated depreciation are not available to debt and preferred equity investors.

Dividends received on debt and other investment structures, such as REITs, are typically eligible for the Qualified Business Income (QBI) deduction, which was introduced as part of the Tax Cuts and Jobs Act of 2017. The QBI deduction allows eligible taxpayers to deduct up to 20% of their qualified business income from their federal income taxes. Here are some of the eligibility requirements:

- The QBI deduction is available to taxpayers who operate as sole proprietorships, partnerships, S corporations, or LLCs.

- The QBI deduction is only available for income generated by a domestic business. Foreign-sourced income is not eligible.
- The QBI deduction is available for income from a qualified trade or business. This includes income from a rental property that meets certain criteria, but it does not include income from certain specified service businesses such as health, law, accounting, consulting, and other professional services.
- Income thresholds: The QBI deduction is subject to certain income thresholds. For taxpayers with taxable income below $181,100 (single) or $364,200 (married filing jointly) in 2021, the deduction is equal to 20% of QBI. For taxpayers with taxable income above these thresholds, additional limitations apply.

The QBI deduction is not unique to private investment markets, so it cannot be considered an advantage of investing in private markets; however, the business structures described above are common with private real estate funds and REITs.

Real Estate Investment Trusts (REITs)

Before proceeding to private equity, including commercial real estate, there is a unique income tax treatment for the special category of assets called REITs. Created in 1960, REITs have flourished and have remained popular with investors, legislators, and tax authorities. Under the goal of democratizing real estate investing for the masses, REITs enjoy significant tax advantages. This includes avoiding double taxation that is always somehow passed through to the end investors.[50] REITs have always received favorable tax treatment in that they do not pay income tax at the entity level despite being a corporate entity.

REITs are required by law to distribute at least 90% of their taxable income to shareholders as dividends. The dividends are taxed as ordinary income, but they may be eligible for the Qualified Business Income (QBI) deduction of 20%, which creates an effective income tax rate much lower than the ordinary income tax rate. REIT investors also benefitted from the 2017 Tax Cut and Jobs Act, placing REITs on par with typical qualified-dividend-paying companies when held in taxable accounts. REITs are allowed to deduct depreciation expenses on their properties, which can reduce their taxable income. The savings from depreciation are passed on to shareholders in the form of higher dividends. Also, when a REIT sells a property for a profit, it may be subject to capital gains tax. However, if the REIT distributes the profits to shareholders as dividends, the tax rate may be lower than if the investor sold the shares and paid capital gains tax on the sale.

According to a recent study, since 1995, 70% of REIT distributions have been classified as ordinary income. Fifteen percent has been considered capital gains, and fifteen percent has been classified as a return of capital.[51] All three categories are tax-favored, considering the QBI Deduction, the lower capital gains rates, and the fact that returns of capital are not taxable. Granted that private REITS cannot be proclaimed to be advantageous to public REITS, but as a general asset class REITS could be argued to have favorable tax treatment relative to dividends of publicly traded stocks.

Specific Income Tax Implications of Private Equity

The returns from private equity funds are typically backloaded in the life of a fund. Stated another way, the main tax benefit from investing in private equity results from a deferral of taxes relative to equity investments in public markets. Income from private equity portfolio companies can be tax-free up until the point of an actual sale of such company.

Let's compare owning a public stock vs a private stock within a private equity fund. Furthermore, assume that the holding period for each is effectively ten years. The public stock may pay dividends over the term of the holding period; such dividends are taxable at ordinary income taxes. When sold, the investment in the public equity would be taxed at long-term capital gains rates. This is assuming that you, as an investor to, do get whipsawed in trading this stock during the ten-year holding period. From a tax perspective, many sad things can happen in terms of rate of return and unintended tax consequences from trading public equities. Now, with private equity, dividends are in the control of the private equity sponsor – capital gains are deferred until an exit event occurs. The deferred taxation benefits of private equity are much more iron-clad than a similar investment in public equity. In summary, private equity funds typically invest in long-term projects, which can result in capital gains over a period of years. These gains are typically taxed at a lower rate than ordinary income and may be deferred until the investment is sold.

The J-Curve in private equity investing is a graphical representation of the returns made by private equity funds through time. The shape of private equity fund performance, when plotted on a line graph, resembles a capital "J," hence the name J-Curve. When a private equity commitment is made, the value of the commitment typically goes down during the early life of the fund. In the graph, if the vertical axis represents the rate of return, typically expressed as an Internal Rate of Return (IRR) in private equity, and the horizontal axis represents time, the graph line curves down and to the right until the investment stabilizes at which point the line starts moving quickly up and to the right as the investment starts to perform and show profitability through time. The graph in Figure 54 below is a model illustration of the J-Curve.

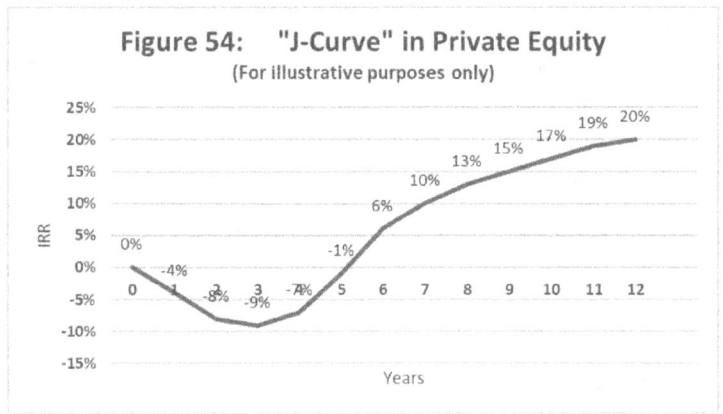

Private equity fund returns are backloaded. Most of the cash distributions from a private equity fund occur in the second half of its life. Even when the distributions start flowing back to the limited partner investors, they are considered a return of capital to the extent of an investor's capital investment. Or, if the fund exits a particular company investment, favorable capital gain treatment will be the result for investors.

Another indirect benefit for investors is the "carried interest" feature with respect to how private equity managers get compensated. Carried interest is a topic that arises every time that tax reform is publicly discussed by U.S. legislative bodies. Private equity fund managers often receive a portion of the fund's profits as carried interest, which is taxed at the lower capital gains rate. This incentivizes managers to generate high returns for the fund, which can benefit investors. How is that for a capitalist twist on the taxation of private equity and how it benefits society?

Commercial Real Estate Common Equity Taxation

Commercial real estate investing has a well-deserved reputation for being the holy grail for tax deferral benefits, providing a major assist to investors in building long-term generational wealth. This is not because real estate investors or bad, greedy, or dishonest. The tax benefits accrue because the IRS Code (IRC) authorizes and incentivizes accredited investors to invest in real estate, funds, and syndications. To describe these tax benefits, we will assume an investor places a $100,000 investment in a multifamily real estate fund syndication with a value-add renovation strategy that estimates net cash inflow over the next five years, a refinancing of the property after three years, followed by a disposition of the properties inside the fund at the end of year five.

The first benefit of this hypothetical investment is the treatment of the annual distributions of net operating income generated by the properties in the portfolio. These distributions can be categorized as a return of investors' capital and not taxable income. Compare this to purchasing a dividend-paying public stock, in which case the dividends would be taxable each year. As the syndicator/operator makes substantial improvements to the properties, the annual distributions to investors may be muted in the early years of the project due to the investments being made to the properties – improving communal areas, modernizing the interior units, or whatever the primary needs that each property requires. These investments add value to each property and, therefore the portfolio, and the sponsor may refinance the portfolio with an increased loan size and return these proceeds back to investors. Since debt transactions are not taxable, investors can potentially get a sizable portion of their investment back within a three-year timeframe. But investors collectively still own the properties, and no tax liability has been incurred at this point. Distributions after this point are infinite in nature since the original investment has been taken off the table. The tax deferral benefits of investing in commercial real estate during the life of the investment are extremely attractive and legal.

Deferred income taxes are further assured due to depreciation. Depreciation is the allowable write-off of the cost of real estate and improvements over time, excluding the value of the underlying land. If the property is non-residential, such as an industrial facility, hotel, or office, or building, the cost of the structures is written off as depreciation over 39 years. If the property is residential or multifamily, the value of the building may be written off over a 27.5-year life. Assuming a purchase price of an apartment building of $750,000, of which the allocation to land is $200,000, that leaves a value assigned to "improvements" of $550,000, called the depreciable basis. Each year, for 27.5 years, there would be a depreciation deduction of $20,000 on average, which may flip Net Operating Income into a Net Operating Loss for the project.

Depreciation is typically allocated to limited partner interests on a pro-rata basis. This depreciation expense can eliminate income taxes entirely, especially in the early years of a project, making it one of the best tax shelters available by law. What does this mean for our hypothetical $100,000 investment? The "net rental income" reported to you on the annual K-1 reporting is typically a net rental loss. At a minimum, this means that an investor will not have to pay income taxes, and potentially can utilize this loss against other sources of earned income. Any losses that cannot be utilized in the current year will roll forward to future years.

The strength of income tax protection can be even stronger with a technique called cost segregation. Cost segregation allows investors to accelerate depreciation even further. Cost segregation is a specialized type of fixed asset review or study that is performed on newly constructed, recently purchased, or significantly renovated buildings. In the absence of a cost segregation study, all non-land costs associated with the building would be lumped into the asset classification of "real estate" and depreciated over 27.5 or 39 years. A quality cost segregation study examines the component costs of the building to determine what assets may have shorter depreciable lives under federal tax rules. Items like carpeting, wallpaper, furnishings, and cabinetry can qualify for faster cost recovery under the rules and generate larger depreciation deductions in the early years of a new building's lifespan. Components like HVAC and specialized wiring may also qualify for shorter depreciation when they are installed in manufacturing facilities.[52]

"Current bonus depreciation rules heighten the value of accelerated deductions because they permit 100% deductions in the year an asset is placed in service if that asset has a depreciable life of 20 years or less. (In short, property with a useful life of less than 20 years can be fully deducted in the year placed in service). Starting in 2023, that percentage is scheduled to drop twenty percentage points each year until bonus depreciation sunsets completely, starting in 2027. Asset balances remaining after bonus depreciation is applied are depreciated starting in the year placed in service under the applicable federal lifespan of 3, 5, 7, 10, or 20 years, depending on the type of property."[53.]

A cost segregation mechanism is at the discretion of the offering sponsor, so you should ask them if they do a "cost segregation analysis" on the real estate purchased in their offerings.[54] Also, cost segregation studies have a cost-benefit aspect since they can be very costly. For a new development syndication in which the sponsor plans to flip the newly constructed building in a three-year term (i.e., one year after completion), a cost segregation study makes less sense.

Finally, upon the sale of properties there will be income taxes to be paid. If not, either money has been lost on the investment, or the investment is able to further defer taxes using what is termed a "like-kind" exchange, which will be discussed more below. When property is sold, there is depreciation recapture and capital gains treatment.

Under Section 1231 of the IRC, gains and losses from the sale of real estate used in a trade or business are treated as long-term capital gains and losses. This means that if you hold the property for more than one year, any gains will be taxed at the lower long-term capital gains tax rate, and any losses can be used to offset other capital gains. Furthermore, Section 1231 of the IRC allows for the netting of gains and losses from the sale of real estate used in a trade or business. This means that if you have multiple transactions in a year, you can offset gains and losses against each other to determine your overall gain or loss for the year. Capital gains treatment is beneficial to investors since capital gains tax rates are generally lower than ordinary income tax rates.

Concurrent with calculating the capital gains on sales, recapture of depreciation is required. What exactly does that mean? This means that when you sell the property, any depreciation claimed will be subject to ordinary income tax rates rather than the lower capital gains tax rate. However, the recapture tax rate is capped at 25%, which provides benefits to higher-income taxpayers. Also, remember that the tax on depreciation recapture is paid only when selling the property, while the benefits of taking the accelerated depreciation deductions occurred each year up to the exit. Another terrific benefit of tax deferral. Of course, if a property is sold for less than its adjusted basis (sales price less cost as adjusted for depreciation), there would be no depreciation recapture. In the U.S., depreciation recapture is governed by Sections 1245 and 1250 of the IRC.

Going back to our example of an investor with a $100,000 multifamily fund syndication. This investor has been deferring distributions from this investment for five years, and now the portfolio is sold for $200,000 at the end of five years. The following assumptions are calculations that demonstrate the framework:

- Purchase price of property or fund: $100,000
- Depreciation deductions claimed in five years: $3,600 per year.
- Sale price in the fifth year: $200,000
- Depreciation recapture tax rate: 20%
- Capital gain tax rate: 15%
- The adjusted cost basis will be $100,000 – ($3,600 * 5) $82,000.

The gain from the sale will be the adjusted cost basis subtracted from the sale price: $200,000 – $82,000 = $118,000. As a result, the investor will need to report $18,000 in ordinary income (depreciation recapture) and $100,000 (total gain less depreciation recapture) in long-term capital gains. The tax liability due will be the sum of the following:

- Since the depreciation recapture tax rate is 20%, the amount of ordinary income tax will be $3,600 ($18,000 * 20%), plus.
- The long-term capital gain tax will be $15,000 ($100,000*15%), equals.
- The total tax liability will be $18,600.

Stepping back, one can see how favorable the taxation framework is for commercial real estate investments. Massive deferral benefits due to the fact that distributions and debt transactions are not taxable, plus accelerated depreciation incentives further reducing taxable income during the early years of an investment. Upon exit, long-term capital gains tax rates will apply to the majority of any gains generated. But as mentioned, further deferral of capital gains from this sale transaction is still possible.

Section 1031 of the IRC is a provision that allows for the deferral of capital gains taxes when a taxpayer sells certain types of property and uses the proceeds to purchase other similar types of property. This provision is commonly known as a "like-kind exchange." In a like-kind exchange, the taxpayer can defer paying capital gains taxes on the sale of the original property as long as the new property acquired is of a like-kind or similar nature. The taxpayer must also follow specific rules and guidelines to qualify for the deferral of taxes under Section 1031. This provision of the tax code is how many billionaires have created their wealth and also why Section 1031 always seems to be a topic in the tax reform discussions in the United States.

There is one final wrinkle regarding how large the tax benefits of early-year net rental losses can be. These passive activity rules have always been confusing to investors (including me). The "cherry on top" for tax benefits of commercial real estate is when an investor can utilize the tax losses created in the early years of an investment against other sources of income, including salaries and wages. This is potentially the ultimate near-term tax shield.

The ability to deduct real estate losses against ordinary income depends on several factors, including your tax status and the nature of the losses. If you are a *"real estate professional,"* meaning you are engaged in the business of real estate as a broker, agent, property manager, developer, or other related professions. To qualify as a real estate professional for tax purposes, an individual must meet two requirements:

1. More than 50% of the individual's personal services during the taxable year must be performed in real property trades or businesses in which the individual materially participates.
2. The individual must perform more than 750 hours of services during the taxable year in real property trades or businesses in which the individual materially participates.

It is important for private-passive investors to understand these rules in order to prevent future troubles with the IRS and to also understand why your tax accountant is asking these questions to you. Because the premise of this book is around passive investing, and delegating the active duties to proven sponsor expertise, it is unlikely that such passive investors will qualify as a real estate professional. If you do spend many hours working in the industry, it is important to research these rules in depth with your tax professional and to keep detailed time records.

If you are not a real estate professional, you may still be able to deduct up to $25,000 in real estate losses against ordinary income **if you actively participate in the rental activity and your adjusted gross income is less than $100,000.** The deduction is reduced by $1 for every $2 of income over $100,000 and completely phased out at $150,000. If you do not meet the requirements to deduct real estate losses against ordinary income, you should be able to carry forward the losses to future tax years to offset future gains. This is the position that I would expect most private-passive investors to be in.

State Taxes

Investors should not completely ignore the state income tax impacts of their decisions, although it should not be the primary economic driver in portfolio construction. There will be incremental tax preparation costs from your tax advisor the larger your investment footprint. The larger an investor's tax pool or overall wealth, tax preparation costs become less of a concern. For most accredited investors, I suggest that you watch the tax footprint of your portfolio.

With all investments, a passive investor should understand the state tax implications prior to making the investment. Again, portfolio diversification (including the geographical aspect) is paramount, but the following are particular concerns that should be around state income taxes.

- How will your state of residency tax the income from real estate activities?

- How will the state where the property is located tax the income from real estate activities?
- How will the investment impact the complexity and cost of your personal income tax return?

As an example, a resident of Massachusetts invests in a multifamily syndication for a property located in Texas. This sounds great because there is no state income tax in Texas. Accordingly, the investor saves the hassle of completing state tax returns in Texas, reducing the cost of tax compliance. However, the Commonwealth of Massachusetts will want to collect state income tax on these real estate activities. It is worth noting that Massachusetts allows taxpayers to claim a credit for income taxes paid to other states on income earned in those states, which can help offset the tax liability for gains from out-of-state property sales. Many high-tax states operate this way, so just be aware. Bottom line, Massachusetts residents will still pay state income tax related to out-of-state properties, one way or another.

A final note is with regard to investment in funds, particularly debt or preferred equity funds. Funds are all different, and understanding if their structure protects the investor from having to file multiple state income tax returns is important. A discussion is warranted with both the sponsor and your income tax professional, even when the language in the prospectus is similar to "the fund to conduct its activities in such a manner that will not cause its Members who are not otherwise subject to income tax in states other than their state of primary residence, to be taxed and subject to tax filing obligations in other states, solely as a result of owning Member interests."

Quick Summary

1. The taxation benefits of investments in private asset classes are at least as good as investing in public equities and bonds. In the case of commercial real estate, the income tax benefits are far superior to investing in public markets.
2. The tax characteristics of any investment are important but should not be the primary reason for making an investment relative to similar investments in any asset class.
3. Investments in private equities can be superior to public equities by the simple fact that tax deferral benefits are inherent in private market assets due to the lack of liquidity and long holding periods. Public market assets can be traded excessively, resulting in unfortunate tax consequences.
4. Investments in commercial real estate have tax benefits that are unmatched by all other asset classes because the U.S. Government has created these incentives for investors. Benefits of investing in real estate and real estate funds include tax deferral, tax-free refinancing transactions, tax-free refinancings, accelerated depreciation, special incentives such as Opportunity Zones, the potential to offset active income with passive losses, and Section 1031 like-kind exchanges.
5. Working closely with an experienced tax preparer and advisor is essential when analyzing investments and subsequent tax filing compliance in the future.

Chapter 17 - Make Investing Enjoyable Again

There is a scene from the movie *Money Ball* where Brad Pitt (playing manager Billy Beane) walks into the Oakland A's locker room after losing another game. Nick Porrazzo (playing star player Jeremy Giambi) is dancing on a table to loud music. Billy asks Jeremy, "Is losing fun?" After a few tense seconds, Jeremy responds with a quiet "no." Billy responds, "So what are you having fun for?" and proceeds to destroy an innocent water cooler. This interchange is simple yet profound. We remember times as children just having fun, and somehow, these moments seem to become rarer in adulthood. Can investing be fun? Should it be fun? For me, it used to be fun. However, over the years of watching my traditional retirement portfolio being whipsawed in 2001, then again in 2008, 2020, and 2022, it has certainly reduced the fun as the stakes have increased. As eluded in *Money Ball*, life should be a quest for meaning, fun and enjoyment, whatever that means to you. The more I have learned about the abundant opportunities in private asset classes, historically the domain of the rich, and the more I have allocated to these markets has made investing more enjoyable for me over the past decade.

Granted that the existing accredited investor framework does not provide investors with access to private markets in a meaningful way. Clearly, this framework is moving in the direction of expanding the ranks of accredited investors in the future. Certainly, there are enough opportunities and platforms for non-accredited investors to get started today. The confluence of these liberalized regulatory frameworks, technology, and crowdfunding has meant that investors cannot afford to remain ignorant about how these massive private markets operate and what the possibilities are. Giving up on expanding your investment horizons because of your current financial situation would be an excuse. For those interested in investing, one cannot ignore private asset classes, and small actions can be taken anytime to become a private market player.

This does not mean I advocate moving all investable funds into the private-passive quadrant. That would be irresponsible and would further eliminate an essential element of diversification that investing in both public and private assets can provide. Private and public markets do not move in lockstep. The correlations are weak in many cases. I do support a reasonable allocation of a total portfolio to private alternatives, depending on your financial sophistication and risk comfort level.

I will address how to make investing enjoyable again by doing a deeper dive into three interrelated and important questions.

Will My Investment Strategy Work Long-Term With Reasonable Confidence So That I Can Achieve My Desired Goals And Lifestyle?

When markets gyrate and the news cycle is unfavorable, it is extremely beneficial to know that your investment plan is solid from a historical perspective and consistent with your values and risk tolerance. Knowing these facts allows an investor to ride out any situation that may come up. Like the Federal Reserve increasing short-term rates from 0.25% to 5.00% in a brief 12-month timespan. As an aside, why were rates at .25% to begin with and for so long?

The public market 60/40 portfolio is not dead, it just can evolve depending on your skills and needs. An investor who sticks with a diversified 60/40 portfolio can expect returns of approximately 7% over a period of many years. It just takes time. The same long-term strategy is true for private asset classes but with less volatility and the addition of approximately 100-200 basis points of return. Yale University is a case in point that private alternatives can be a successful long-term strategy. Granted, portfolio construction for a private portfolio is not as simple as with a public market portfolio. The common element is that investors must develop a logical plan and execute it religiously over a lengthy period of time. Allocation of a portion of your overall portfolio to private markets is the optimal plan because now you are adding more diversification (with less correlation between private and public assets) and higher potential returns.

Having the confidence that your foundation is strong will allow investors to survive difficult macro environments coupled with the continuous Federal Reserve policy oscillation, enabling long-term success. If you are a proficient public market investor, then there will be a learning curve involved with designing a private market carve-out for your overall portfolio. Education around private markets is scattered at best and mostly driven by sponsors who want your money. Just like you evolved and educated yourself on public stocks and bonds, investors have the capacity to learn and experiment with the private-passive approach.

Is The Process Of Investing Fun And Consistent With My Values In Generating Wealth?

Investing in public indices checks the box as a solid long-term strategy for growing wealth. There is no doubt about that. But does it further an investor's understanding of how companies operate, grow, and succeed? Invest $100,000 in a real estate syndication or private equity fund, and I guarantee you will watch it like a hawk and learn a lot about main-street capitalism. Investing directly or indirectly in private equities is all about investing and operating main-street businesses. As an investor, you will be able to follow projects from beginning to end, regardless of investment strategy be it ground-up development, value-add, or venture capital. Wall Street is more analogous to a casino. How many investors actually read the annual reports of companies they invest in? Warren Buffet does, and it provides him a competitive advantage over the public. Private-passive investing is more closely aligned with learning the details of capitalism, in my opinion. Public market investing is a form of anesthesia; it slowly impairs your ability to think and reason.

Investing in private markets can be significantly less psychologically and emotionally taxing. The public markets with real-time pricing and discounting can wear on investors over time. There are infinite examples of rapid dislocations in public markets that can immediately jeopardize an investor's long-term confidence and investment plans. From February 1, 2023, to May 4, 2023, the regional bank ETF (Ticker KRE) fell from $63 to $36, a 42% decline in three months. This is even more troubling given that a systematic bank run would have dire consequences for many sectors of the economy. At the outset of COVID-19, the S&P 500 index dropped by 20% in a brief period of time. Employees were calling me up to find out the most conservative investment option available in our 401K Plan because they could not take it anymore (at exactly the wrong time). Investors cannot enjoy times like these, watching their 401K statements as the balances fall off a cliff. Enjoying life during these times may cause your spouse or friends to ask, "Is losing fun? What are you having fun for?"

Investing in private markets requires a change in mindset. Investors in private deals will be focused on a few investments a year – a handful of larger investment decisions each year for new deployments that fit into their long-term asset allocation. No excessive trading and no kneejerk reactions to what is happening in the markets. It is a smoother ride for investors. There is still stress since factors impacting public markets are impacting the valuation of private assets; however, there is nothing an investor can do about it, and usually, what goes down will go up again. Private market investing activity is about scouring the landscape for deals that meet your objectives and portfolio allocation at the present moment in time. Having some "dry powder" available at all times allows private investors to be opportunistic as well.

This shift in mindset from public market investing to private markets will require time, experience, and confidence. Initially, investors need the courage to be imperfect to make this mental shift. On a net basis, investing in private markets is more fun if one follows the conservative principles described in this book. For me, investing in private real estate companies or private equity is more interesting since you are communicating directly with the owners of these businesses, evaluating deals based on formal business plans, and continuously advancing your education based on experiences with these asset classes and with particular sponsors.

How Do I Avoid Stupid Investing Mistakes That Will Negate #1 And #2 Above?

In this respect, successful investing in any market or asset class is predicated on one simple rule – avoid making stupid investing mistakes. Mistakes are unavoidable to some extent, and those moments we learn the most from. Advancing your education in private markets is a cheaper way to go about it. Learning from experience is expensive. Making unforced errors will negate any progress made with the above two questions – is my plan appropriate, and is it enjoyable? Is losing fun? We can all agree the answer is no. Legendary investor Charlie Munger is quoted, "It's remarkable how much long-term advantage people like us have gotten by trying to be consistently not stupid, instead of trying to be very intelligent."

Summarizing the key lessons or takeaways from this book will produce the opposite list of stupid mistakes to avoid. I hope this book has piqued your interest in a private market, passive investment strategy.

Stupid Mistakes of Accredited Investors

1. **Investing in Private Markets Without a Plan**: Many investors just wing it. Trust me, this does not work. This would be analogous to a baseball manager picking nine names out of a hat to determine the starting lineup. Determine your goals and first tolerance first, and then design your target asset allocation, no different from a rational approach in the public markets.
2. **Bet Too Large on a Single Private Offering:** This is an effective way to lose excessive amounts of money and destroy your confidence in investing in private markets. Diversification is key, and investing in funds is an attractive way to protect against the losing positions that are bound to occur in any

diversified portfolio. Small (minimum) investments with new sponsors or funds are the preferred approach. Especially if you value a good night's sleep.

3. **Investing in Single Business Ventures:** Wouldn't it be great to invest in a new fintech startup, brewery, or clothes-sharing start-up? Unless you are active in a particular business sector or work for this particular venture (inside knowledge), do not attempt this. Instead, invest in private equity, commercial real estate, or venture capital funds.

4. **Overweight Your Portfolio with the Common Equity Component of the Capital Stack:** Even for younger or more aggressive investors, it is suggested that there be a portfolio allocation to debt and preferred equity tranches of the capital stack because these securities act differently than common equity during extremes in market conditions. Having the allocation to debt funds and a roster of "go-to" sponsors will provide you more flexibility to adjust a portfolio on short notice as the business cycle changes. Invest across the capital stack for cash flow, stability, and flexibility.

5. **Implement a Private-Passive Strategy Using a "Do-It-Yourself" Approach.** Throughout this book, the importance of developing the necessary team and network has been stressed. The network is your list of contacts and sponsors you build and cultivate over time to identify great opportunities with trusted sponsors and operators. The supporting team includes that network plus tax, legal, and financial advisers that can assist with their professional knowledge and experience to assist with developing and executing your plan.

6. **Invest in a Private Offering Because You Saw an Advertisement on Instagram or Facebook:** This is not the type of advertising channel that well-breed sponsors utilize. There may be reputable, emerging sponsors trying to build up their investor roles, but there are plenty of others who have no clue what they are doing. This is a recipe for disaster. Sponsors should be corroborated through other trusted resources and interviewed in depth. The only thing worse than these type of advertisements is to take a tip from a co-worker around the water cooler (just don't take it out on the water cooler).

7. **Over concentrate the Portfolio with Just a Few Positions:** This is a close relative to #2 above, but with the more general point that private investors should diversify their portfolio along as many dimensions as possible, consistent with the parameters of their overarching plan. Granted, you may have an awesome private equity fund in the portfolio, but why not add a second with a different strategy, such as venture income? Five real estate syndication funds can be better than one, especially when you can achieve diversification around geographical regions, investment profiles (value-add, development), and place in the capital stack. Investors who were overly concentrated in hotel and office property syndications back in 2020 wish they spread their exposures more widely.

8. **Invest in Asset Classes or Sectors When Everyone is Making Money:** This is easy to say and much harder to do. In retrospect, investing in SPACS (public market "special purpose acquisition company") or cryptocurrency in late 2021 was a horrible mistake. I am by no means an expert, but I have learned not to invest at the top. However, I tend to get back in too early after seeing Bitcoin fall by 25%; what a

bargain, right? Then it falls another 50% from there. A more constructive way to look at this is to learn how to recognize dislocations in the market at times of distress. Maintaining dry powder to invest in sectors that are clearly distressed is an important skill to develop. There are typical opportunities somewhere, such as hotels in 2021 or office properties in 2023. Did you hear anyone in 2023 saying that office property investment is a good idea? That may be a cue.

9. **Ignore What the Professionals or Your Network are Telling You**: Instead, listen to your network of proven sponsors and synthesize what they are saying into a cohesive picture of the market environment.

10. **Neglect Maintaining Dry Powder / Emergency Fund of Atleast 15% of the Private Portfolio Value**: Another yardstick would be to maintain liquidity of at least 5% of total net worth. This is a frustrating mistake for many reasons. Economic or market conditions can deteriorate quickly, and not having the liquid reserves to take advantage of temporary dislocations is aggravating. There also may be extremely exciting offerings that come to market that are a perfect fit in terms of your plan and asset allocation. With zero liquidity available, private investors lack the flexibility to invest in great opportunities and may also leave investors vulnerable to capital calls. Liquid reserves are also important to cover income tax liabilities that may emerge in the future. Investors receive many upfront tax shields with commercial real estate, but eventually, the taxes will have to be paid.

11. **Ignore Investments Post-Acquisition:** Yes, the money is made on the buy when the investment is made. But to ignore the investments post-purchase would be missing a tremendous opportunity to further your education in private markets. Especially when operating in cyclical real estate markets, the experiences of the sponsor are highly informative of the real estate conditions that are impacting other operators in that market and, in some cases, macro factors that are impacting operators nationwide, such as the impact of changing interest rates. This continuous feedback will help you in placing your next position.

12. **Do Not Listen to or Trust Your Gut**: It is hard not to get excited after discussing a new private offering with a sponsor or listening to the offer webinar. If you wait two or three days, what naturally happens is that you are not so excited anymore. You are more rational. At this point, it may still be a nice investment if it fits into the overall plan. The key is to closely listen to your mind and any dissonance around this investment decision. I purchased a small business about fifteen years ago, excitedly going through the due diligence and dreaming of some degree of future independence. The entire night before the closing, I had an exceedingly tough time sleeping, and my mind was racing. I have learned from this experience that this is a clear warning sign. It is better to say no and walk away than to suffer for a period of years. Listen to your gut. Sleep on any new decision an extra night. Do not ignore significant anxiety when entering a position. There will always be another deal coming down the pike.

13. **Build a Private-Passive Portfolio Inside of a Qualified, Self-Directed Individual Retirement Account (SDIRA):** A SDIRA is effectively a partnership between you and the Government. Forty percent or so of the income and gains generated inside the SDIRA will eventually be paid to the IRS.

That can be avoided by using a Roth SDIRA, but to get the money into a Roth, you have to pay all the taxes upfront. Taxes aside, the complexity of compliance and costs involved with operating a SDIRA are extremely daunting. You might as well distribute the funds to a taxable brokerage account, especially if you are over the age of 59.5, thus eliminating the 10% penalty. Avoiding self-directed IRAs to invest in private markets unless (a) you really have no other choice given where your investable funds are, and (b) you are thoroughly educated about the tax and other consequences of housing complex investments in an SDIRA. Most folks will not meet both of these tests.

14. **Assume Nothing Will Go Wrong with Private Investments:** Just as in your personal life, a business entity will face challenges. Can you imagine any entity in life never facing tough times? It is part of life. Does this mean you will lose money at the first sign of trouble? Absolutely not. It is important to recognize that these problems are principally the problems of the managers of the real estate or private equity business. You are going along for the ride to learn and understand how managers can (or cannot) solve these problems to build your understanding of how these businesses operate and whether you want to invest with a sponsor in the future, given the alternatives in the market. For every windstorm, there is insurance. When interest rates rise, there should be rate caps or swaps. Bad property management can be changed out. To be a successful private-passive investor, get rid of your mindset of unrealistic expectations and be prepared for challenges. These challenges will resolve themselves over a 5–10-year period and 20+% IRRs can still be achieved. You must play "the long game" in private markets.

The hope is that this book serves as a gateway for investors to participate in private investments and to continue to advance their education and understanding of all the factors that impact the successful navigation of these asset classes. Access to private market alternatives is expanding at a very rapid pace, so all stakeholders need to accept this fact. There will always be market pundits who claim that private investments are bad and that households are not sophisticated enough to navigate alternatives. But the cat is out of the bag, and education coupled with mindful action is the only realistic solution. Everyone can expand their knowledge about private investments. Like everything else, efforts to learn over periods of time create expertise. I have learned more about the markets and myself while compiling the information herein. I hope this is the beginning of a successful journey for readers as well.

Notes

Chapter One

1. (n.d.). Yale Endowment Reports. Yale University. https://investments.yale.edu/reports *Yale University Annual Reports*, Yale University website.
2. Orr, L. (2019, July 31). David Swensen Is Great for Yale. Is He Horrible For Investing? Institutional Investor
3. Brown, R. (2021, June 2). How to Invest Like a Legend. Forbes. *How To Invest Like A Legend.* June 2, 2021
4. Cerulli Associates, January 8, 2022, further referenced in Fortune Magazine.
5. Boyd Wealth Management, as further referenced to Morningstar Direct's Asset Class Returns Quilt.
6. Cambridge Associates, LLC. *U.S. Private Equity Benchmarks (Legacy Definition) Q2 2020 Final Report*, page 8.
7. National Council of Real Estate Investment Fiduciaries (NCREIF), Second Quarter 2022 Press Release at https://www.ncreif.org/news/npi-2q2022/.

Chapter Two

8. Securities and Exchange Commission of the United States (n.d.). Definition of Accredited Investor. Retrieved June 30, 2023, from https://www.sec.gov/education
9. Posner, C. (2019, May 6). What happened at the Small Business Capital Formation roundtable and Advisory Committee meeting? Cooley PubCo. Retrieved September 23, 2023, from https://cooleypubco.com/2019/05/06/small-business-roundtable-and-committee-meeting/
10. *SEC (2019, June 26). SEC Concept Release on Harmonization of Securities Offering Exemptions. 84 Fed. Reg. 30,460, 30,470.*
11. Department of Commerce (2021, September 30). Income and Poverty in the United States: 2020. U.S Census Bureau.

Chapter Three

12. *SEC (2019, June 26). SEC Concept Release on Harmonization of Securities Offering Exemptions. 84 Fed. Reg. 30,460, 30,470.*
13. Zanki, T. (2019, August 13). Changes to Accredited Investor Rules Take Priority at SEC. LAW360. https:////www.law360.com/compliance/articles/1188099.changes-to-accredited-investor-rules-take-priority-at-sec.
14. Department of Commerce (2021, September 30). Income and Poverty in the United States: 2020. U.S Census Bureau.
15. Department of Commerce (2021, September 30). Income and Poverty in the United States: 2020. U.S Census Bureau.
16. Department of Commerce (2021, September 30). Income and Poverty in the United States: 2020. U.S Census Bureau.
17. Crenshaw, C. (2020, November 2). Statement on Harmonization of Securities Offering Exemptions. Securities and Exchange Commission.
18. SEC Release Nos. 33-10824; 34-89669; File No. S7-25-19
19. Fletcher III, C.E. (1988), *Sophisticated Investors Under the Federal Securities Laws*, Duke L.J. 1081.

Chapter Four

[20] Pensions and Investments, *Number of Hedge Funds Remains on the Upswing*, October 2021.

[21] BarclayHedge, Assets Under Management, www.barclayhedge.com/solutions/assets-under-management/

[22] Scaramucci, A. (2012), *The Little Book of Hedge Funds*, John Wiley & Sons.

[23] Khajuria, S., *Two and Twenty* (p. 39). Crown. Kindle Edition.

[24] 2020 NACUBO-TIAA Study of Endowments.

[25] 2020 NACUBO-TIAA Study of Endowments.

Chapter Five

[26] SEC Office of Investor Education and Advocacy.

Chapter Six

[27] Market value of the NCREIF Property Index, 4th Quarter 2022. NCREIT.ORG. Retrieved April 30, 2023, from https://www.ncreif.org/data-products/property/

Chapter Eight

[28] Figure 14. Yale University Annual Reports.

[29] Figure 15. Reproduced from Moonfare.com. From 1Q86 to 4Q20, where data is available, deemphasizing 2008 and 2009 returns at one-third the weight due to the extreme volatility and wide range of performance, which skewed results. Using MSCI AC World Gross USD for Listed Equities; Barclays Global Agg Total Return Index Unhedged USD for Fixed Income; Cambridge Associates Global Private Equity for Private Equity; HFRI Fund Weighted Composite Index for Hedge Funds; and Barclays US T-Bills 3-6 Months Unhedged USD for Cash. Source: Bloomberg, MSCI, Cambridge Associates, KKR Global Macro & Asset Allocation analysis.

[30] Figure 16. Based on the Burgiss Private Equity Benchmark (the "Burgiss PE Index") as of Q1 2021, which consists of funds that pursue a global private equity strategy. The number of funds included for each vintage year from 2000-2020 ranges from 75 to 4,400 funds per vintage year. The Burgiss PE Index is based on a since inception IRR and is net of all fees and carried interest.

[31] Icten, T. (2021, December 8). Increased Access To Private Markets Expands The Opportunity Set For Financial Advisors. Forbes.com. Retrieved April 30, 2023, from https://www.forbes.com/sites/tayfunicten/2021/12/08/increased-access-to-private-markets-expands-the-opportunity-set-for-financial-advisors/?sh=4ae883403296

[32] Fratto, N. (n.d.). Fund Distributions. Svb.com. Retrieved April 5, 2023, from https://www.svb.com/emerging-manager-insights/starting-a-fund/cash-flow-management-fund-distribution

Chapter Nine

[32] Client Relationship Summary, CrowdStreet Capital, LLC, December 2022.

[33] Cummings, Douglas; Johan, Sofia; Reardon, Robert. "Governance and Success in U.S. Securities-Based Crowdfunding," Florida Atlantic University, December 14, 2021.

[34] Jensen, Marlin; Marshall, Beverly; Jahera, John. "Can Non-Accredited Investors Find and Invest in the Next Unicorn?" Auburn University, March 31, 2017.

[35] Walthoff-Borm, X., Vanacker, T.R. & Collewaert, V. (2018). Equity Crowdfunding, Shareholder Structures, and Firm Performance. Corporate Governance: An International Review, 26(5), 314-330.

Chapter Ten

[36] All returns from January 2005 through December 31, 2021. The yield on private real estate debt is estimated based on personal experience and target returns of funds in this sector. High-yield bonds is based on Bloomberg Barclays High Yield Index; Corporate bonds are based on the Bloomberg Barclays U.S. Corporate Bond Index; Investment grade bonds are based on the Bloomberg Barclays U.S. Aggregate Bond Index; Treasury bonds are based on the Bloomberg Barclays U.S. Treasury Index.

[37] The returns on private credit compared to private equity and venture capital reference to Preqin in "The Case for Credit," a 2022 whitepaper by Moonfare.

[38] Knickerbocker (October 24, 2022), *What is Private Debt?* Pitchbook.

[39] Private debt is the third largest asset class. Source Preqin.

[40] Preqin.

[41] Cambridge Associates, as of December 31, 2021. Private credit returns expressed net of fees. Past performance does not guarantee future results, which may vary. Outperformance of public loans on a public market equivalent (PME) basis. PME returns reflect the performance of the S&P LSTA Leveraged Loan Index ("index") (for public loans) and the Bloomberg Global High Yield index (for High Yield) expressed in terms of an internal rate of return and consider the timings of the private credit strategy's cash flows.

Chapter Eleven

[42] Armour, B., Jackson, R., Boyadzhiev, D. (September 2022), *Morningstar's U.S. Active/Passive Barometer*.

[43] Burke, B. The Hands-Off Investor: An Insider's Guide to Investing in Passive Real Estate Syndications (p. 221). BiggerPockets Publishing. Kindle Edition.

[44] Startup Business Failure. Startup Genome - the 2019 report claims 11 out of 12 start-ups will fail.

Chapter Fourteen

[45] Champion, H. (2023, March 22). Yieldstreet Review 2023. Finder.com. https://www.finder.com/yieldstreet-review

Chapter Fifteen

[46] UBS (March 2022), "UBTI in IRAs - FAQS".

[47] Matt Fellowes, Jason Fichtner, Lincoln Plews, Kevin Whitman, "The Retirement Solution Hiding in Plain Sight: How Much Retirees Would Gain by Improving Social Security Decisions," United Income.

[48] Alicia H. Munnell and Anqi Chen. 2015. "Trends in Social Security Claiming." Center for Retirement Research at Boston College, IB Number 15-8.

[49] Social Security Administration, "Annual Statistical Supplement to the Social Security Bulletin", 2019.

Chapter Sixteen

[50] Thomas, B. (2020, February 15). The Taxman Cometh: REITs and Taxes. Forbes. https://www.forbes.com/sites/bradthomas/2020/02/15/the-taxman-cometh-reits-and-taxes/?sh=4b7863614c0d

[51] Thomas, B. (2020, February 15). The Taxman Cometh: REITs and Taxes. Forbes. https://www.forbes.com/sites/bradthomas/2020/02/15/the-taxman-cometh-reits-and-taxes/?sh=4b7863614c0d

[52] Knutson, L., Powell, J. (January 12, 2023), "Updated IRS audit guide helps taxpayers improve cost segregation studies," Plante Moran.

[53] Knutson, L., Powell, J. (January 12, 2023), "Updated IRS audit guide helps taxpayers improve cost segregation studies," Plante Moran.

[54] Burke, B. "The Hands-Off Investor: An Insider's Guide to Investing in Passive Real Estate Syndications." BiggerPockets Publishing. Kindle Edition.

www.ingramcontent.com/pod-product-compliance
Lightning Source LLC
Chambersburg PA
CBHW060748050426
42449CB00008B/1322